Chevrolet Summers, Dairy Queen Nights

Books by Bob Greene

Chevrolet Summers, Dairy Queen Nights (1997)

The 50-Year Dash (1997)

Rebound: The Odyssey of Michael Jordan (1995)

All Summer Long (1993)

To Our Children's Children: Preserving Family Histories for
Generations to Come (with D. G. Fulford) (1993)

Hang Time (1992)

He Was a Midwestern Boy On His Own (1991)

Homecoming: When the Soldiers Returned from Vietnam
(1989)

Be True to Your School (1987)

Cheeseburgers (1985)

Good Morning, Merry Sunshine (1984)

American Beat (1983)

Bagtime (with Paul Galloway) (1977)

Johnny Deadline, Reporter (1976)

Billion Dollar Baby (1974)

Running: A Nixon-McGovern Campaign Journal (1973)

We Didn't Have None of Them Fat Funky Angels on the Wall
of Heartbreak Hotel, and Other Reports from America
(1971)

Chevrolet Summers, Dairy Queen Nights

BOB GREENE

VIKING

VIKING
Published by the Penguin Group
Penguin Putnam Inc., 375 Hudson Street, New York, New York 10014, U.S.A.
Penguin Books Ltd, 27 Wrights Lane, London W8 5TZ, England
Penguin Books Australia Ltd, Ringwood, Victoria, Australia
Penguin Books Canada Ltd, 10 Alcorn Avenue, Toronto, Ontario, Canada M4V 3B2
Penguin Books (N.Z.) Ltd, 182–190 Wairau Road, Auckland 10, New Zealand

Penguin Books Ltd, Registered Offices: Harmondsworth, Middlesex, England

First published in 1997 by Viking Penguin, a member of Penguin Putnam Inc.

1   3   5   7   9   10   8   6   4   2

The selections in this book first appeared in the *Chicago Tribune*.

Chevrolet and the 1955 Chevrolet Bel Air Emblem and Body Design are trademarks
of Chevrolet Motor Division, General Motors Corporation, and used under permission to Bob Greene and Penguin Putnam Inc. This book is not licensed, endorsed,
or sponsored by Chevrolet Motor Division or General Motors Corporation, nor does
it necessarily represent their opinions or views.

Dairy Queen® is a registered trademark used with the kind permission of
American Dairy Queen Corporation.

LIBRARY OF CONGRESS CATALOGING IN PUBLICATION DATA
Greene, Bob.
Chevrolet summers, Dairy Queen nights / by Bob Greene.
p.   cm.
ISBN 0-670-87032-3 (alk. paper)
1. United States—Social life and customs—1971—Anecdotes.
2. United States—Social life and customs—1945–1970—Anecdotes.
3. Popular culture—United States—Anecdotes.   4. United States—
Description and travel—Anecdotes. I. Title.
E169.04.G745   1996
973.9—dc20   96–12912

This book is printed on acid-free paper.

∞

Printed in the United States of America
Set in Bembo
Designed by Junie Lee

For Gary Griffin

CONTENTS

INTRODUCTION

Once, a long time ago, an editor said something to me that, as the years go by, seems more and more insightful.

The real truths of our lives, he said, don't make the morning paper or the six o'clock news.

That has become a thought I have carried with me for the more than twenty-five years I have been writing a newspaper column. The stories that earn the banner headlines in each day's paper, that lead the network newscasts, more often than not fade to insignificance and are long forgotten by the time the seasons have changed. Meanwhile, the small moments of our lives—the things no respectable editor would ever think to feature on the front page—grow in importance as time passes, resonate ever louder in our memories and in our hearts.

Much of my life has been spent wandering the country in search of those stories and those moments. In this book you will find very little about national politics or government policy or economic crises. Rather, you will meet a man in middle age who, facing personal troubles, finds in the junkyard behind an auto-parts store the car he used to drive when he was seventeen and hopeful—the same car, not just the same model—and who repairs it and drives it around his city, all those years later, doing his best to recapture the person he was, the boy whose life once seemed to stretch out in front of him like the most perfect and endless two-lane highway ever built.

You will meet a theater audience full of World War II—

generation men and women watching a matinee performance of the musical *Guys and Dolls*, an audience whose collective unspoken story, at least on that day, seemed more evocative than anything transpiring up on the stage. You will take a private walk through Yankee Stadium on a day when it is locked and closed; will sit with a man who retired at the age of forty-four and declared silent whimsical victory over all the strivers still grasping their way up the ladder; will feel the common thread between a family of Ohio farmers who take quiet pride in the blue ribbons they have accumulated over a lifetime invisible to the outside world, and a high school string quintet in a small Midwestern town who, through their music, hold at bay the coarse forces that sometimes seem to be unraveling the fabric of the land.

There are famous people here: Frank Sinatra in a chance encounter; Jack Benny in a solitary hotel room near the end of his life; Michael Jordan during his most solemn spring; Stan Musial teaching a lesson today's big-league athletes might have trouble understanding. There are stories about parents and their children —stories that seem more moving and complex and multilayered to me than I ever would have imagined when I first set out writing columns. There are three stories that combine the two themes—fame and family—in ways bittersweet and curious, stories that caught me unawares and that made me think: the tales of the daughter of the man who played Sergeant Bilko, the son who was named for the man who was football's most celebrated quarterback, the daughter—now seventy years old—of that most puzzling and melancholy of forgotten American heroes, Jim Thorpe.

Not all of the stories here will make you smile. There are many aspects—aspects of meanness and cruelty—that darken our national life, and some of those are here, also. For a better part of the last seven years I have spent an inordinate amount of time covering for the newspaper stories of how the courts have terribly failed the voiceless children who count on them the most. Because people don't read a book like this one to be depressed, I have for the most part left those stories out. But we must never let ourselves forget what is being done to these children in all of our names, and so, to keep them in our minds, I have included two stories that illustrate this tragedy most vividly. One—"Who Will Say, 'You Have a Home'?"—is a story that eventually ended happily, with the judges ruling in the child's favor. The other— "Please . . . Don't Send Me Away"—is the story of what happens when judges do not consider children to be human, but treat them as parcels, as pieces of property. The child in this story is a boy about whom I wrote more than sixty columns. This story is the one I have chosen to include here, because this is the one that shows in the most indelible and awful way what is done to children whose faces the judges never even choose to see. Since the day I reported this story, I have never once slept all the way through the night.

The theme that connects all the stories in this book—the stories of cloudless and carefree American days, the stories of troubled times—is the theme that has given the book its title. It often seems to me that what we all may be searching for are those elusive Chevrolet summers and Dairy Queen nights we once knew and that once, at least in memory, made us and our country feel fine and special and right. It's not a case of nostalgia, or of unrelenting yearning for times now gone. Rather, it is a feeling that what we want the most is what we—as a nation and as individuals—once had. It's a sense that the answers we all may be looking for are out there, always have been, and that we'll find them if we keep looking hard enough. The Chevrolet summers and Dairy Queen nights are ours for the taking—they're waiting for us.

My gratitude, as always, to the people who have let me spend my life this way, especially to the editors of the *Chicago Tribune* and its newspaper syndicate, who make space in their pages for these kinds of stories. I hope you enjoy taking this journey with me. Thanks for choosing to come along.

Bob Greene

Chevrolet Summers, Dairy Queen Nights

ONE

Sunday Morning

It was just after seven-thirty on a Sunday morning, and the streets were silent. Jack and I walked past the elementary school building and Jack noticed a pile of furniture stacked by the side, where the bike racks used to be.

"Look at those chairs," Jack said. "The little ones."

We veered off the sidewalk to approach the pile.

"Do you think they could be ours?" Jack said.

"If they are, they're at least forty years old," I said, picking up a chair and holding it in one hand.

The chair was wooden. The style was old-fashioned. The chair was so small that it could not comfortably hold a person much older than seven or eight.

"I'll bet you these are the same chairs that were used when we went to school here," Jack said. "They're pretty sturdy. They could have lasted all this time."

The elementary school was being remodeled. On this August Sunday morning, the little wooden chairs awaited Monday pickup by a salvage crew. Jack and I, best friends all our lives, both of us half-a-century old now, were walking the streets of the town where we grew up. Neither of us lives there now. We had flown in with nothing much more important in mind than to do just this: walk around and see things.

To us, the pile of elementary school furniture was like a prized find at an archeological dig. Soon enough the streets would be filling with people on their way to church, but we were still pretty much alone as we left the furniture and headed toward Main Street. A police officer, cruising, waved, and we waved back. In a town of 15,000, that kind of thing can happen.

On the other side of Main Street was Paul's Food Shoppe. "I wonder if it still has the wooden floors," Jack said. In the middle of a block we crossed without a traffic light because there was no traffic. The store was closed, but through the front windows we could see that the floor was still made of well-worn wood, the nailheads visible.

"It was always so much smaller than the Kroger's across the street," I said. "But it always did good business."

"People liked the service," Jack said. "Paul's gave personal service. You could call Paul's with your grocery list and they'd deliver to your house."

Across the street, the Kroger's supermarket was gone, a chain pharmacy in its place. Paul's remained. We saw the food on the shelves, and Jack, who knows about the twists and vagaries of business now, mentioned the name of a giant national food manufacturer that he noticed on one label through the window and said, "They're such a slimy outfit," and began to explain to me about the national conglomerate's low business practices.

But I didn't want to hear it. I'm willing to listen to just about anything Jack wants to talk about, always have been, but a silent Sunday morning in front of Paul's grocery windows was not the time to remind ourselves that we now knew secrets and shames of the real world. "Paul's really did have good service," I said, cutting him off. "My grandmother had them deliver her groceries all the time."

The record shop where Jack and I each bought copies of *Meet the Beatles* the day it arrived in our town is now a store that sells sheets and towels; we looked in that window, too. Connell's Flowers is bigger than we remembered; Seckel's 5 & 10 is gone. We took a right and passed the house where my mother used to live when she was a girl. We stopped on street corners and debated which way to turn next.

Each of us had been back here many times before; each of us

has thought, more times than we can tell, about what the streets and buildings mean to us. We hadn't done it together, though, not like this, and the Sunday morning grew later and the streets began to fill.

In the nicer sections of town the homes were still lovely, but very few had the names of their owners displayed on address signs in front, the way they used to. Instead, the signs on the lawns bore the names of security firms, announcing to would-be burglars that the homes were wired and connected to the police station. It's like this everywhere now, all over America, in our new age of fear and discretion. Don't let strangers know your name; just tell them you are wary and well-protected. Security on those streets we walked was once something that was taken for granted, and the security was of a sort that people did not have to order from a company and pay for once a month.

"Do you think they're just going to haul those little wooden chairs away?" Jack said.

"My mom's old house was really beautiful," I said, looking in the sky for Sunday-morning rain clouds.

TWO

Loving Ronnie

When a baby boy was born to a Rhode Island couple named Joseph and Emma Horbert in 1947, it did not take long for them to sense that something was amiss with the child. The baby—his name was Ronald, and his parents always called him Ronnie— did not develop quickly. By the time he was eighteen months old, he was still not sitting up or expressing much alertness.

Joseph Horbert was a meter reader for the Providence Gas Company. He and his wife took Ronnie to a succession of doctors. Ronnie, it turned out, was severely retarded.

"Back then, they didn't have many of the things we have today," Ronnie's father said the other night. He was referring to sophisticated schools and programs for disabled children. "We had no place to go, really."

Friends and neighbors whispered that Ronnie should be institutionalized—"put in a home," to use the common term of the era. His parents wouldn't hear of it. "I wouldn't even consider it," Joseph Horbert said. "Back then . . . it would not be the right place for my son to be loved. Would they take care of him and look out for him? I couldn't be sure that they would."

An incident that took place when Ronnie was ten years old cemented that decision. "There was a day camp for children who were retarded or who had physical disabilities," Joseph Horbert said. "We sent Ronnie to it. One day Ronnie wandered away from the other children at camp and he sat in a car. A man who worked at the camp saw Ronnie in the car, and he slapped him. He slapped Ronnie in the face.

"I suppose it was to discipline Ronnie. But Ronnie told us about it, and he never forgot it. Even thirty years later, when Ronnie was forty years old, he talked about what the man had done. No . . . he belonged with us."

And with his parents is where Ronnie stayed. He never developed a vocabulary, and the few words he did say were hard for outsiders to understand. A cousin of Ronnie's, Kathy Keenan, said: "He was always so loving and sweet. He was so enthusiastic about things he had enjoyed. If I had spent Christmas Day with the family, he would bring it up every time he saw me for the next year. He would see me and say, 'You here Christmas!' "

Ronnie grew into a man; his father and his mother bathed him and shaved him and helped him dress. Ronnie had no brothers or sisters. Then, in 1984, Emma Horbert died at the age of seventy-two.

"So it was just Ronnie and me," Joseph Horbert said. He was retired from his job; each morning he and his son would get up together. In the afternoon they would go for a drive, down by the water. Then, early in the evening, they would sit in the house together and watch one of Ronnie's favorite television programs, *Sanford and Son*.

Ronnie's parents had always been worried about what would happen to Ronnie after they died. Who would take care of him? With Emma gone, this became even more of a concern for Joseph. Earlier this year Joseph Horbert had a gallbladder operation. He hired a housekeeper to stay with Ronnie: "I had to pull through that operation, because I knew that I had to go home to Ronnie." By this time Joseph Horbert was eighty years old; Ronnie was forty-two.

Then, early one morning last April, Ronnie came into his father's room, as he did at the beginning of each day.

"He would always say the same thing," Joseph Horbert said. "He would come into my room from his room. He would be carrying a pillow. He would say, 'Daddy, I come over.' That's when he would come over to my bed and kiss me good morning. Sometimes he would get in the bed for a few minutes, and then we would get up and start the day."

On this particular morning, Ronnie appeared in the doorway. He said, "Daddy, I come over." But he didn't make it all the way to kiss his father. Just before he got to the bed, Ronnie collapsed to the floor.

He did not move. By the time the paramedics arrived, Ronnie was already dead—dead at forty-two of a massive heart attack.

So now Joseph Horbert lives alone. He misses his son terribly, but he knows that the day will never come when Ronnie has to depend on strangers.

For years, friends told Joseph Horbert that he ought to give himself a vacation—that he ought to fly down to Florida.

"But Ronnie said that he would be afraid to go on an airplane, and I certainly never would have gone without him,"

Joseph Horbert said. "As a matter of fact, I have never been in an airplane myself. I never wanted to, without my son."

Now the friends are urging him to finally fly to Florida for that vacation.

"Maybe I will," he said. "It's just me now. Maybe I'll fly on an airplane. I don't know, though. I really don't know."

THREE

"She Can See"

"I don't think the doctor even knew I was in the room when he came in," Cleo Canty said.

Mrs. Canty, sixty-nine, is a patient at the University of Chicago Eye Clinic. Within the span of a month she had two operations for cataracts, and is receiving treatment for glaucoma. She is far from wealthy; Medicare enabled her to have the surgery.

The day after one of the operations, Mrs. Canty returned to the Eye Clinic for a follow-up evaluation. She was sitting in an examining room, speaking with one of her physicians—Dr. Kimberly Neely, thirty-three, a resident who is doing her specialized training at the Eye Clinic.

"Dr. Neely had assisted the main surgeon who had operated on my eye the day before," Mrs. Canty said. "The surgeon is a professor at the medical school. All of a sudden, he came bursting through the doorway. I know he didn't notice that I was there right away.

"Across the hallway, in another examining room, was this very old wheelchair patient, in her eighties or nineties. I had seen her before, at the clinic. She just sits in her wheelchair and doesn't say very much. That's who the surgeon had been examining.

"He came into the room where I was, and he said to Dr. Neely: 'I just examined her. And she can *see*. The operation was a success. She passed the test one hundred percent.'

"He was so excited that his voice shook. His face was glowing, and he was smiling so happily. He was almost jumping around. Whenever I had seen the doctor before, he was very staid and dignified. But he was so thrilled—you would have thought he had won the Nobel Prize."

Mrs. Canty said that Dr. Neely joined the senior surgeon in his elation; Dr. Neely's face broke into a big smile too. "The joy and excitement of the two doctors was so wondrous, I began to cry," Mrs. Canty said.

The main surgeon was Dr. Ramesh Tripathi, fifty-five, a professor of ophthalmology and visual science at the university. He was born in India, and has been associated with the school for sixteen years. Here is one of the reasons Mrs. Canty was crying at what she was seeing:

"We hear so much about hatred and racial troubles in this sad old world," she said. "I'm a black woman. The patient in the other room was old, black, indigent, and obviously very ill. The surgeon was of Indian descent. The younger physician was Caucasian, and a woman. And everyone was just so happy that the patient could see.

"That's why Dr. Tripathi was so excited—from knowing that what he and his colleagues had done had let that woman see again. He was feeling something that the rest of us will never have the honor to feel—because of him, another person was given her sight back. I don't think I've ever been as moved as I was when I watched him burst into that room."

I spoke with Dr. Tripathi. He was grateful for what Mrs. Canty had said, but surprised that anyone thought his reaction was exceptional. "I get very excited with most of my patients who do so well," he said. "That is the gratification that comes with what we do. That is the reward we get."

He said that many clinic patients, especially the elderly, are impoverished or have only government assistance available to them. "Many feel they are going through life not being taken care of," Dr. Tripathi said. "They feel that no one cares about them. But they deserve the most expert care, the same as if they were wealthy people."

Dr. Neely too—she grew up on a farm near Emlenton, Pennsylvania—said that one of the great satisfactions of her work is knowing that people with little money and no connections can have a chance to see well again. "The woman in question that day had gone into surgery because her eyesight was extremely, extremely poor," Dr. Neely said. "As I recall, it had gotten so bad that she could barely make out the shape of her hand in front of her face. So yes, we get excited when someone like her comes out of surgery with her vision greatly improved."

Cleo Canty doubts she will ever forget the look on Dr. Tripathi's face when he burst into that examining room.

"We're not important people," she said. "We have no money. I heard his voice that day, and I knew that in this crazy world of hate, there's hope for us all. There are people who truly do care.

"Everyone is not consumed by thoughts of race or of money. The excitement in those two doctors' faces and voices—you see something like that, and you think that maybe our world is not doomed, after all. I wish I could re-create for you the joy and trembling in his voice. I'll never forget how he said those three words: 'She can *see*.' "

FOUR

Jack Benny's Way

There was a network television tribute to Jack Benny that was broadcast last week; maybe you saw it. It was a lovely look at Benny's life and his talent.

A friend and I were talking about the TV special, and we also were talking about some of the people currently in public life who specialize in outrage and calculatedly crazed behavior (professional athletes, TV and radio performers, comedians), and the thought occurred that the two subjects—Jack Benny, and the present-day purveyors of outrage—are not entirely unrelated.

Because the reason people still talk fondly of Benny, still consider him almost a member of their families, is that day after day, year after year, he let the public see that talent and dignity are not mutually exclusive qualities; that if you treat people the way you'd like to be treated yourself, not only will they appreciate it, but they will accept you into their lives not just for a hot season or two, but for the long run.

It's an idea that seems to be all but outmoded in public life today, where the loudest and the most abrasive get all the attention. You wonder whether a Jack Benny, were he to come along now, would even be given a chance to shine. Where are the headlines in Jack Benny's demeanor? Where are the news flashes in a career built on taste, and impeccable timing, and respect for one's audience?

And yet—this is what is being lost today—those are the things that stick. People remember.

I certainly do. I met Jack Benny only once. I was twenty-two years old, a beginning reporter, and Benny, then seventy-five and near the end of his remarkable career, was performing in the Empire Room of the Palmer House hotel in Chicago. I had called the hotel's management to arrange an interview, and had been told to show up one evening at a certain time.

When I did, there seemed to have been a mixup. From the house phone, I called Benny's room; there was no answer. I rode the elevator upstairs, knocked on his door. No answer there, either.

I kept knocking, for a minute or more, and finally there was that unforgettable voice: "Come in!" In the middle of the hotel room, sitting at a room-service table eating dinner for one, wearing a blue bathrobe over a white T-shirt, black slippers covering black knee-length socks, was Jack Benny.

"I don't know anything about any interview," he said, peering through his eyeglasses. "No one told me."

He was one of the biggest stars and greatest talents in the world; I was some kid trying to do well in his first full-time newspaper job. Anything I might write about him, he didn't need; he had been written about for half a century. "I have to go downstairs and be on stage in fifteen minutes," he said. "I've got to finish eating, I've got to shave, I've got to put my makeup on. . . . Can you come back in the daytime sometime?"

I couldn't, because that's when I had to be at the office. The interview with Benny was something I was attempting on my own time. "Oh, come on then," Benny said. "Finish dinner with me, and then you can come down and watch the show, and we can come back up and talk some more afterwards if you like. Sit down."

And so my evening with Benny began. He treated me like a young relative; he sat and talked with me in the room, he took me down to the Empire Room with him, he whispered something to the maître d' so that I would be given a seat where I could clearly see the stage. He invited me back up afterward, sitting around with me until after midnight, treating someone he'd never met and would never see again with absolute courtesy and graciousness.

"I hope I've given you enough for a story," he said when I finally left to go home. Whatever I would write would have no effect on his life, but he understood that doing the story was important to me.

He lived for five more years, and we never spoke again. There must have been thousands of people who passed through his life whose names and faces he inevitably forgot. But watching the television tribute to him last week, I understood the legacy of people like him—the people who do things right, who realize that soft voices echo longer than strident shouts. All this time later, and I'm telling you the story of that night. That's the legacy— the legacy is that people never forget.

FIVE

To Serve and Protect

WHITEHALL, Ohio—When the police officer came to the trailer, the man and woman inside said they had only two children.

Officer Rex Adkins of the Whitehall Police Department was responding to an anonymous tip phoned in to the Franklin County child welfare agency. The caller said that there was a child being brutally abused in the trailer.

The man and woman who lived there—Robert Jeffery, thirty-four, and his wife, Rita, thirty—pointed to the two children with them in the trailer: their thirteen-year-old daughter and ten-year-old son. The caller to the child welfare agency had said there were three Jeffery children. The caller had said that one of the children—a boy—had blackened eyes, was scarred on his face, and suffered from a severe speech impediment. The two children that Adkins saw appeared "clean and well cared for."

So he left the trailer. But something kept sticking in his mind. Something just didn't seem right.

"He could have just let it go," said Whitehall Police Chief James Stacy. "He could have just filed his report."

But he didn't. Adkins, accompanied by four other White-hall police officers, returned to the trailer that night. They knocked on the door and told Mr. and Mrs. Jeffery that they wanted to examine the trailer thoroughly. When the Jefferys tried to hurry them out, one of the officers said, "We have all night."

In fact, the assignment of the five officers to revisit the trailer was a big commitment on the part of the Whitehall police. White-hall is not a large community—the entire police force consists of forty-two officers, spread over three shifts. But the five showed up, and told the Jefferys that if it took a search warrant to look around the trailer, then they'd just wait there until a warrant could be obtained.

The Jefferys, realizing the officers weren't going to leave, reluctantly allowed them to look around. At first they didn't find much.

Then an officer named Dan Wardlow looked in a drawer underneath a water bed that Mr. and Mrs. Jeffery slept on.

"When he opened that drawer he at first could not believe what he was seeing," Chief Stacy said.

Stuffed in the drawer, covered with blankets, was a twelve-year-old boy. He was the Jefferys' other son.

"We may be police officers, but our hearts beat too," Chief Stacy said. "Police officers have children. I don't think there was an officer who looked at that boy in the drawer who didn't think: What if he was my son?"

The boy was bruised, scarred and filthy. Six of his teeth were chipped, he had a human bite mark on his back and his speech was extremely difficult to understand.

"He was very frightened," Chief Stacy said. "He had been put in the drawer so no one could find him." According to an investigation, the boy had been beaten routinely virtually since the time of his birth. Although all three of the Jeffery children had allegedly been abused, the twelve-year-old boy was the one singled out for punishment.

"He had never been sent to school," Chief Stacy said. "His life consisted of being beaten in that trailer. His parents ridiculed him and made fun of the way he talked and beat him in front of his brother and sister as an 'example.' He was made to stand in the corner for hours and sleep on the floor with the dog. When our officers asked the father why the boy had never been enrolled in school, the father said, 'He ain't been sent to school because he talks funny.' "

The children were removed from the trailer and placed in foster homes; last week a Franklin County grand jury indicted the Jefferys on eleven counts of child abuse. If convicted, Robert Jeffery could be sentenced to eighty years in prison; Rita Jeffery could be sentenced to sixty-five years.

"These people moved around the country a lot in that trailer," Chief Stacy said. "If Officer Adkins hadn't returned to the trailer that night, they probably would have been gone by morning. No one would ever have known about that boy."

Officers learned that some residents of the trailer park had seen the boy being beaten by his father, but did not report it to the police because they weren't sure it was important enough.

What the chief had to say about that is a lesson that deserves to be heard far beyond Whitehall, Ohio:

"If you ever suspect a child is being abused, please place the call. You may be worried that if it turns out to be groundless, you'll be bothering us or inconveniencing us. Please—bother us. Inconvenience us. When it comes to something like this, we want to be bothered and inconvenienced. Please—let us check it out."

SIX

Blue Ribbons

EATON, Ohio—The nature of ambition and self-fulfillment is no different here than in the canyons of Wall Street or the boardrooms of Hollywood.

"That pumpkin pie fainted," a woman said to her husband. This was in the Household Arts Building of the Preble County Fairgrounds, right around 7:00 P.M. on Day Six of this year's fair. On a sultry August night, the white frame building was mostly empty. A representative from the office of Ohio Auditor Thomas E. Ferguson sat at a table, ready to take entries in a free lottery that would award one flag (your choice of Ohio or United States) to the person whose name was drawn at the end of the fair, but traffic was slow.

The pumpkin pie that had appeared to faint was one of the winners in the Preble County Fair's baking competition; the winning piece of pie had collapsed in the heat, but its blue ribbon was still attached to the plate beneath it.

The building was full of winners. There was the winning bale of alfalfa, entered by Bill Rushbush of West Alexandria. There was the winning bale of clover, entered by Christine Howard of Somerville. The best chocolate pie—actually the "best chocolate pie baked from scratch"—had been entered by Shirley Fisher, also of West Alexandria; the best tender-sweet carrots had been grown by Roger Gebhart of Lewisburg.

The men and women weren't here on this night; just their winning entries, for all to see. And even if there were hardly any of us present at the moment, the effort that must have gone into putting together submissions for the contests was more than impressive. The Preble County Fair is local in scope—the Ohio State Fair, over in Columbus, is the big event of the summer, and it was starting on this very same day—but here in rural Preble County, the men and women had obviously cared enough to prepare and submit their best work.

I noticed that one man's name appeared on quite a few ribbons. He was Gib Harris, who, according to the tags, lived in the town of Eldorado. He had taken second in the alfalfa; he had won an award for his shelled corn (displayed in a large jar); he had done well in the wheat competition. The Harris last name, with various first names, was prominent in other categories too; apparently the Harris family of Eldorado was diligent in its devotion to excellence.

I left the Household Arts Building, and stopped to talk with a man named Emil Lipps, proprietor of the Emil Lipps Home Improvement Company, who was manning his firm's fairgrounds display. Lipps was from Eldorado, also, and I asked him about Gib Harris.

"He's a friend of mine," Lipps said. "He has a farm in Eldorado; he's around sixty, I would say. His real name is Gilbert Harris. I haven't seen him tonight, but I think he'd be happy if you were to call him."

So I did, when I got to the place where I'd be sleeping that night. I asked him how many awards he had won at this year's Preble County Fair.

"Well, just a minute," he said. "I'll go get my book and check." When he returned to the phone he said, "I believe I won at least eleven prizes."

He said he has been submitting entries to the Preble County Fair for more than twenty-five years. "It's a lot of work, but it makes me feel proud when I win," he said. "It makes me feel I've accomplished something in my life."

Farming is hard and getting harder, he said: "There are

younger people in some farm families who are deciding it's probably not worth the trouble." But he finds the work immensely
satisfying, and each year puts together his county fair entries.

"I hope my winning entries inspire other people," he said.
"Maybe a person will see my hay entry, and say, 'I can grow hay
that well,' and then try to do it."

The other Harrises among the winners were, indeed, members of his family: "My son got a first and a second in corn and
soybeans. My wife, Anna Belle, baked the grand champion coffee
cake. My daughter-in-law got a first in noodles. And this year,
for the first time, my grandson showed a pig. He's seven years
old, and his pig got tenth place, and he got a ribbon for it."

There are no ceremonies to announce the winners of the
contests Gib Harris enters: "You just go look at your entries after
the judging, and the ribbons tell you whether you've won." He
said his success at the Preble County Fair over the years has made
him feel that his farm career has been well spent.

He keeps his quarter-century of ribbons in a box, because he
doesn't know what else to do with them.

"But my wife tells me she may make a quilt of them," he
said.

SEVEN

A Father, a Son and an Answer

Everyone's always looking for the answer to what's gone wrong.

Sometimes the answer is right in front of our eyes.

The crime, the violence, the murderous soullessness that
seems to be taking over the lives of so many young people in this

country. The lowering of educational standards, the increase in public use of vile obscenities, the disappearance of simple civility. We look to studies and polls and government programs for the solution, and nothing works.

And then you look in front of you and it's right there.

I was in the giant Atlanta airport on a recent Saturday morning, preparing to return to Chicago.

I got onto one of the trains that take travelers from the main terminal to the various boarding gates. The trains have become commonplace in many American airports; they're free and sterile and impersonal.

All day long, the trains run up their tracks and then return. In Atlanta, a computerized voice enunciates instructions from the ceiling. Not many travelers I know consider the trains to be anything resembling fun.

On this Atlanta morning, though, I heard laughter on the train. Right at the front of the first car—where a person could look out the window at the tracks and tunnel that lay ahead—a man and his son were having a wonderful time. I'd say the boy was five years old, the father in his early thirties.

"All right!" the father said to his son. We had just stopped to let off some passengers, and now the doors were closing again. "Here we go! Hold on to me tight!" The boy made sounds of sheer delight.

I know that you're supposed to avoid making racial distinctions in print these days, so I hope no one will mind if I mention that the vast majority of the people on the airport train were white, apparently middle-class travelers, dressed as if they were returning from business trips or heading on vacations, and that this father and son were black, and dressed in clothes that were just about as inexpensive as you can buy. Everyone else in the car was lugging carry-on suitcases or briefcases or backpacks; the boy and his father had no luggage of any kind.

They were having a great time on the ride; the rest of the travelers were simply enduring another airport. "Look out there!"

the father said to his son. "See that pilot in the hallway? I bet you he's walking to his airplane." The son craned his neck to look.

I got off, then realized that, absentmindedly, I had forgotten to purchase something back in the main terminal. I was early for my flight, so I decided to ride the train back and do my shopping.

I did—and just as I was about to reboard the train for my gate, I saw that the man and his son had returned, too. They hadn't been heading for a flight.

"You want to go home now?" the father said.

"I want to ride some more!" the son said.

"More?" the father said, mock-exasperated but clearly pleased. "You're not tired yet?"

"This is fun!" his son said.

"All right," the father said, and when a door opened we got onto a train car.

"How fast do you think we're going, Daddy?" the boy said as we pulled away.

"Very, very fast," the father said.

There are parents who can afford to send their children to Europe or to Disneyland, and the children turn out rotten. There are parents who live in million-dollar homes and give their children cars and swimming pools, yet something goes wrong. Rich neighborhoods, poor neighborhoods, black and white, so much goes wrong so often.

"Where are all these people going, Daddy?" the son said.

"All over the world," the father said.

It was a Saturday morning, and the father had brought his son out here so that they could spend the time together and see something new. The other people in the airport today—they were leaving for distant destinations, or arriving at the end of their journeys. The father and son, though, were just riding. Riding this train together. It was free and they were making it exciting and it was something they could do to share each other's company.

So many troubles in this country; so many questions about

how to fix the troubles. Here on the train was a father who cared about spending the day with his son, and who had come up with this plan on a Saturday morning. The answer is so simple: parents who care enough to spend the time, and to pay attention, and to try their best. It doesn't cost a cent, yet it is the most valuable thing in the world. The train picked up speed, and the father pointed something out, and the boy laughed again, and the answer is so simple.

EIGHT

"The Body of a Mortgage Broker . . ."

The message said to call my sister. I was in a hotel room on the road. When I reached her, the sound of her voice registered the terrible news even before the three words could sink in.

"Leon was murdered," she said, that last word pronounced with a combination of mourning and fury and pure despair.

She didn't say his last name, and she didn't need to. She lives in California now and I live in Illinois, and it has been thirty years since we were kids on the streets of the peaceful central Ohio town that we both love so much, love so much now and in memory. When you're kids in a town like that, it's as if everyone you know is a member of the cast of characters in some long-running, free-form stage play. It's a stage play that's never supposed to end—at least you don't think of it ever ending when you're young—and the characters require no last names. Tim asked Sherry out for Friday night. Rick broke his arm at football practice. Wendy got a job as a lifeguard at the pool this summer.

Leon was murdered.

That's not supposed to be a part of the stage play. "Police Find Broker Shot to Death." That was the headline above the brief story about the murder of Leon in the *Los Angeles Times*. Broker? "The body of a mortgage broker who had been shot to death after returning from a Clippers game was discovered Thursday morning, authorities said." So Leon was a mortgage broker. That somehow didn't seem any more right than the murder itself. Is this how it's destined to end? With a newspaper headline that says you were a broker, and that the police have found your body?

The part about the Clippers game at least made sense. Every basketball game, every football game, every pro wrestling match, Leon was always there. The arenas had changed; had the year been 1965, Leon would have been watching a basketball game in the high school gym in the town where we lived instead of at the Los Angeles Sports Arena in the town where he died—but at least that much about Leon hadn't changed. He loved to watch sports, and he loved to listen to music. "The body of a mortgage broker . . ."

The shocking thing is that it isn't shocking. In the most recent year for which figures are complete, there were 23,760 murders in the United States. It's quite common. The day is fast coming when everyone will probably have known someone who was a victim of murder. The details of Leon's murder—what an awful phrase, "Leon's murder," as if it's something he possesses—may offer clues to what happened to him, but very few clues to what has happened to us. Found dead in his own garage, police said. May have been followed home, police said. Shot once in the upper body, police said. Car missing—stealing the car may have been the motive, police said.

I called my friends from the town where we all grew up— the fellow actors in the stage play that was supposed to go on forever. Not believe it? Not believe a murder? Of course we believed it. As peaceful and safe as our world always seemed— always was—Leon's murder wasn't even the first murder of a man who had once been a boy in the neighborhood. Safe neighborhood, safe town. The boy who lived in the house right next door to mine also grew up to be a man who was murdered. He was murdered a few years ago, a few miles away from the neighborhood; Leon was murdered in his garage in California. Big country; no escape.

Who is supposed to solve this, make sense of it? On the day of the murderous bombing at the Oklahoma City federal building, the FBI agent in Oklahoma giving briefings to the press was another one of us, another boy from our old town—another character from our stage play that once seemed so easy. Friend of mine, friend of Leon's. First name Dan. Now an FBI agent trying to explain what is unexplainable.

My friends back home were crying as we talked about Leon. Crying for him, crying for all of us, in every town. A story in a Los Angeles paper said that Leon, on his way to the Clippers game the night he was murdered, was playing a collection of oldies he had just bought. "He was listening with fond memories," a friend who had ridden with him to the game said. Going to a basketball game, just like when the stage play was new. Listening to the same songs as when the fond memories weren't memories, but were forming and being acted out, lived out, every cloudless day.

NINE

The Sky's the Limit

WAPAKONETA, Ohio—We were driving up the highway, and off to the side of the road were telephone wires bare and black against the leaves of autumn. Winter wheat had been planted, and the cornfields remained. There was a barn constructed of gray wood.

I saw the sign saying that the next exit was Wapakoneta, and I said that we should stop and look around.

So we did. Wapakoneta is a town of 9,214 in northwestern Ohio. It looks like so many small Ohio towns—its borders are invisible, but it is a self-contained universe, and a person can be born here, go to school here, work his whole life here, and be buried here. If you didn't know anything about Wapakoneta, you might get the impression that a person who grows up here is pretty much destined to stay in Wapakoneta forever.

Yet no town on the globe may be more representative of the power and grandeur of the human dream. Many of the people who are born in Wapakoneta do stay here, and lead good lives here, and are happy here. One man who grew up in Wapakoneta decided that the boundaries around his town—around any town —are not permanent and not constraining. He left Wapakoneta and he went to the moon. In the history of the world he was the first man to step upon the moon, and this is where he got started. This is where the dream was allowed to be born.

Neil Armstrong grew up walking these Wapakoneta streets. He attended Blume High School here in the 1940s; at the age of fifteen he began taking flying lessons at an airstrip north of town. He received his student pilot's license before he got his driver's license. On July 20, 1969, as commander of the Apollo 11 spacecraft, he stepped onto the moon, something no one else had ever done.

On this bright autumn afternoon we drove slowly through Wapakoneta. School had just let out; there were children on the sidewalks, heading for home. The day's edition of the Wapakoneta *Daily News* beckoned readers from vending boxes on corners; the Farmers Insurance Group branch office was open for business. At the corner of Wood and Bellefontaine a house bore a "For Sale" sign; at the Zip Stop convenience store, Mountain Dew and Dr. Pepper were being featured.

You can do anything. If you want it badly enough, you can do anything that anyone ever dared to dream, and some things that no one ever dreamed. On this October afternoon, people worked on their cars on the streets of Wapakoneta, and three men sat and talked on a front stoop, and leaves were on the ground. You can do anything in the world.

On the outskirts of town, there was an air and space museum named in Armstrong's honor. I went inside; there weren't many visitors today. I looked at his spacesuit, and I studied the pictures of him that were on the wall. I asked if there was any biographical information available on him, and a woman who worked in the museum directed me to a skimpy four-page pamphlet printed on blue paper, which she said cost twenty-five cents a copy. "That's the story of his life, what there is to tell," she said.

I bought a copy. "You don't have anything more complete?" I said.

"There's not much written about him," she said. "He's a very private man." She said that he now lives elsewhere in Ohio, and does his best to avoid publicity.

"Does he ever come back to Wapakoneta and look around your museum?" I asked.

"The last time he was in here was twelve years ago," she said.

"Did he like the museum?" I asked.

"He didn't say he didn't," she said.

Encased in plastic, attached to the wall, were newspaper front pages from around the world—front pages from the day after Armstrong walked on the moon. There were papers from Italy and from Thailand, from England and from Germany; there was *The New York Times*, recording for history the day a man did what no one had ever done before. And then there was the Wapakoneta *Daily News*, the edition of July 21, 1969. The headline: "Neil Steps on the Moon."

You can do anything. You don't have to be from a big town or a famous town; you don't have to be from New York or from London or from Los Angeles. You can do anything you want, and you're the only one who can decide to do it.

On this autumn afternoon the Auglaize River flowed gently

through Wapakoneta, and a woman walked past the United Methodist Church holding her child's hand, and at the Wapa Theater *Sneakers* was showing and tickets were three dollars apiece. The highway runs right past this town, and most travelers speed by without giving it a second thought, and you can do anything. You can do anything you dream.

TEN

"I Was Just Playing"

Because the occurrence was not all that rare—a so-called drive-by shooting in which an innocent child was hit by a gang member's bullet intended for someone else—what happened to Ricardo Hernandez, eight, rated only four paragraphs in the newspaper. Ricardo didn't die, which was a factor arguing against large headlines.

So a week after the shooting, it was as if the incident had never occurred as far as the rest of the city of Chicago was concerned. Ricardo lay motionless on a bed in the pediatric intensive care unit of Mount Sinai Hospital Medical Center, his eyes large, his voice soft and high-pitched as he spoke with a visitor.

"My stomach kind of hurts," the child said.

Above his bed were a balloon with a picture of Mickey Mouse on it, a poster with a rainbow drawn by children from his school, a photograph of a kitten. They were the kinds of things you would want any eight-year-old to have over his bed.

"I was just playing in front of my house," he said.

On August 14, the night of the shooting, Ricardo and some other children had been standing in front of his house on West

Cullerton Street. According to police, a car containing young men drove by the house; the men were said to be looking for other men involved in some sort of gang-related dispute. The men in the car saw the other men standing near where Ricardo and his playmates were standing; police said that bullets were fired from the car toward the other men.

"The other children knew to dive down to the ground," said Ricardo's older sister Elvia. "But Ricky stood back up too quickly. Because he stood up too fast, he got shot."

The boy was rushed to the hospital. "The bullet had hit him in the midsection," said Dr. Patrick Paxton, who helped perform the surgery on Ricardo. "The bullet divided his pancreas right in half. We operated for four hours. Essentially, we had to take out half of his pancreas. We took his spleen out, too. We're watching to see if there are kidney problems. One of the kidneys may have to come out."

A .38-caliber bullet does terrible insult to the human body— especially when the body is that of an eight-year-old. But Dr. Paxton was surprised that, even as Ricardo was being carried into surgery, he was frightened not about his injury or even about the possibility of death. He was frightened about something else.

"He kept telling us, 'Please don't make me say anything,'" Dr. Paxton said. "He was begging us not to make him tell. It took us a moment to realize that he thought we were going to make him say who shot him. We told him that we were here to help him get better, not to ask him questions he didn't want to answer."

And now he lay in the hospital bed, with that voice not much louder than a whisper.

"The other kids stayed down on the ground, so they didn't get hit," he said.

And then:

"It felt like pure air. That's how I knew something was wrong with me. My stomach felt like pure air after the bullet hit it."

Like pure air. The child said it as if by putting what happened into words, he could give some meaning to it. "He's a little scared," said Mary Ann Urban, a nurse in the pediatric intensive care unit. "He's afraid that the people are going to come back and hurt him.

"He knows that he didn't do anything wrong, and that the men in the car were aiming at other men and not at the children, and that it was a mistake that he got shot. But he's still scared. We reassure him that there are guards down at the front desk, and that no one can get in here who isn't supposed to get in here. I think he's worried about what will happen when he eventually goes home. Here, I think he feels safe."

One of Ricardo's physicians had ordered a kidney scan; it was time for the boy to be wheeled to another floor so that the procedure could be performed.

The attendants lifted him onto a cart, and wheeled the cart out into the hallway. Ricardo seemed very small as the men rolled him down the corridor.

His big sister was standing out there. Seeing Ricardo being wheeled toward the elevator, she tried to smile for him as he was rolled past her.

Ricardo, flat on his back, saw his sister. His eyes were wide and damp.

"Hi, Ricky," she said to him with as much cheer as she could put into her voice. "Where are you going?"

He looked up at her, his voice barely audible.

"I don't know," he said.

ELEVEN

All Aboard

ABOARD THE LAKE SHORE LIMITED—There's a man on a roof, nailing down a tile. We roll past him in an instant. A woman is driving her auto out of a long car-wash shed. She takes a left, maybe toward home, but we are going the other way.

What was it that the late Tip O'Neill, Speaker of the House of Representatives, once said? "All politics is local"? So is life. Sometimes we forget that.

The train is on its daily run from New York City to Chicago. It has left the East Coast in darkness, and now, in the morning light, it is on the long stretch through Ohio, Indiana and Illinois. This country of ours seems so big at times. You can rent a bedroom on a cross-country Amtrak train, look out the window, and make life small again.

That house out there—someone has painted decorative flowers on the side of the front porch. Next door, one of the neighbors has rolled up the bright-green garden hose into a tight coil and hung it on its rack, no slack at all. There are dandelions dotting the lawn of the house next to that, and suddenly there is a pond, not a big one, with a short wooden pier that looks like someone has built it with diving in mind. There's Kelley's Diner, here and now gone.

Every street in every city, each with its own touches, each touch created by one person on that block. Often it seems that everything in our world conspires against the thought of this country ever becoming truly local again. From the television networks to the chain restaurants to the famous-name discount stores, everything seems nationwide, everything seems standard. If you want to, you can ride on a train with a cellular phone in your pocket; if you wish, you can dial anywhere in the world from your compartment.

Or you can choose not to. Those telephone wires by the side of the track—someone once strung them, someone climbed those poles to do the job when telephone wires represented distance and scope. A telephone wire—or a cross-country train—seems not very racy these wireless days. Telephone wires and cross-country trains are around, in case they are needed, but many don't seem to need them. Every blade of grass out there, planted by someone in the towns.

You can look out the window in Indiana and see the inter-section of County Road 47 and U.S. 6. There's only one structure at the intersection: one red barn. Not much else in the vicinity, and the train hurries by, but for the owner of that barn, the corner of 47 and 6 is likely the most important in the world. Farther along the tracks, there is a business bearing a sign that announces it is a humane center. You can see the dogs in their outdoor pens, but inside the train you cannot hear a thing.

Worlds clash. In the tiniest of towns, satellite dishes point toward the skies. Trucks are proudly painted with the names of local businesses; a man in suspenders and a tie, his suit jacket removed, stands behind a factory having a private smoke in the middle of the day as the train goes by.

The street signs have different colors. The train passes from one town to the next, and the signs change from blue to white to green. You can read the street signs even when you don't know what towns you are hurrying through. The corner of Middlebury and Willard, wherever it is, looks like a place where you wouldn't mind spending some time; the corner of Best Street and Van Vleek looks kind of lonely. In Millersburg, Indiana, there is a light-blue water tower proclaiming the town's name—and attached to it is a light-blue microwave TV dish, sucking in the rest of the world.

The flags are at half staff in every town, lowered for thirty days at the order of the President to commemorate the death of a national leader. Red letters on a gray building announce the headquarters of the Concord Township Fire Department. The President of the United States may have to worry about putting out fires all around the world; here, in a town with flags at half staff, the men in the gray building deal with smaller fires closer to home.

Life is local if you let it be. The sun moves in the sky. A bus pauses and one man gets out. The Lake Shore Limited rolls past the bus and the man. From somewhere in the train, a voice announces that the dining car is finished with its service for the day. The voice says, "Remember, God loves you, and we're trying, folks."

TWELVE

In the Chapel

All the technologically awe-inspiring equipment in a modern hospital, all the rooms full of computerized monitors and heroic machines, yet at moments like this one you always end up in the chapel.

The chapel was on the fifth floor. One floor below, on four, my mother was in surgery. I knew that in the operating room she was surrounded by medical professionals. In the chapel I was alone.

Right up until the moment the call had come, so many things had seemed so overwhelmingly important. A new President was preparing for his inauguration; urgent front-page stories awaited developments; projects I had begun demanded my attention. All of it so important.

"Mother is in the hospital," my father's voice on the telephone said. "She was having some chest pains. . . ."

In the chapel on the fifth floor I looked up toward the empty pulpit with wet eyes. I hadn't had an abundance of time to get from Chicago to Ohio. By the time I knew that the surgery would be in the morning, I had missed the last possible airplane. It was almost eight hours in the snow and ice over the highways to Columbus. I had finally gotten to bed after 2:00 A.M., arisen a few minutes after 4:00 A.M., and arrived at Mount Carmel Medical Center before the sun rose.

My mother was in her room. Our family has always hidden everything with jokes. No jokes this morning. "Thank you for being here," she said. The nurses were already coming in and out, getting her ready.

The news broadcasts were reporting on the events that were going on involving the most powerful men in the world. A man I had never met before—Dr. Randy Miller—entered the room and explained the surgery he would be performing. He was thirty-seven years old, born in Dayton, and twenty-four hours before I had never heard his name. Now there was no person on Earth I needed to put more faith in, more trust.

Coronary bypass operations, if not routine, certainly are commonplace now. They are no longer uncharted territory. Until it's your mother who will be the person on the operating table. Dr. Miller talked to us, and I figured it out: The year my mother turned thirty-seven years old, this man was born. Thirty-seven years later, her life was in his hands.

My father arrived, and the nurses said my mother would be taken to surgery in five minutes. I got out of the room so my father and mother could talk privately. A son is always his mother's child, but at a moment like this a husband and wife should have some time alone.

They allowed us to accompany her as she was wheeled to surgery. You say a lot of goodbyes to your parents during the course of your life, most of them said without giving it much of a thought: leaving in the morning for school, going out at night with your friends, ending countless telephone conversations. On a morning like this one, you avoid that word. "Goodbye" is not something you want to say.

The waiting room on the surgical floor is not the happiest of places. Every set of lonely eyes in that room, looking toward the door, waiting for a doctor with an answer. My brother arrived from Colorado, and my mother's own brother was there, and the three of us sat with my father and after a few minutes I got up and said I would be back.

The lights in the chapel were dim, and I was just as glad that no one else was there. I knew that the doctors and nurses and technical personnel were relying on their years of training and experience, and I was relying on their training and experience, too, but I was also relying on something else. I bowed my head in the chapel and tried to put myself in the operating room.

Three hours later she was in the surgical intensive care unit, and Dr. Miller was saying that the bypass had gone well. A man in surgical scrubs said that he had been a part of the team that ran the heart-lung machine during my mother's operation. Meaning that while her own heart was stopped and out of service, he and his colleagues were her heart. "I think she'll be fine," he said.

The other doctors and staff members at the hospital, the nurses in the surgical intensive care unit and in the coronary recovery unit—they do this every day, and I suppose it becomes almost standard for them. I wonder if they have any idea how indelibly their faces and their voices will stay in the minds, the memories —the hearts—of so many families.

Days later, when the doctors said she was going to be all

right—when they said she was going to be cleared to go home
—I left her hospital room and said I'd be back in a few minutes.
I rode the elevator to five one more time. The chapel door was
open. It always is.

THIRTEEN

A Clean, Well-Lighted Place

BLOOMINGTON, Minnesota—I think I was somewhere around
the fourteenth hole of Golf Mountain when I looked beneath me
at the ludicrous sprawl of the Mall of America and realized that
this thing just may work.

Golf Mountain is about as high as you can get inside the Mall
of America; it's a miniature golf course, but like everything else
inside the mall it is built to outsized proportions; "miniature" is
a word that just doesn't apply here. So somewhere on the back
nine, I gazed out beyond the green—down toward the ground
floor of the mall, down past the corridors jammed with customers
(the mall is averaging 120,000 a day), past the seven acres of
amusement park rides, past the portion of the 333 retail stores that
were within my range of sight—and I figured there's a good
chance that people will keep showing up here.

You can do as much business-world analysis of the mall as
you like; you can ponder what the fate of the Mall of America
will mean in a troubled economy. My first day at the mall, that's
what I did—tried to guess at how a development on this scale
can possibly make a profit during a time when Americans are
afraid to spend their money.

But after a while, you begin to believe that the mall may make it for the simplest of reasons: People may love to come here. The scale of the place (4.2 million square feet set on 78 acres, 13,000 parking spaces, the Knott's Camp Snoopy amusement park sharing the same roof with those 333 stores inside the enclosed structure) at first glance strikes you as intimidating and far too huge. That's because you are conditioned to think of it as a shopping mall. My hunch—this is being written at the end of my second full day here—is that the developers don't want you to think of it as a mall at all.

They want you to think of it as a city. A new city, started from scratch. Sealed off from the outside world, with everything you would ever need inside its walls. Wealthy neighborhoods, not-so-wealthy neighborhoods, trees, shrubbery, a police force, a play area for the kids, nightclubs for people who like to stay up late, early-morning strolls before the stores open for people who crave quiet exercise . . . the thought seems to be: Whatever it is you have in the town where you live, we have it here, too, only it's newer, cleaner, safer.

No one is saying any of that out loud. But the message is unmistakable. The Mall of America advertises itself as "the largest fully enclosed combination retail and family entertainment complex in the United States," and points out that it is "five times the size of Moscow's Red Square." The true selling point, though, is that once you're inside, the real world seems locked out, held at bay.

At least it does from up on Golf Mountain. The comment you hear most often from clerks in the stores is that they started working here the day the mall opened, and they still have not even seen many parts of the structure.

What would seem to be a drawback of the mall—it's just too large to get a handle on—may turn out to be its main lure. The Mall of America is like a town you can't claim to have visited every part of; one group of people may gravitate to Bloomingdale's and another group may gravitate to Sears, some may shop at Brooks Brothers while others choose the Everything's $1.00

rock–bottom–remainders shop. You can spend a goodly amount of money for lunch at Tucci Benucch; you can grab an ice cream cone at a stand with no name. You can see movies on fourteen screens and you can go to the doctor or the dentist. In the back of your mind you have a hunch that the place has a mayor.

Once in a while you are struck by something small and quirky, something that doesn't seem to fit in here. One such place was a little room on the top floor of the mall where, for a couple of bucks, you could go inside and watch ten model trains whiz around on different sets of tracks. Nothing was for sale; the place seemed to be run by a model train buff. It didn't appear to be doing great business—I was the only spectator during the fifteen minutes or so I spent inside—but I liked it a lot. The model train room had the feel of a tiny candy shop in some old-fashioned downtown somewhere, tucked behind that city's most prominent department store. A modest and unassuming cubbyhole on Main Street.

The Mall of America is a new kind of Main Street, though —and Broad Street and High Street and just about any other street you want to name—and in this new sealed and self-contained city, the small and the quirky may have cut out a place or two, but not many more places than that. The model-train room may represent a piece of the Mall of America, but it's not really representative. Golf Mountain—now that's representative. From the fifteenth tee, you can see forever.

FOURTEEN

Full Circle

BEXLEY, Ohio—With all the sensational worldwide developments demanding front-page space and precious minutes on the evening news this summer, the fact that Marc Levison found his 1960 Ford Galaxy convertible all these years later probably doesn't rate headlines.

"I feel like I'm in heaven," Levison, forty-seven, said the other evening.

Levison's life never has been all that glamorous a one, and lately things have been determinedly downbeat. "I enlisted in the Navy right out of high school," he said. "What happened was, I graduated, went down to Ohio Bell to apply for a job, and they took my application and said they'd call me. I walked across the street and joined the Navy instead."

When he was in high school, he had owned the '60 Galaxy. "My dad and I had bought it used in 1963," he said. "Remember that little used-car lot on East Main Street? Right across from the Grill and Skillet? That's where we got it."

The car was painted a color called Yosemite yellow, with a white, black and yellow interior, which was visible to all when the top was down in the summer. "Only car I've ever loved," he said. "Eighteen feet long and drove like an absolute dream."

When he was at sea in the Navy, on an aircraft carrier off Vietnam, his father sold the car. "It didn't seem like all that big a deal at the time," he said. "It was cluttering up the garage, and he assumed I'd get another car when I got home."

Which he did. He worked as an electrician in central Ohio, married his high school girlfriend and raised two sons. Four years ago he began to have trouble walking. He was diagnosed with amyotrophic lateral sclerosis—Lou Gehrig's disease. As the illness has progressed, he has had to stop working.

He was at an auto-parts store—"JC Radiator and Auto Parts, you know, out on Williams Road"—looking for some hardware when he saw, in the back lot with some other old cars, a 1960 Ford Galaxy convertible. Yosemite yellow.

"It was like all the years peeled away," he said. "I can still drive—it's walking I have some trouble with. I had to have that car."

He bought it, assuming it was merely a car similar to the one he had driven. But on the inside of the driver's-side door he found a serial number.

His father, now dead, used to repair watches. He had left for his son a box of his watch-repair tools. In that same box, Levison kept all his own important papers.

"I looked in the box," he said. "There was an old piece of paper that said 'Car,' and a serial number. They matched."

So in this summer more than thirty years later, he is driving the car he was driving in the summer of 1963. "People see me, and they remember when I used to drive the car," he said. "When I'm driving that car, there's nothing in the world that can make me feel sad. I'm in a different world. I can't explain it. I turn on the radio, I head down the streets, I drive to places I haven't driven in thirty years. I drive around Virginia Lee Circle for no reason at all."

I mentioned earlier in the column that Levison finding his '60 Galaxy convertible was not front-page news. Actually, in Bexley, it was—he drove the car in the town's Fourth of July parade this summer, and the weekly *Bexley News* printed a story on page one. "What a feeling," he said. "Driving through town on the Fourth of July in that same car, and seeing the same people from all those summers before . . ."

I said I knew. I'd watched him in the parade. I said he and his car had looked great.

The prognosis of his illness is uncertain. He knows that one of these days he most likely won't be able to drive a car any longer. "My gait when I walk is not good now," he said. "But I'm doing okay."

One of his sons is about to enter law school; another is in college. He has been married to his wife, Eileen, for twenty-seven years. They live in south Bexley, past Main Street.

"I guess the reason I had to buy the car again was that it gave me the chance to find a little of the sixteen-year-old boy in me," he said. "It gave me the chance to have part of him back. The chance to have a little bit of 'Eileen, let's go cruising.' "

Scientists, from time to time, have debated whether people dream in color. It turns out that, beyond any question, they do.

Yosemite yellow. Over all the years.

FIFTEEN

"Why Weren't You His Friends?"

Curtis Taylor was a boy whom other boys liked to push around.

"Some kids, it happens to," his father, Bill Taylor, said the other night.

It was happening to Curtis Taylor a lot this year. He was fourteen, an eighth-grader at the Oak Street Middle School in Burlington, Iowa.

"Curtis was bullied for at least the last three years," his father said. "He was a very needing boy. He never really knew where he might fit in."

His dad said that Curtis would come home from school in tears on virtually a weekly basis. "He would tell us that the kids were picking on him again," his dad said. "He was very unhappy with himself. He blamed himself for the other students not liking him."

According to his father, a group of boys at the school took pleasure out of making Curtis's life awful. "Curtis told us that the other students had grabbed his head and kept banging it into a locker," his father said. "They gathered around and tripped him in the hallways. When he was walking in the hallways, they would come up to him again and again and knock things out of his hands, and when he'd pick the things up they'd knock them to the floor again."

Curtis, his father said, didn't have many people he could turn to. "He really didn't have any friends," his father said. "He tried to make friends with some boys from another neighborhood. But then they joined up with the group of kids who were tormenting Curtis, and they ganged up on him, too. So he was alone again."

On numerous occasions in the last three years, Curtis's father said, he went to Curtis's school to talk to administrators about what was being done to his boy. "I didn't get much of a response," Bill Taylor said. "I tried to let them know what all of this was doing to Curtis, but I don't think they understood."

In many ways, it's an old story: Some schoolchildren, sensing weakness and lack of confidence in another student, take glee in making the weaker student's life agonizing on a continuing basis. In most cases, the tormented students somehow manage to get through it.

"He came home crying after a particularly bad day," Bill Taylor said. "It was getting worse. His bicycle had been vandalized twice at school. The name-calling had increased. He had broken his foot, and it had been in a cast, and they'd kick the cast. He had two books that meant a lot to him, and they stole the books from him. He had a sweatshirt that he liked, and they poured chocolate milk on it in front of other students.

"He was crying and he said he just didn't want to go back to school anymore."

Bill Taylor wanted to talk to the administrators again, but his boy asked him not to: "He said it would only make things worse. He said that if people found out we were complaining, they would hurt him more and the harassment would increase."

Although Curtis's life was lonely, his father said that the boy tried to do good things. "He was on the honor roll," Bill Taylor said. "He interviewed Vietnam veterans in this area about their lives. He volunteered to help disabled students during first period at school."

On March 22, according to both Curtis's father and school officials, Curtis went to a school counselor, extremely upset—so much so that he was talking about suicide. The counselor reportedly talked with Curtis until he seemed calmer, then sent him home with some literature and the telephone number of a suicide hot line. Curtis and the counselor were supposed to meet again the next morning.

That night, at home, Curtis went into a bedroom and shot himself to death. He was found by his five-year-old brother.

"You can't go back and change what happened," said Bob Cameron, the principal at Oak Street Middle School. "Could all of this have been handled differently? Obviously, it could have. Would it have made any difference? That, I don't know."

But people need to stop closing their eyes to the kind of meanness that has long been condoned as an inevitable part of the school experience—it's long past time to stop pretending it's somehow excusable. Parents, teachers, other students—it's time for all of them to start comprehending the kind of indelible pain this can bring. Curtis Taylor was the third teenager in the Burlington area to commit suicide in a four-day period. "We are all trying to figure out what all of this means, and what can be done," said Bill Mertens, editor of the local paper, the *Hawk Eye*.

"When my boy died, there was a memorial service held for him, and at the school a big piece of paper was placed on his hall locker for the students to sign and say goodbye," Bill Taylor said. "A lot of them wrote that they thought Curtis was a nice person. But I could only think, where were you kids? Why weren't you his friends?"

SIXTEEN

Radio Days

Sometimes progress can be vastly overrated.

Panasonic, the electronics company, is vigorously marketing a new product that, by all objective criteria, is technologically remarkable. The product is a car radio.

It's not called a car radio, though—it's called the CQ-ID90. With the CQ-ID90, you punch one of six buttons. The buttons represent six different kinds of radio stations: rock, jazz, country-and-western, easy listening, classical and talk.

Then, wherever you drive in the country, your radio automatically finds the kind of station you prefer.

"This is a very sophisticated system," a Panasonic spokesman said. "We have identified more than ten thousand radio stations. We have classified them by program format, by location and by call letter. We've put all of this information on a computer chip inside the radio.

"So let's say that you're a rock fan. You're on a long trip. The rock station you're listening to starts to fade out. All you have to do is punch in the direction you're going—say, north— and instantly you'll get the strongest rock station in whatever town you're closest to. Plus, the call letters of the station and the name of the town will be displayed on a screen."

Well, it sounds nice. . . .

"It is nice," said another Panasonic executive, national marketing manager Rick Del Guidice. "What could be more convenient than this? You know what kind of music you like, and no matter where you drive, you automatically get that music on your radio. It's the ultimate in convenience."

Maybe that's the problem. The CQ-ID90 does, indeed, reduce music on the road to a convenient science.

But there's a quality that is more seductive than convenience. That quality is mystery.

One of the great treats of being on the road has always been the mystery of leaving the town where you live, heading off for somewhere you know nothing about, and hearing your hometown stations gradually getting softer and softer. And that's when you start to look for new stations.

It always happens suddenly. Your favorite disc jockey fades to silence, and you start twisting the dial, and right there on your radio there's a new voice, louder and, at least seemingly, fresher. You're out of town, all right; you're twisting that dial, and a new voice is talking to you. And you keep twisting, hearing the voices, deciding which ones you want to keep you company in the car.

"This is the same thing," said Rick Del Guidice. "Only more convenient."

But it's not the same thing. It's not mysterious, and it's not romantic. It's a computer chip that's dedicated to finding your favorite kind of music.

"It saves you so much more time," Del Guidice said. "In the major markets, you can have up to a hundred radio stations on the band. Who wants to spend all the time listening to all of them, trying to find something you like? With our radio, the radio finds what you like for you."

"How old are you?" I asked Del Guidice.

"How old am I?" he said. "I'm forty-six. Why?"

"When you were a teenager, did you ever used to take trips with your friends during the summer?" I said.

"Sure," he said.

"What did you do about radio stations?" I said.

"Oh, it was a great thing," he said. "The radio station I grew up with was WABC, which used to be the giant rock station in New York City. But one summer my friends and I drove all the way across the country. And somehow, without even knowing where we were, we were able to find the best rock station in every town.

"One of us would be driving, and one would be twisting the radio knob, and we'd listen for a few seconds and then one of us would say, 'Find another one.' We didn't know where we were, but we were always able to find the music we wanted."

See? That's exactly the point. What would the romance of that have been had the radio in the car been a CQ-ID90? What would he and his friends have felt like if a computer chip inside their car radio was constantly seeking out the strongest rock signal in every city and town?

"I enjoy using the new radio," Del Guidice, a loyal Panasonic man, said. "I enjoy how the radio finds the stations for me."

"Does it really find the best rock stations for you, like you and your friends used to do?" I asked.

"Actually, I don't program my radio to look for rock," he said.

"You don't?" I said. "What do you program it for?"

There was just the slightest hesitation before he gave me the answer.

"Easy listening," he said.

SEVENTEEN

Ties You Wouldn't Wish on a Dog

During what turned out to be an ill-fated attempt to buy some fashionable clothes, I made a startling discovery.

The startling discovery came in the minutes after I realized that if a man wants to buy a pair of fashionable pants these days, the pants are going to look like a pair of huge, billowing parachutes hanging from the man's waist. I knew that there was no way I was going to buy the parachute pants, but the sales guy had spent a lot of time bringing parachute pants over to me so that I could stand in front of a mirror and let them billow, and I felt bad just walking out.

So in this high-fashion men's clothing store, in an effort to give the sales guy some business, I said, "I don't think I'm going to get any pants after all. But maybe I'll buy some ties."

"Fine," he said. "I'll bring some over. What kind of ties were you looking for?"

"Oh, nothing special," I said. "Just some striped ties."

"We don't carry striped ties," he said.

"You're out of them?" I said.

"No," he said. "We don't carry them."

I thought this was bizarre: a men's clothing store that didn't carry striped ties.

"Your owner have something against striped ties?" I said.

"It's not just our store," the sales guy said. "There is no demand for striped ties generally. Men don't wear them anymore."

He then disappeared to the place where the store kept its ties, and brought me back a selection to choose from. I don't mean to be indelicate here, but the design on all of the ties looked like varying patterns of dog vomit.

"Don't tell me that men really wear these ties," I said.

"What do you think they wear?" he said.

"I don't know," I said. "Striped ties."

"Look around you on the street," the sales guy said. "This is what they're wearing."

And in the ensuing days, I took his suggestion. I looked around on the street. And he was right. Men are wearing ties with patterns that look like dog vomit.

Not flashy men; not boisterous men; not men who laugh loudly in public places. Regular men are wearing the dog-vomit ties—men you would expect to automatically wear striped ties.

(To be fair, some men are not wearing dog-vomit ties. They are instead wearing ties with patterns resembling exploding amoebas.)

There is an obvious reason for this. Men are going into clothing stores and asking to see the ties. What they are looking for is striped ties. They are being unilaterally told that men do not wear striped ties anymore. So they are obediently purchasing the dog-vomit ties or the exploding-amoeba ties, and they are obediently wearing those ties to work every day.

You don't believe this? Turn on your TV set and look at the men who appear on television. Even the news shows; even the business shows. Distinguished-looking, conservative-looking, somber-looking men. With dog-vomit ties. If you peer into their faces closely enough, you can see the pain. They don't want to be wearing dog-vomit ties. They want to be wearing striped ties, just like they've always worn, just like their fathers before them wore. But they have been told that there are no more striped ties. So they swallow hard and go with the dog vomit.

In all likelihood, even their elderly fathers are now wearing dog-vomit ties.

Men love striped ties; of this there can be no doubt. Ties

were meant to be striped. Somehow, though, the leaders of the men's clothing industry, for perverse reasons we probably shouldn't even think about, have decided that men shall wear dog vomit instead of stripes.

There's a happy ending to this, by the way.

I might have been unable to buy striped ties at fashionable men's clothing stores, but I found a place that had them in plentiful supply.

It wasn't exactly a clothing store.

Actually, it was the airport newsstand at Port Columbus in Ohio.

I was passing through my home state, and I was at Port Columbus to catch a flight, and there, right next to the cashier's counter, was a rack of striped ties for sale. Don't ask me what they were doing there.

Beautiful ties they were. And as cheap as a magazine.

I bought a Columbus *Dispatch*, a pack of Wrigley's Spearmint, and three striped ties. One red with blue stripes, one blue with red stripes, and another red with blue stripes.

The second red with blue stripes was identical to the first red with blue stripes, but I didn't know when I'd be back to the newsstand again, and I was afraid to the point of panic that they'd be sold out.

EIGHTEEN

Those Ties Refuse to Play Dead

This is the single greatest honor of my life. I am overwhelmed with pride.

In Abilene, Texas, the other day, an advertisement ran in the

Abilene *Reporter-News*. The advertisement was placed by an Abilene menswear store called F&S Clothiers. The advertisement featured several items. Sansabelt cotton pants were being sold for $35 a pair. Botany 500 blazers were on sale for $134.50.

And, displayed prominently in its own section of the ad, was this:

"The Best Selection of Dog-Puke Ties in West Texas. One-Third Off."

I felt as if I had just won the Academy Award, or the Nobel Peace Prize.

As many of you know, I am destined to go down in history as the Dog-Vomit Columnist, a fact that pleases me immensely. Ever since this column introduced the concept of dog-vomit ties, the phrase has been creeping into the national lexicon. Dog-vomit ties, of course, are ties that look like dog vomit. Might as well insert the customary disclaimer here—i.e., sorry for the indelicate phrase. But that's what they look like. Dog vomit. Because clothing-store owners for some reason love these ties, it has become close to impossible to purchase a simple striped tie anymore. All you see on the tie racks is dog vomit.

The story of the dog-vomit ties has been spreading by word of mouth—sorry—from coast to coast. But this advertisement in the Abilene paper broke new ground. "The Best Selection of Dog-Puke Ties in West Texas. One-Third Off." The spirit sings.

F&S Clothiers in Abilene is owned by Bill Standly, fifty-four, and managed by his daughter, Karla Brown, twenty-three.

"We ran the ad because so many people were coming in here and asking us, 'Do you carry those dog-vomit ties?' " Brown said. "They told us that they had read about the dog-vomit ties in a newspaper column, or that they had heard people talking about them."

Brown said that, like many men's clothing stores, hers carried dog-vomit ties almost exclusively. "It is an accurate description of that kind of tie," she said. "They do resemble dog vomit."

So when she and her dad were making up their next ad for the *Reporter-News*, they decided to feature the ties.

"It was my decision to use 'dog puke' rather than 'dog vomit,' " she said, taking full responsibility. "I know that 'vomit' might be a better word than 'puke' to run in the newspaper, but I went with 'puke.' "

Accompanying the ad were pictures of two dog-vomit ties, and a photo of a dog sitting on a chair.

And the response?

"It's been great," Brown said. "People have been calling and coming in, asking if we still had any dog-puke ties left. They're afraid they may be too late. Most of them know what it means —you don't have to be too observant to know that these ties look like dog vomit. But some people who saw the ad have called and asked what a dog-puke tie is. And I tell them, 'It is a tie that is multicolored and has designs on it, what looks like dog vomit.' "

Since the ad ran, she said, business has been heavier than usual. "Some people come into the store holding the ad in their hands," she said. "They point to it and they say that is what they want. They ask me what they can wear a dog-vomit tie with. And I tell them: 'Your dog vomit is very versatile. You can wear dog vomit with a wide range of suits and sport coats.' "

The irony, of course, is that the entire purpose for the original dog-vomit columns was to protest the proliferation of those ties, which have driven out stripes. Now, at least at F&S Clothiers, dog vomit is being used as a label of distinction.

"Here in Abilene, we're about two years behind Dallas, as far as clothing goes," Brown said. "So the columns about the dog-vomit ties, plus our advertisement, have helped people feel fashionable. It gives them a hint about what to wear. Although I must say, ladies who are buying ties for their husbands or boyfriends really like dog vomit, but men still ask for stripes."

At the *Reporter-News*, Pam Deffenbaugh, advertising account representative, said: "When the ad copy came in, I double-checked with the store to make sure they wanted to say 'dog puke.' They confirmed that they did. Which was fine with us."

Any complaints from readers?

"None at all," Deffenbaugh said. "Everyone knows what those ties are. They are ties that look like dog vomit. It's obvious."

At F&S Clothiers, Brown said the store plans to extend the ad campaign.

"You can see it in the customers' eyes as soon as they come through the door," she said. "They've come here for one reason. And if they hesitate and ask what I think about a particular tie, I say to them: 'That dog vomit will look good on you.' "

NINETEEN

Rubber Match

Two recent stories in the news about American life offer a bizarre look at what our world has become.

The first story is out of Akron, Ohio, and concerns what has happened to that once-mighty producer of tires.

The second story is out of San Francisco, and concerns a new fashion trend for stylish young women and men.

Let's start with Akron. The tire industry there is just about dead. The legendary Goodyear Plant No. 1 closed back in 1975; now Bridgestone/Firestone, Inc. has just relocated to Nashville. The last auto tire to come out of Akron was made in 1977. The last truck tire was made in 1981. The last aircraft tire was made in 1988. Akron, which used to proudly call itself the Rubber City, essentially doesn't manufacture tires anymore; only racing and experimental tires are made there.

It's a huge blow to a city that defined itself by being the world capital of tire making. Akron's economy was built on rubber; at the University of Akron, the football stadium is called the Rubber Bowl. All of that is ending.

Now, to California.

National news stories have reported a hot new fashion craze: People like to wear clothing and accessories made out of tires.

"We make handbags, we make belts, we make wallets, we make jewelry, we make shoes," Cameron Trotter, thirty, told me the other day. "All of this is made out of old tires. We sell them ourselves, and we also sell them through high-fashion stores."

Trotter is a partner with Mandana MacPherson, twenty-six, in a company called Used Rubber U.S.A.

"People just seem to love wearing things made from tires," Trotter said. "We've even made miniskirts from tires. We're talking to Bloomingdale's about carrying our line."

There have been reports of rubber clothing for several years now—pants, dresses, shirts. Among a certain high-style set, women are even said to wear rubber underwear—rubber bras and other rubber undergarments. Apparently there is a certain erotic aspect to this.

I wouldn't know about that, but MacPherson of Used Rubber U.S.A. said most people who wear tire rubber are doing so just because they like the way it looks.

"We have a real mix of customers," she said. "There's a funky crowd, and very high-fashion people. Many people seem to like it best when their rubber items actually show the name of the tire manufacturer. We're proud of our work. We use all-aluminum rivets."

Now, there would seem to be an old-fashioned American can-do solution in all this.

In Akron, the economy is hurting because the great rubber factories aren't making tires.

In California, apparently there's this big new demand for tires. Not to put on cars, but to wear on a dinner date.

What if the Akron rubber factories started manufacturing clothes instead of tires?

"I can't see it," said John Mesko, treasurer of Local 7 of the United Rubber Workers union in Akron. "First of all, I can't imagine people really adorning themselves with a tire. On a hot day? I mean, rubber is very heavy.

"And even if this fad did catch on, there are millions upon millions of scrap tires all over the country. You don't need new tires to make these clothes, I would guess. You can use the old ones. We'd love to have the work, but I just don't think the clothing business is the answer."

Over at the international headquarters of the United Rubber Workers, Curt Brown, a union official, was equally skeptical.

"If we were to make clothes?" he said. "It would be piddly. Just piddly. What the city of Akron could use is a plant turning out fifty thousand or sixty thousand tires a day. That's what it used to be like here. Clothing wouldn't do it."

He tried to understand why people would wear old tires as clothing. He just couldn't.

"I guess the only rubber clothes I might wear would be the heels of my shoes," Brown said. "I don't want to question the people you say are wearing rubber tires—but, you know, rubber doesn't have a terribly good odor. I don't see it. People in California will try anything, I guess, but I don't see this having any big effect in Akron."

Out in San Francisco, the owners of Used Rubber U.S.A. say that making clothing out of old tires is not only environmentally sound, but also provides a vagabondish sense of roving: People who wear clothes made out of tires can think about all the places those tires have been.

"And we keep coming up with new fashion items," Mandana MacPherson said. "We make an absolutely beautiful rubber briefcase."

TWENTY

Life Story

The funeral service was held at the Broad Street Presbyterian Church, back in my hometown. I flew to Ohio for the service not only because I had been close to the man being memorialized, but because I admired him so much.

He was ninety-five years old when he died last week; his name was Leigh Koebel, which probably doesn't mean much to people outside of the town where he lived. He was in the real estate business, and that, too, is not unusual. He closed his office only in the last year; at the age of ninety-five he was still going to work. His health was such that he could not drive a car downtown, so he stood at a bus stop on Broad Street. He wore a suit every single day.

He was married to the same woman for seventy-three years. I never heard one person even intimate that he was ever dishonest in a business dealing, or mean-spirited in a personal relationship. He went out of his way to make strangers feel comfortable; if a person walked into a room and that person seemed to feel a little alone or a little ill-at-ease, he would approach the person and introduce himself and ask some questions to draw the person out. This was at the age of ninety-five, mind you; at ninety-five he seemed to feel a responsibility for others in the room.

When I say that I never heard a person say a bad word about him, that is no exaggeration. And I would have heard such words if they were being spoken. Instead people marveled at him. Not because he was the wealthiest man in town; he wasn't, although

he did very, very well for himself by conducting his business honestly. Not because he was the most famous man in town; he
certainly wasn't, in fact he was a model of self-effacement, he
seemed to enjoy seeing other men and women flourish. What
people who knew him marveled at was the one quality that seems
to be vanishing so quickly in our world: an absolute and overrid-
ing sense of decency.

I meet so many people who take shortcuts on their way to
success. In some quarters of this country, that has almost become
a badge of honor: the easier the path someone takes in amassing
a fortune, the more that person is admired. It is as if by putting
something over on less sophisticated citizens, a man or woman
today has shown how smart he or she is. The theory seems to be
that the money is out there for the taking, and only a sucker has
to work diligently for it. Speed is what counts; why waste time
when you can "do a deal" on the telephone, or hit some computer keys and move some cash around?

I know so many people like that; so many people who have
all the angles figured. Those people would undoubtedly find
something very foreign in a man who, at ninety-five, waits for
the bus to take him downtown to his office; who, at ninety-five,
puts his suit on every morning because that is the way a man is
supposed to dress when he is conducting business.

The Broad Street Presbyterian Church is a majestic old building, a building that invites a hushing of the voice as soon as you
enter its doors. The men and women who filled the pews of the
church the other morning were not there because they had to be;
when a man dies at the age of ninety-five he has few contem-
poraries still alive, and there will be few people to chastise you
for neglecting to show up at the funeral service. So the men and
women who filled the pews were there because they wanted to
be; they were there because—and this is another phrase that may
be going out of style—it was the right thing to do.

I have read thousands of obituaries, and by necessity the obituary writers attempt to sum up the most important aspects of a man's life or a woman's life in the first paragraph: president of this, chairman of that, winner of this award, recipient of that honor.

What you don't often see in the lead paragraph of an obituary is this: that the person who has died could look in the mirror every morning of his life and never be ashamed of the person he saw looking back. I think that is what drew the people to the church: the knowledge that they were saying goodbye to a person who never had to apologize for who he was, or how he lived, or the way he treated other people. To a person who somehow, at some point, had determined that yes, a life can be lived that way.

The service was not long; the morning was exceedingly warm. I know that every person in the church was glad that he or she had come to say goodbye to Leigh Koebel, who was married to the same woman for seventy-three years, who was ninety-five when he died in his sleep, and who, every morning, looked into the mirror and saw looking back at him a man he could respect and like. Wearing a suit, every day, even at ninety-five, because that is what a man wears when he goes off to work.

TWENTY-ONE

"I Tell Her That She Is Beautiful"

The judge, who has seen many terrible things, cannot get this little girl off his mind.

"I think about her, and I don't know what's going to happen

to her," Cook County Circuit Judge Richard Neville said the other morning. "She has had such a tough road, and I'm afraid that it's going to get even tougher for her."

The prosecutor deals with meanness every day. This is a kind of meanness that haunts her when she goes home at night.

"It is just now that Delenna has started to get really brutal teasing from other children," assistant state's attorney Jennifer Borowitz said. "I don't know what can be done to help make her life happier."

The part that can be handled in a court of law has been handled. That part is almost over.

Delenna Williams, who is seven, was horribly burned when she was a baby, in a fire that killed her mother. The disfigurement of her body, including her face, was devastating.

Then, in March 1993, two of her aunts were looking for an apartment on South Marshfield Avenue in Chicago. Delenna was with them. They were walking down a dark gangway, trying to find the right address.

Four men were looking for a drug dealer with whom they had had a disagreement. They saw Delenna and her two aunts. They opened fire.

Three bullets struck Delenna. One of the bullets remains in her chest. Delenna's pet dog, Pup Pup—the one thing in her life she cherished—was with her that day. The gunmen also shot the dog. The dog, bleeding heavily, walked to the injured girl and began licking her face. "They shot Pup Pup," Delenna reportedly called out. The dog died in the alley.

The story of the shooting went quickly in and out of the news. This winter, before Judge Neville, the four alleged gunmen went on trial. Deron Jones, twenty-four, was convicted of attempted murder.

Later this month Judge Neville will sentence Jones. What happens to Jones doesn't really matter; he should be sent to prison for as long as the law allows, and then forgotten. But what of

Delenna? We have a system of justice, but where will justice be for her?

Her life has been filled with such unrelenting cruelty. After she was shot and her dog was killed, Chicago firefighters presented her with the gift of another puppy, which she loved.

But on Easter Sunday of 1993, as Delenna played with the new dog in front of her house, some young people approached her and pretended to befriend her.

"They made her believe that they wanted to play with her," her great-aunt, Rose Doyle, said the other evening. "But after about ten minutes they picked up the dog and ran off with it. That's why they had talked to Delenna—to steal her dog. We never saw the dog again."

Many people are casually horrid to Delenna, Doyle said. "It's so unkind, what people say to her on buses," Doyle said. "Delenna and I were riding one bus, and a woman looked right at her and told her she looked like a monkey."

Almost all of Delenna's hair was burned off in the fire when she was a baby. It will never grow back. Her great-aunt bought her a wig to wear to school. Last summer, when Delenna was in a corner store buying a soft drink, a teenage boy walked up to the child and set fire to her wig. It was pulled from her head before she could be injured, but now she does without it. In school, in court, she appears with just a few tufts of hair.

"She is such a nice, friendly child," Judge Neville said.

"I tell her that she is beautiful, and not to let anyone ever make her believe that she isn't," Rose Doyle said.

They live in an extremely rough neighborhood. Her elementary school is on a dangerous street. Medically, Delenna seems to be receiving good care; the Shriners Hospital for Crippled Children is treating her without charge. The question is, what will become of her? What can be done—by any of us, by all of us— to salvage her life?

Her great-aunt speaks of her most fervent wishes for Delenna.

That the child could live in a safer neighborhood, that she could go to a school in a place where she felt secure.

But the main wish her great-aunt holds for her is one that seems all but impossible. When she says it out loud, it is spoken with a wistful, faraway tone, like whispering a secret dream:

"If people would just be nicer to her."

TWENTY-TWO

After Hours

It felt like snooping around some huge office tower late at night, when no one was there. It felt like sneaking into a hundred private offices and seeing what was what. But it felt different from that, too, because the only clues were the voices.

It was a Sunday evening, and I had dialed one of those 1-800 numbers in an effort to place an order for something. Apparently I had gotten one or two digits of the phone number wrong; a mechanical voice on the other end said that I had reached the headquarters of a corporation. I have no idea what the corporation was; its name consisted of three letters of the alphabet.

The mechanical voice instructed me to punch in my corporate code number. This did not seem to be a 1-800 number for the public to use; this was a number for the employees of the corporation. Instead of hanging up, I hit a few buttons, just to see what would happen.

The mechanical voice told me my code was invalid. I did it again. Again, no good. I kept doing it, wanting to find out how this would end up. After a few minutes I realized that I was entering only three digits, which weren't enough. So I started hitting four buttons, to provide four-digit codes.

The machinery continued to reject me. But after six or seven minutes, a second mechanical voice came on. It welcomed me to the corporation's internal communications network. It instructed me to dial the extension of the person I wanted.

So I was inside; I was authorized to connect with the people who worked there. For almost thirty minutes I punched buttons at random, and listened to voices of greeting, inviting me to leave messages.

The voices were mundane and bizarre at the same time. Whatever this corporation was, it had offices in many cities. I heard voices from San Diego, Los Angeles, San Francisco, western Canada. All of these people seemed to work on the western edge of the continent, all of them for this firm.

The impulses behind the voices were what was fascinating. These men and women, if my supposition about the internal nature of this communications system was correct, knew that their taped messages would be heard only by fellow employees of the corporation. They knew they were talking to their bosses and colleagues.

As impersonal as large corporations are supposed to be—as impersonal as electronic voice messaging is supposed to be—the voices told a different story. There was a human element here that was almost poignant. I knew none of these people, but their voices sounded as if they were trying out for something. Their voices made it clear that they had each rehearsed this—not only the words, but the presentation—before committing it to the internal network.

There was a man who was gruff beyond possibility; he was intent on letting his colleagues know how busy he was. There was another man who was attempting to be willfully paternal— every syllable he spoke gave off the underlying message: Come to me with your problems and I'll fix them. There were men who had secretaries say their names for them; it was as if they felt that by leaving their own voices in the system, they would seem less important.

One woman sounded angry; why would a person deliberately choose to present a furious welcome to any colleague who called? Another said, "Have a good day," at the end of her message. She was the only one who did that—she seemed to have missed the decree that there should be no frivolity here. Some men and women were forceful in keeping their greetings as short and blunt as possible. We're here for serious matters and we don't want to fool around, those curt voices let the rest of the company know. Other voices seemed almost desperate for the internal caller to like them and to leave an optimistic message.

These were like résumés, these were like studied presentations at an ostensibly casual corporate retreat. These were like finger-prints. I found myself thinking about all these men and women before they had joined the corporation; I thought of them as chil-dren. Children who had yet to consider that someday they might be digit-coded stopping points in this corporation's internal web. Defining their days by their duties at the corporation, and trying to make their messages make a point about them.

I had no business doing this; I was not a part of the corpo-ration, I should never have punched into the system. An outsider is not supposed to do that. An outsider is not supposed to snoop around an office tower late at night, when everyone has gone home. I had no business doing this, but I did. I didn't leave any messages. I just switched from voice to voice, from life to life. When I finally hung up, I realized that I had no idea what any of these people did for a living.

TWENTY-THREE

Bilko's Daughter

Bilko had a daughter.

Actually, he had five of them. A recent column I wrote about the old *Phil Silvers Show*—the 1950s TV series that starred the late Silvers as Sergeant Ernest Bilko—prompted a lot of responses from readers who agreed that the show was the funniest in TV history, and that Silvers was the funniest actor. Of all the responses, the most gratifying was from one of Silvers's daughters —Nancy Silvers, thirty-two, of Los Angeles.

"My father was twenty-five years older than my mother," Nancy Silvers said. "So when my sisters and I were little, our dad seemed sort of like a grandfather with a million stories. You know how grandpas will sit in a chair and just talk? That was our dad."

I guess I had never realized that Silvers had children; the persona of the Bilko character was so strong that the idea of Bilko with kids didn't register. "In terms of discipline, he never raised his voice to any of us," Nancy said. The exception, she said, was when her dad would go into the "Bilko bark"—the Army commands made famous on the TV series, when Bilko would snap orders to the soldiers in the motor pool.

"He'd do that as a joke," she said. "He'd tell us to go clean our rooms or something, and he'd do it as Bilko."

Her father's voice around the house, she said, was much gentler than the one on TV—a "smaller voice," she said. "With us, that's the way he talked. But let anyone at all walk into the house—the gardener, the milkman—and he was immediately on.

The voice would turn right into the Bilko voice. Even when his friends came over. He only dropped it when it was just the family."

She said her father had a depressed side. "He was like a lot of comedians in that sense," she said. "It seems to come with comedic genius. All his comedian friends were like that—they all seemed to have a dark side. It's no secret that my dad gambled— a lot. All of the TV sets and radios in the house were always turned on, because he always had to know the sports results. There was probably never a day when he didn't have a bet down."

The girls didn't like to watch him on TV. "It was too weird to have him in the room and on TV at the same time," Nancy said. "We would see him on the screen with the actors who played the motor pool soldiers. We said we were watching 'Daddy and the dirty men.' I guess because the soldiers on the show were always smoking and gambling and doing dirty tricks."

Even though Silvers was not conventionally handsome, his daughter said she has heard stories all her life about how women fell in love with him. "His first wife was a Miss America," Nancy said. "My mother was his second wife, and she was the Revlon Girl and a Miss Florida. He always had these gorgeous women falling for him.

"I've said to my mom, 'What was it about him?' She said he was very sexy, and that all the women adored him. He was my dad, so when I was five I would have married him in a second. But over the years I've heard so many stories about the women who fell for him—I mean, Grace Kelly. I don't think it was just a case of him being funny—you can't make love to a sense of humor. I think it was a combination of things. I think women loved him because he was very safe and paternal. And at the same time he had this enormous command—he exuded confidence. Pretty powerful mixture."

Silvers wrote one song in his life—"Nancy (With the Laughing Face)," made famous by Frank Sinatra. "He didn't write it for me," Nancy said. "He wrote it for Sinatra's little daughter, Nancy. It was before I was born. My dad was at Sinatra's house, and there was a birthday party for Nancy Sinatra, and my dad hadn't brought a gift."

So Silvers and the composer Jimmy Van Heusen ducked into a back room and when they emerged they had written "Nancy (With the Laughing Face)" as a gift. Sinatra loved it and recorded it. When Nancy Silvers was born, she was named after the song. "It was the song I chose to be played at my wedding," she said.

Now that she is old enough to appreciate her father's talent, "I am in awe," she said. She has some old scripts from the Bilko show. Something she has found in those scripts makes her understand just how good a performer her dad was.

"Remember, that show had some of the best writers in the world—Neil Simon was one of them," she said. "I look at the scripts. The specific dialogue for each character is written out. And all through the script there would come certain times for my dad to speak, and the notation would be: 'BILKO: Says something funny.'

"He was making it up as he went along. And the writers knew to give him the leeway. 'BILKO: Says something funny.' I love that."

TWENTY-FOUR

Victory

The guy in the next seat on the airplane could have been a character in a movie about big business and ambition. He had picked up the in-flight telephone even before he fastened his seat belt, and by the time we taxied away from the gate he had already made three calls.

He didn't waste a word. His secretary had provided him with a printout of calls to make, and as we took off from Newark Airport, heading west, he worked his way down the list, by time zones. East Coast first, to catch people in their offices before they went home for the day. He kept punching in the numbers, announcing his name and company, going into his pitch.

He was aggressive and he was combative and he was nonstop, and here, five miles in the air, it didn't even matter. I leaned back and blocked out his voice, because something I had seen back in the airport had already made the day a good one.

It had been at the ticket counter in the main lobby at Newark. This had been a broiling, muggy, oppressive day in New York, and everyone heading out of town seemed to be in a foul mood.

All of us were lined up in one of those queues that snake their way back and forth between metal stanchions, separated by thick colored ropes. When you get to the front, dragging your luggage, you look up and down the length of the counter, waiting for an agent to be free.

These airport transactions are done mechanically and by rote most of the time; both the travelers and the ticket agents have been through all of this on too many occasions before, and there is seldom the impulse for a human connection to be made. Everyone has somewhere they're supposed to be, and the goal is to keep moving.

Today, though, I sensed that something out of the ordinary was going on. It took me a few seconds to figure it out.

I had advanced to third in line. Up ahead, at one of the ticket-counter stations just to my right, a woman who appeared to be in her twenties was speaking with an agent. The woman gave every appearance of being what used to be referred to as retarded, and now is more often described, with more compassion, as developmentally disabled. I am not certain if a nonphysician can make a sure observation of Down's syndrome from a distance of ten or fifteen feet, but that appeared to be the case.

She was working on exchanging a ticket. I knew because I could hear her parents talking about it.

They were right next to me, her parents were, waiting on the other side of the ropes. They appeared nervous and hopeful and maybe a little bit frightened; if you have ever sat in a high school football stadium next to the parents of one of the players, you know what their frame of mind was as they watched their daughter.

This was hard. This was a big moment. This meant something.

I listened to them talk to each other. She, and they, had decided that this was the day she was going to try this. She was going to do it on her own. She would succeed or fail on her own, without their help.

And she was working at it. That much, looking over at the counter, I could see. I could see this, too:

I could see that the ticket agent was not rushing her. I could see that, on this hectic airport day, the agent somehow understood just how monumental this bit of business was. The ticket agent worked with her, and the woman did her best to carry out her transaction the way she wanted to—the way she had practiced it—and this mattered. This was part of one person's, and one family's, history.

The other travelers did not complain at the wait. Some knew what was transpiring and some didn't, but no one said anything unpleasant in an effort to hasten the progress of the line, no one gestured at the ticket agent. The grown daughter worked to make sure that she transferred her ticket correctly, and this meant something.

Her parents . . . I wish you could have seen the look in their eyes. I don't know their story; how can you ever know the story of a family like this one? But I know this: When the transaction was complete, when their daughter came back to them bearing the ticket, I thought they were going to cry with pride. With pride, and with happiness for the smile on their daughter's face.

You never know when you'll find a moment. Now, next to me five miles in the air, the fellow on the telephone barked a strategic insult at some business associate somewhere down on the ground. I didn't care. Let the guy snarl. I was still seeing the look on that woman's face. She did it. Yes she did.

TWENTY-FIVE

A Shortcut to the Finish Line

I received a shocking piece of news about a boyhood friend:

He retired.

"He retired?" I said.

"He retired," I was told.

The guy in question is forty-four years old.

The news suddenly changed everything. The man who retired was once a sixteen-year-old kid in whose company I drank my first beer, a kid who had a ready laugh and absolutely no idea of what he wanted to do for a living when he grew up. Now I was being told that he had retired.

This was one of those moments during which you realize that the old rules of envy no longer apply.

People—at least people with even a marginal level of ambition and human frailty—often go through life with one eye on men and women their own age, especially men and women who work in the same field they do, or with whom they grew up. It's a contest, mostly a silent contest, that generally starts when people are in their twenties.

Does he have a better job than I do? Is she making more money? Did he just get an impressive new title? Was she promoted to manager? Did he just buy a house? Did she and her family move to a better suburb?

As people grow older, this tends only to intensify. Did he just make vice president? Was she named partner? Did he receive a national award? Was she written up favorably in the newspaper?

People may hate themselves for doing it, but they can't help it. The contest is beyond their control, and they're always measuring themselves against the accomplishments of others. It has probably been this way since the beginning of time. Make more money; get a bigger office; be named to the board of directors; show everyone you're moving up.

It seems that the contest will never end, that there's no finish line. People who are lagging behind in the race set their eyes on the people ahead in the distance, and think, "I'll get there someday. He's winning right now, but if I try a little harder . . ."

"He retired," I was told.

My goodness. My childhood buddy apparently declared the race over. He proclaimed victory for himself. He's no longer working. He retired.

At forty-four?

This is a man who's had extraordinary good fortune in the world of business. He has made so much money that he never needs to work again. None of us could have guessed that he would have been the one—can anyone, ever?—but he, indeed, was.

And he has long had all the trappings of his success. Beautiful house, frequent trips to exotic destinations, great cars, you name it. Everything for people to envy. I suppose I never thought about what could possibly come next for him.

"He retired," I was told.

I called him. Same voice as the kid who drank his first beer and laughed at the idea of being drunk for the first time.

"You retired?" I said.

"I retired," he said.

The story is a long one, and involves more than a little executive-suite intrigue. But the basic detail is, one morning in March he decided it didn't make sense for him to work anymore. He retired that day.

He isn't looking for a new position somewhere; "retired" isn't a euphemism, it isn't some fancy way of saying "between jobs." He has no plans to work again.

He is aware that many will frown on the idea of a forty-four-year-old man retiring. He's already hearing some of the remarks. He repeated some of them to me—when I heard them, I realized that they must undoubtedly have been uttered with the same tinge of jealousy with which people comment on others' salaries, or titles, or mansions.

But this is new. If you can be envious of a man's paycheck or his real estate, think of how you might feel about a man who has given himself the greatest luxury item of all: the rest of his life without work.

And without, of course, the need to work. Some of us get up in the morning and head for the office or the factory. Some of us get up and worry about getting a job in a dismal employment environment. Most of us know people in both of those categories.

This, though, is different. I've never known anyone my age who up and retired.

"What do you do every morning?" I said.

"Read the paper," he said. "Go work out. There are some men I've been exercising with. They're good guys, but I just wish some of them were younger."

"How old are they?" I said.

He laughed. "I asked in the sauna the other day," he said. "One of them is eighty-four. The other is eighty-two. The youngest guy I exercise with in the morning is seventy. I guess there aren't a whole lot of retired people our age."

This may take some getting used to.

TWENTY-SIX

Alma Mater

"We're doing this because the world is changing," said Roy A. Haberstock, president of the educational products division of the L. G. Balfour Company.

The name of the company may sound familiar to you. Balfour, with headquarters in Attleboro, Massachusetts, is one of the nation's largest manufacturers and purveyors of high school class rings; you may have bought a Balfour ring when you were in high school.

"Things just aren't the same in the class ring business as they once were," said Haberstock, fifty-eight. "When I was in high school in the early 1950s, the history teacher would stand up and announce that he was taking orders for class rings. We'd all wrap bands around our fingers to measure them, and he'd tell us to bring in our $24.95 the next day. It didn't occur to anyone not to order a high school ring. It wasn't required, but it might as well have been."

No more. Class rings are a harder sell in American high schools than they were forty years ago. Which goes a long way toward explaining what the Balfour company is doing.

Namely, selling class rings from the fictional West Beverly High School of the television series *Beverly Hills, 90210.*

Correct. Balfour is launching an advertising campaign designed to sell young Americans class rings from a TV high school that doesn't even exist.

"We have every expectation that the West Beverly High class rings will quickly become our biggest seller," Haberstock said. "Certainly a bigger seller than the class rings of any real high school."

Class rings are supposed to provide their wearers with lasting memories of the wonderful times they had in high school. After discussing it among themselves, Haberstock and other Balfour executives came to the conclusion that a huge number of young Americans would probably rather remember the good times of West Beverly High than the times they're experiencing in their own schools.

"Let's face it," Haberstock said. "I'm sure that most high school students look around the hallways and realize that their friends at school are not nearly as exciting as the characters on that TV show."

So Balfour, in addition to selling class rings at real high schools, has just begun to market the West Beverly High rings. They're black and gold, they sell for $48, and they are being advertised in national magazines. Balfour couldn't be any more serious about its plans for these rings.

"At a real high school, even the biggest high school, we would do well to sell five hundred or six hundred rings to a graduating class of perhaps a thousand," he said. "And that would be one of the largest high schools in the country. With these West Beverly High rings, we will be very surprised if we don't sell at least a hundred thousand rings. And we could very well do much better than that.

"I don't think there's any question about it—these rings from that TV high school will appeal to young people who would prefer to be going there than to their own high school."

He said he does not think young people will consider the rings to be a joke: "Kids want to be part of a group, and from

what I understand the group of characters on *Beverly Hills, 90210*
is a very desirable group to be a part of. So our customers for this
ring will feel good that they can wear the ring from the school
where Luke Perry is a student."

Is Luke Perry the name of the actor, or of the character he
plays? "I think it's the name of the character," Haberstock said.
"Is that right?"

The interviewer was not sure.

"In any case, we think that the West Beverly High ring is a
good value," Haberstock said. "For forty-eight dollars, it's a high-
quality ring. It's not as high-quality as our class rings for real high
schools—those go for around two hundred dollars—but it's a real
piece of jewelry that we believe people will wear and keep."

So Balfour's corporate position is that the class rings from the
fictional TV high school will end up in dresser drawers decades
from now, the same way that real class rings from real high schools
traditionally have?

"We think so," Haberstock said. "After all, why do people
keep their high school rings? They keep them to remind themselves of good times when they were young—football games,
dances, friendships.

"We're living in a new era. Today's teenagers, when they
look back at the time when they were young, will remember,
among other things, watching a lot of TV. So yes, they'll keep
the ring. It will bring back many fond remembrances of high
school activities, even if those activities did happen to take place
on television."

TWENTY-SEVEN

Moonstruck

The answer is so simple, it's shocking that no one has thought of it before.

Our country is in terrible financial trouble. The national debt is soaring, manufacturers are laying off workers by the thousands, foreign economies are making ours look weak and pitiful . . . and we don't seem to know how to turn things around.

And the answer is just so simple.

"We ought to cash in on the most valuable piece of property there is," said Robert Marrs, a high school social studies teacher and learned philosopher who lives in Athens, Ohio. "It's rightfully ours, and we ought to start putting it to work for us."

And that piece of property is?

"The moon," Marrs said.

His point is well taken. This country spent an astonishing amount of money in the sixties and seventies in our effort to go to the moon; we succeeded, and we still are the only nation whose citizens have actually walked on the moon. Six American flags are planted in the moon's surface.

Yet we make no money on it. Zero. Zip.

"How could we have let this happen?" Marrs said. "People seem to have forgotten that we conquered the greatest natural resource there is. The way I figure it, the moon is ours. Let's make it start earning a living!"

It's hard to tell Marrs that his idea is foolish. At NASA head-quarters in Houston, spokesman Brian Welch said that between

1962 and 1973, the United States spent $20 billion on the effort to send Americans to the moon. He said that would translate to $95.3 billion in current dollars.

There were nine moon missions; on six of them men actually walked on the moon. The last moon mission was in December of 1972. Then we left the moon, never to return.

Twenty billion dollars and all that genius and courage. And what did we get out of it?

"Tang," Marrs said. "Tang, and Teflon."

His idea is that we officially claim the moon as American property, and then make it pay off.

"If you own something valuable, you can make a bundle," he said. "As far as I'm concerned, we own the moon."

There are international legal experts who would disagree with him. In 1968—before Americans stepped onto the moon for the first time—a United Nations statement of intent proclaimed that the moon was a resource that belonged to all the people of the Earth.

"Nonsense," Marrs said. "Look what Christopher Columbus did. He got to America and took it over from the Indians. When we got to the moon, there weren't even any people there. We have nothing to feel guilty about. It's ours."

He has several potential ways to make money from the moon—all of which would be applied to our national debt and pumped into our economy:

• Charge other countries money to go to the moon. "The Japanese just paid ninety million dollars to send one of their people into space aboard the *Endeavour*," he said. True enough: The Japanese did, indeed, pay that much toward mission costs in order to send nuclear scientist Mamoru Mohri along on the trip. "If riding around in the space shuttle is worth ninety million, think what going to the moon would be worth," Marrs said.

• Trademark the moon, and make foreign companies pay every time they use a photograph of it. "You take a picture of the moon and you're not an American, you write our government a check," he said. "Hey—we're the ones who spent all the money to go up there."

• Charge royalties every time the word "moon" is used in a song lyric or a poem. "It's private property, subject to tariffs," Marrs said.

• Encourage foreign countries to fly spaceships to the moon —and then charge them hefty landing fees. "What's wrong with that?" Marrs said. "We charge foreign airlines to land at American airports; think of the moon as simply another American airport."

The biggest moneymaker of all, of course, is the obvious one: We should sell the moon.

"Why not?" Marrs said. "We're not using it. I think the Japanese would love to buy the moon."

He has a point. Japanese investors have shown an affinity for purchasing prestigious American property—high-rises, golf courses, film companies.

"The greatest piece of property there is is rightfully ours, and we're not doing anything with it," Marrs said. "It was nice when we could afford it. But let's face it—we need the money."

TWENTY-EIGHT

Applause

The show was terrific, but the audience was the real treat.

The national touring company of *Guys and Dolls* had been in town for a while, and toward the end of its run I went down to the Shubert to see it. I was expecting something midway between wondrous and corny—*Guys and Dolls* is one of the legendary musicals of the American stage, but there's something inherently otherworldly today about the prospect of seeing men and women speaking loudly in Damon Runyon vernacular, and belting out "I've got the horse right here, his name is Paul Revere . . ."

Anyway, after arriving at the Shubert I started making my way to my seat, and I had an inexplicably good feeling. The orchestra hadn't begun warming up yet, so it couldn't have been the sound of their music. Then I realized: It was the people.

This was a World War II–generation crowd. Earlier in the summer, around the anniversary of D-Day, there were a number of stories about the men and women of the World War II generation, the generation that is starting to leave us. It may have been the most remarkable generation in our history; certainly it has been the most remarkable generation of this century. Coming of age in the Depression, winning the battle for freedom during the war itself, building a prosperous and civilized nation for their children in the years after the victories in Europe and Japan . . .

Not that they're all gone yet—in fact, one of the things I've learned is that they mightily resent sometimes being thought of in the past tense. If you wanted to spend a couple of hours enjoying something with them, a Saturday matinee of *Guys and Dolls* was the place to be. Certainly not all the audience members were in their seventies and eighties—but I'd say that *Guys and Dolls* had about as great a proportion of World War II folks in the seats as any entertainment you might name.

No barking their approval like dogs for these audience members; no cut-off jeans and backward baseball caps. No obscenities lacing their conversations; no pumping of fists or hooting at acquaintances a few aisles away. Among the many qualities of the World War II generation is an instinctive understanding that there are certain ways to behave in public. I don't know if they were taught it when they were kids, or whether they figured it out on their own. But if you've been to a beer-soaked outdoor popular music concert lately, or to a ball game where you're tempted to buy earplugs for every child in the vicinity so they don't have to hear the language in the stands . . . well, you would have liked sitting in the audience at the Shubert, watching Sky Masterson and Nicely-Nicely Johnson on stage while silently appreciating the men and women on all sides of you.

The show? All it was promised to be. There is a touch of inadvertent bittersweetness to *Guys and Dolls*; maybe in 1950, when it first went to Broadway, there was something racy and forbidden about the stage world of gamblers and streetwise Manhattan archetypes. Today, if Harry the Horse or Nathan Detroit were on the streets of an American city after dark, they're the ones you'd fear for and be protective of; in our stark and modern United States, they'd be far from cool and jazzy: They'd be easy pickings.

Which is part of the charm of seeing *Guys and Dolls* today. And though it wasn't planned this way, a bonus came with the price of the ticket—a chance to see the musical with the audience that it attracted, at least on this particular Saturday. "Adelaide's Lament," and "A Bushel and a Peck," and "Sit Down, You're Rockin' the Boat" . . . all were a pleasure to see and hear.

But, truth be told, not as big a pleasure as observing the men and women around me in the audience—those World War II men and women out on dates with the partners they seemingly had been married to forever. Among the many things they know how to do is have a good time. At the end of the show—after the reprise of the title song—the audience rewarded the cast with warm applause. I was cheering just as loudly as the rest—and my ovation was for the people in the seats, the people who won't be coming to theaters like this eternally. Guys and dolls indeed.

TWENTY-NINE

Courtesy Month

"Give compliments here and there and now and then. It's amazing how this will help create a pleasant working environment!"

What's that, you ask? Why, it's just one plank from Tom Danaher's platform in his effort to establish National Courtesy Month. Danaher, sixty-seven, of Las Vegas, has been trying to persuade Congress to authorize National Courtesy Month since 1977.

"Yes, I have been doing this for years, sir," he said to me. "But I am afraid I have had no luck at all."

National Courtesy Month, in Danaher's view, is needed because guns are not America's leading problem. Neither is crime, nor unemployment, nor drugs. What is the Number One ill that ails us?

"Impoliteness," Danaher said. "If people were more polite, all the other problems would go away."

He said he has beseeched news organizations with his pleas for National Courtesy Month, but no one appears to be interested. "I am getting the feeling that a person like me is considered to be a twit," he said. "But I do not think I am a twit. I think I am merely a polite man."

He distributes little posters, which he hopes will be hung in people's homes and offices. The messages are not exactly controversial or cutting-edge, which is probably why so few people display them. For example, here are a few of his slogans. Have you ever seen them hung on a wall?

- "Let's Watch Our Language. Thank You!"
- "It's Nice to Be Nice."
- "This Is National Courtesy Month. Please Participate."
- "Courtesy Is the Golden Rule in Action!"

"I am trying to get my point across," Danaher said. "But I seem to be doing something wrong."

He also hands out pamphlets, devoted to trying to persuade people to mend their ways. From a recent issue:

"What is our super special project? It's cultivating the habit of saying 'Thank you.' Whatever happened to 'Thank you'? How come we don't say this vital expression when it is required? Tsk! Tsk! Are we becoming a little *too* careless? Oh, I know! We're just a wee bit forgetful and a tad complacent."

Because courtesy is not the sexiest subject in the world, not the most passion-driven social movement, Danaher believes he may never succeed in his crusade.

"I am retired now, but I used to be a real estate agent in California, and when I would drive around I would observe people being impolite to each other," he said. "I thought to myself: 'Gee, this is terrible, really. Maybe I can do something. Formulate a program. Persuade people to be polite instead of upset.'

"But so far, I must admit, I have failed."

He continues to distribute his pointers for a more polite world:

- "Can we refrain from being uncomplimentary, telling tales or talking about our co-workers?"
- "In a conversation, everyone has equal time."
- "If we are 'Mr. Funnyman,' the jokes are on us, not someone else."
- "What sweeter sound to hear than the sound of our name. Let us get into the habit of addressing everyone by name; *no name, no existence!*"
- "The boss told us something? Let's do it, don't argue. Also, let's answer our superiors this way: 'Yes, sir,' or 'No, ma'am.' "
- "We must get into the habit of using the following expres-

sions if we are to be regarded as civilized: 'Hello or goodbye.' 'Good morning or afternoon.' 'Please.' 'Thank you.' 'I apologize.' 'Pardon me.' 'May I?' 'You're welcome.' I do not know why so many of us have difficulty in saying them. Also, *gasp!,* can we do *our best* to use a civil vocabulary and express ourselves in a civil manner?''

Despite his best efforts, Danaher feels that Americans are becoming less polite by the year. "People are discourteous even to members of their own households," he said.

He sounds just the slightest bit down these days. Perhaps this is because of what he sees when he looks at the calendar. For, in his dreams, National Courtesy Month falls in September. That is what he has been pushing for all these years—the designation of September as the big month. And once again September has passed, and October is with us, and still there is no National Courtesy Month.

"Perhaps they are right," he said. "Perhaps I am a twit."

"You're not a twit, Mr. Danaher," I said.

"Thank you," he said.

THIRTY

The Most Vivid Picture

I have just found my favorite clergyman.

He is the Reverend Phil Blackwell, pastor of the Trinity United Methodist Church in Wilmette, Illinois. Why do I admire him so much?

Because of a courageous stand he has taken on one of the most vital issues of our time.

Reverend Blackwell performs many wedding ceremonies; part of his duties consists of counseling the couples before the day they are married. He meets privately with them and discusses all kind of issues.

Because ours is an age in which people do not like to be told what to do, even by a clergyman, there are certain topics on which Reverend Blackwell does not offer unsolicited advice to the couples. Unless they ask, he does not discuss bedroom practices with them; he does not discuss their personal finances; he does not discuss their political beliefs.

But on one subject, he gives them very strong advice, in the most vehement terms.

"I tell them that they should not videotape their wedding," Reverend Blackwell said.

During the last decade, he said, he has seen a vast increase in couples videotaping their wedding ceremonies. At Reverend Blackwell's church, as at many churches, this is permitted. But the reverend does his best to talk couples out of doing it.

"I tell the couples in our counseling sessions that videotape is unforgiving," he said. "It preserves every twitch, scratch and frown. Our memory is a much better judge of reality. Our memory evaluates, edits and enhances.

"The power of the marriage comes from what we carry inside of us, not from the rerun of a pageant we are forced to watch from the outside. Videos distance us from the actual event—and eventually become the substitute for it."

Reverend Blackwell said there are certain exceptions: times when he thinks it is all right to videotape a wedding. "If a beloved member of the family is unable to attend—if a grandmother is in a nursing home, or a brother or sister is serving in the military—then videotaping the ceremony for them could make sense. Otherwise, I think it's a mistake."

The reason is that we are beginning to live in a society that is observed not with our eyes alone, but through the lens of a

camcorder. Go to a high school football game or a grade school
graduation; the parents are watching their children through a
video camera mechanism. Remember those weird and funny photos from the fifties, the ones that show audience members at a
movie theater gazing toward the screen wearing 3-D glasses? We
laugh at that scene now, but a parallel picture from our own era
would show a crowd of people at a public event, each person
with a camcorder held up to his or her face.

Which is why the brave Reverend Blackwell's stance on wedding videos is so heartening. "When I counsel the couples, I ease
into the subject gently," he said. "We'll be discussing a number
of things, and then I'll say, 'There's a matter I would like to discuss
with you . . .' And then I tell them how I feel about wedding
videos."

Reverend Blackwell practices what he preaches, by the way.
He has been a pastor for twenty-five years; he estimates that he
has given more than a thousand Sunday sermons. None of them
has been recorded on videotape; he has no video record of his
sermons.

"I don't think I'm missing anything," he said. "A sermon is
supposed to be an experience of the moment. It is supposed to
happen at a certain moment, and not be repeatable. A videotape
of something that happens in a church overrides the memories.

"What you should take away from your wedding is what you
remember in your heart. What's inside of you. Those moments
are yours to keep. They are not intended to be stored on a shelf
above the VCR."

Reverend Blackwell said about half of the couples he advises
against videotaping their weddings reject the advice; they go ahead
and do it anyway. "But the other half seem almost relieved that
they don't have to videotape it," he said. "There is such pressure
these days to videotape everything—many couples seem grateful
when I tell them they're not obliged to tape the wedding."

The pastor feels that he is probably destined to lose this battle

eventually; every day, camcorders become more and more popular, and soon people simply may not understand that you can
decline to videotape the important moments in your life.

"I'm just as glad that videotapes didn't exist during biblical
times," Reverend Blackwell said. "If the Sermon on the Mount
had been available on video, people would have been paying so
much attention to how Jesus looked, no one would have ever
noticed the words he was saying."

THIRTY-ONE

Musial's Thanks

ST. LOUIS—"When I saw the look in their eyes, part of me felt
happy," Stan Musial said. "But mostly I felt sad."

In St. Louis last week, the Cardinals organization, realizing
the terrible situation in which baseball finds itself during the players' strike, decided to hold its annual Fan Appreciation Day even
though there would be no game. The people of St. Louis were
invited to Busch Stadium so that the club could say thank you.

No one knew what to expect. Who would come to a baseball
park without the lure of a baseball game?

Amazingly—all right, thrillingly—almost 50,000 men, women
and children showed up at the ballpark near the Mississippi River.
They ran the bases, ate hot dogs, batted toy balls around, participated in throwing contests. They walked on the field where the
Cardinals play, and had such a wonderful time that the four-hour
event was extended to five.

It was the Cardinals' way of saying thanks to the fans, all right.

That's why the 50,000 came. And how many of the present-day Cardinals—the members of the current team—do you think bothered to show up?

Oh, you know the answer to that.

Zero.

"We would have welcomed the ballplayers with open arms," said Brian Bartow, a Cardinals spokesman. "Because of the strike situation we couldn't formally ask them to attend, but we would have been happy to see them.

"I told the St. Louis *Post-Dispatch* the day before the event that the players would be welcome. They wouldn't have had to participate in the activities—we would have been pleased for them just to wander around the park with their families, if they had wanted to."

Zero. Some of the players do not live in St. Louis, and left town when the strike began—but, as we have seen, major leaguers are willing to commute back to the United States from foreign countries if they have a union meeting. Apparently not for Fan Appreciation Day.

Which brings us to Stan Musial. One of the most magnificent players in the history of baseball, the best Cardinal there ever was, Musial is seventy-three years old now. On Fan Appreciation Day, he came to the ballpark to thank the people of St. Louis.

No one had to pay him a penny. The Cardinals organization asked him if he'd like to come, and he said of course. He posed for pictures with fans, he talked with them, he pulled out a harmonica and played a few songs for them. Stan Musial, lifetime batting average of .331, member of the Hall of Fame, retired from baseball in 1963. He has provided so many glorious moments for so many people—there is no need for him to thank any of us for anything. We are the ones who ought to thank him.

But there he was, saying thank you to St. Louis. On a day when no current Cardinals took the time to appear, there was Musial telling the fans: I am grateful to you.

"It's true," Musial told me when I spoke privately with him later. "I am grateful. The fans were always so supportive of our teams—they love our game. We all love baseball. I wanted to let them know."

He played his entire career in St. Louis—from 1941 to 1963. "Maybe that's why I feel such a strong connection with the fans," he said. "The only big-league uniform I ever wore was a Cardinals uniform. I don't know if that will ever happen again—players staying with the same team for so long. But when it happens, you feel something for your town."

Musial said that what is happening with baseball makes him profoundly sad. "It's just a catastrophe," he said. "It's the fault of both sides, but the main thing is it's just awful. That's what I mean about the look I saw in the eyes of the fans—they seemed happy to be at the ballpark, but you can't really be happy about baseball these days."

He said he is always heartened by how strongly baseball fans react when they see him. "It's been a long time since I've played, but they still seem to remember."

Yes, they do. They saw him in the ballpark here the other day, and they will remember Stan Musial forever.

And the current-day players—the players who didn't show up at Busch Stadium, the players who went on strike all across the major leagues?

Oh, they'll be remembered too. No one will ever forget them. They can count on that.

THIRTY-TWO

Honked Off

PARKERSBURG, West Virginia—You, like many of us, may have grown up in an era during which there were certain rules about what you did when you wanted your friends to join you for the evening, or when you picked up a girl at her house for a date.

Actually, there weren't "certain rules," plural. There was one rule, singular:

You didn't honk.

You didn't honk because it tended to drive parents crazy. If you were a teenage guy standing around the house in the evening, and your buddies pulled up and leaned on the car horn to summon you, you could look at your father's face and see it turning purple. And—especially—if you were a girl, and your date came to pick you up and honked the horn instead of knocking on the door, your dad was likely to threaten to forbid you ever to see the guy again.

Honking was rude. Honking outside the house was forbidden. People did it all the time, of course. But just because they did it didn't make it any more acceptable with your parents. "If that kid comes to this house one more time and honks on that horn . . ." You knew the routine.

"My own father was adamant on the subject," said Bob Hattman, the principal of Parkersburg Catholic High School in this Ohio River town of 33,000. "My father drilled it into us: If you wanted someone, you were not allowed to honk for them. You went up to the door and asked for them. My father said that car horns were for honking at other cars, not for getting people to come out of their houses."

Hattman, forty-six, was explaining this in the context of something that happened recently with his own teenage son. To put it in perspective, he was talking about how his dad would react back in 1964 when there was the sound of a honk outside the Hattman house.

"My dad would not permit us to go outside," Hattman said. "The rule was that if someone wasn't polite enough to come up to the door, then we were not allowed to respond to the honk. It was bad enough when we knew it was our buddies waiting for us out there, and we couldn't go out. But when it was a girl . . ."

That was worse?

"Of course," Hattman said. "In 1964, girls were usually much too shy to come knock on a boy's front door. They might work up the nerve to honk outside your house, but they would be embarrassed to come knock for you. And it killed me to know that a girl was honking for me, and that I wasn't allowed to go out to her car."

Nevertheless, the lesson that Hattman's father taught him— honking for someone is rude—stuck with him. "To this day, I won't honk at someone's house," he said. "Even at the house of a close friend or relative, I will get out of the car and go up to the front door."

He has imposed the same rules on his own children: No honking. If a Parkersburg teenager pulls up in front of the Hatt-man house and honks, the Hattman kids are not supposed to respond.

"And all of my children's friends know it," Hattman said. "They know the no-honking rule."

Which brings us to what happened recently. It is one more example, as if one were needed, of how the world we now live in is different from 1964.

"I was standing in the kitchen," Hattman said. "The phone rang.

"I picked it up, and a voice said, 'Mr. Hattman, can you tell Mike to come out?' "

Hattman was confused. Mike is the name of his sixteen-year-old son.

He looked out the window into his driveway. There was a car idling there. Inside the car were two teenage boys.

"It was the Prieto twins," Hattman said. "Daniel and David. They knew about my no-honking rule. They were calling me from their car phone."

The Prieto twins are friends of Hattman's son. "I was dumb-struck," Hattman said. "I'm standing there with the phone in my hand, and I'm looking at the Prieto twins talking to me from their Subaru station wagon. In my driveway."

Hattman said he called his son to the phone. "Mike just got on the phone, said hello to them, said he'd be right out, walked outside to their car—and they drove away."

What did Hattman do?

"I just stood there and looked," he said. "The no-honking rule has been such a good idea for such a long time."

But was this really a violation of the no-honking rule? Was calling from the car phone just as rude as honking? Or was it better than honking? Was it the same as coming to the door? What was it?

"I don't know," Hattman said. "I haven't figured it out yet. If I'd figured it out, I would know how I felt about it. But I don't know. If you have the answer to how I should feel, let me know."

THIRTY-THREE

What Do You Say to the Naked Guy?

The Naked Guy is no longer going to his college classes, a fact that has made national news and launched a thousand jokes.

There's a serious side to the Naked Guy's story, too, and while the serious side is probably not worth devoting undue amounts of time to, it ought to be addressed, however briefly.

The Naked Guy is a fellow named Andrew Martinez, who until recently was a junior at the University of California at Berkeley. Since the fall term, Martinez had made a practice of walking around the campus naked, going for jogs naked, sitting in classrooms naked, and eating in campus dining halls naked. He said his refusal to wear clothing on campus was his way of protesting the sexually repressive traditions he felt Western society observed.

In late January, Martinez was finally expelled from school. This seemed to surprise some people, and seemed to strike others as proof that society is, indeed, just as repressive as Martinez claims it is.

The truly intriguing thing, though, is not that Martinez has been kicked out of school—but that it took the university all fall and into the winter to do it. The presence of the Naked Guy— that's how he was popularly referred to—on campus all fall became something of an accepted part of the college routine. Students would walk to class, and there would be the Naked Guy, naked. No one in authority seemed able to figure out what to do about him.

This may be the ultimate example of contemporary society

being afraid to tell anyone that anything is wrong and off-limits. It doesn't matter whether you believe that the human body is a beautiful and sacred temple, or whatever—the fact is, a man went to classes naked for much of the fall semester at a major university, and the university couldn't seem to find the proper loophole in its regulations to make him stop.

Say you're a parent who sends your son or daughter off to college, and you read in the newspaper that there's a naked man who regularly walks around campus and even attends classes naked with your child. Would you accept the university officials' explanation that they can't figure out a valid reason to make the naked man get dressed?

There was a time, of course, when a naked man walking around a college campus would be locked up immediately, put in jail or sent to a mental facility. That kind of punishment is currently regarded as being out of fashion and excessively harsh. So while the Naked Guy roamed the campus, months went by as the authorities tried to come up with a reason to get rid of him that would hold up in court.

Indeed, the rights of the Naked Guy were vehemently defended by some students who could not understand why anyone should have the right to suggest that he put some clothes on. A seventeen-year-old first-year student named Michelle Murray told the San Francisco *Chronicle*: "He has the right to express himself however he chooses. If people don't like to see him naked, they can just turn their head away."

Chandra Griffin, a junior at the university, took the debate out of the realm of the purely philosophical when, discussing the Naked Guy's naked attendance in classrooms, she told the *Chronicle*: "There is the seat issue. I wouldn't want to go sit where he had. It's just not sanitary."

Yet during the months when the Naked Guy walked the campus naked, every precaution was taken not to hurt his feelings or violate his rights. Indeed, back in November, the university banished him from campus under a new policy forbidding public nudity—but immediately rescinded the ban when school officials discovered they had erred by not securing a vice chancellor's approval for the order. A university spokeswoman said at the time: "The university recognized that its procedures hadn't been followed. Mr. Martinez can come back on campus."

Even when the press reported late last month that Martinez would, indeed, be kicked out of school, a university spokesman at first would not give a reason for the expulsion, citing confidentiality rules.

Thus, a man was permitted to wander around naked on campus all fall—but the university was not permitted to violate his privacy by saying that he was being booted out for being naked. (Eventually the university did give a reason: The Naked Guy was expelled for failing to wear "proper attire.")

Now the university must prepare to defend itself for its thoughtless actions. The Naked Guy is said to be readying a lawsuit against the school. If he wins, he'll probably end up owning the place.

THIRTY-FOUR

The Naked Guy Speaks

"She wanted to know *what?*" the Naked Guy said, laughing.

"Your grades," I said. "She wanted to know your grades."

Our recent commentary about the Naked Guy questioned why it took the University of California at Berkeley so long to order him to put his clothes on—and then to toss him out when he refused to do so. But one reader of the column—Amy S.

Cohen, of New York City—had a specific question about the Naked Guy:

"I couldn't help but wonder—what kind of grades did this guy get? Is anybody else curious about this, or am I just weird?"

Her point was that if the Naked Guy was going to classes naked, he must be taking tests and handing in papers naked, too. How was he doing before he got expelled?

The university would not answer that question; school officials said that the Naked Guy's grades were confidential information.

But we called him, and, after expressing puzzlement that a woman in New York would be curious about his grades, Martinez did his best to answer.

"I had about a 2.5 grade-point average before I started going to classes naked," he said. "I would almost never wear a shirt, but I don't count that as naked. I assume that I'll get all F's for the semester when I was naked, so I guess that's the answer."

The semester when he was naked was the semester just past; he was expelled at the end of the term.

"I was taking four classes last semester," he said. "Russian History, Rhetoric of Legal Discourse, Racism in U.S. Law, and Rhetorical Theory."

He said he had attended each of those classes naked, but hastened to add that he did not attend every class naked every time.

"Sometimes I would wear, like, underwear," he said. "Or a bandanna hanging down to cover my [private parts]."

Anyway, back to his grades . . .

"I would not say that being naked directly affected my grades," he said. "It may have affected some other people's grades. This one guy complained that because of me, he couldn't stand to come to class. Couldn't deal with it."

And his professors?

"It didn't seem to bother them that much," Martinez said. "If I was a few minutes late to a class, I would hear people whispering, 'Oh, there he is, he's naked again.' Or, 'Look at him, he's so rad.' "

Did his classmates sit right next to him?

"Not usually," he said. "Unless I knew someone. I'd watch people's eyes. They'd usually look down and then look away. The women especially would move their heads 180 degrees away. Some of them would hold their hands over their eyes."

But we were talking about academics here.

"I took a couple of midterms," he said. "I think I was naked those days. In Rhetorical Theory, I got a B-plus on the midterm. In Russian History, I got a D."

Does he think he got the bad grade on that one because his professor penalized him for being naked?

"No, I just didn't know the material," he said. "I think it was an essay test. Something about comparing and contrasting the Kievan political culture with, like, feudal culture. I blew it, basically."

And he always sat with empty chairs on each side of him?

"Well, a couple of times people chose to sit next to me," he said. "I don't think women ever came up to me and said, 'How you doin', sweet thing?' One guy did sit down and say, 'Hi, dude.' "

Speaking of sitting down: When the Naked Guy was sitting in class naked, what were the chairs made of? Wood?

"There was a pretty wide range of chairs," the Naked Guy said. "There were some plastic ones, and some wooden ones, and some upholstered ones that were sort of roughed-up and had grungy-looking fabric. I'd bring a sweatshirt and sit on it."

Wait a minute. He'd bring a shirt to class not to wear—but to sit on?

"Oh, yeah," the Naked Guy said. "Some of those chairs, you wouldn't want to sit on them unless you put something between you and them. Not if you have any common sense."

THIRTY-FIVE

A Wedding Place

PORTLAND, Oregon—Scottie Pippen paused to sign an autograph in the lobby of the Bulls' hotel, and B. J. Armstrong walked toward the elevator pursued by excited young fans. Phil Jackson ate lunch by himself at a table near the window, and Bill Cartwright headed out the revolving doors for a late-afternoon stroll.

These were all little moments during the week just past in Portland, where the Chicago Bulls were playing in pursuit of a National Basketball Association championship. But for me, the time I spent here had a resonance I had not expected, a resonance that had me walking the hallways of the hotel and thinking of something far more personal than basketball.

This began the day the Bulls arrived. I called my parents long distance to see how they were doing, and when I told them I was in Portland they asked where the team was staying. I said the hotel was the Benson.

And my father said, "That's where your mother and I were married fifty years ago."

I'd never known that. I had been aware that my father had been serving with the Army and was in infantry training in Oregon during the early months of World War II, and that he had married my mother before being shipped overseas. But I hadn't known that the Benson was the place where the wedding had been held.

"Go down to the front desk and ask them," he said. "Tell them to look it up. Say that their records should show that a dashing young second lieutenant checked into their hotel on November 7, 1942."

"I don't think you'll be in their computer, Dad," I said, playing along with the joke.

But the next time I did walk past the front desk, I couldn't help looking over and trying to imagine my father signing the register on his wedding day fifty years ago. Last week, of course, many of the faces in the lobby belonged to famous athletes, to Horace Grant and Craig Hodges and Michael Jordan. The hotel has been refurbished to look as elegant as when it opened in 1913—all Circassian walnut and soaring ceilings and sweeping marble staircases—and I stood among the passing people this year and thought about two people checking in on a November's day in 1942.

"We didn't even stay the night," my mother told me on the phone. "We were married in a suite at the Benson, and we left that same night so that your father could go back to his unit."

"Mother got an apartment in Medford," he said. "I was with the Ninety-first Infantry, and we were stationed out on the desert. The Benson was a beautiful, beautiful place."

Fifty years. I thought about all that has happened in the world since 1942. In 1942, the nation was trying to persuade itself that the Depression was finally over, while living with the new and churning fear of what would happen in the terrible fighting in Europe. Franklin Roosevelt was president on the day my mother and father were married at the Benson; in the years since that day, their marriage has survived the presidencies of Roosevelt and Truman and Eisenhower and Kennedy and Johnson and Nixon and Ford and Carter and Reagan and Bush. Radio was king the day they were married; the nation grew from forty-eight states to forty-nine and then fifty, and airplanes took over most of the business of the passenger trains, and the interstate highway system was dreamed up and then built, all in the years since their wedding day at the Benson.

It must be so difficult at times for men and women of my

parents' generation, to have all that history, and to understand that to their children's generations the history means nothing. Had they told me about the Benson under other circumstances, I might not have given the particulars of their wedding day much thought. I'd heard parts of it before—about their best friends, Lois and Harry Hofheimer, coming to Oregon for the wedding, about the liquor bottle breaking in my mother's suitcase and spilling all over her bridal clothes—but if I hadn't been here, I wouldn't have felt what I was feeling.

"I think we had a meal before the wedding in a grill room in the basement," my mother said. I went down there; the room is called the London Grill now, but I was told that in 1942 it was called the Oak Room, and that the Oak Room was undoubtedly where my parents had dined that day. I stood in the doorway, looking in.

There was no National Basketball Association in 1942; that was one of the many developments in American life that came along later. Last week in Portland, I, along with much of the country, was caught up in the drama of the NBA Championship series. Before I left Oregon, I took one last walk around the hotel. Fifty years of marriage. There is more than one kind of championship in this life.

THIRTY-SIX

The Games People Play

I've been carrying two documents around with me for the last couple of weeks. Each of them has to do with sports.

The first is a brochure I picked up at a McDonald's restaurant in Greenfield, Indiana. Greenfield is in the eastern part of that state. I'd never been there before. Late at night I was riding on the interstate, and we pulled off, and the McDonald's was the only place we could find that was open.

We got our food, and I noticed a stack of the brochures on the counter. They were free, and they were sixteen pages long: "High School Basketball . . . Hancock County" the legend on the cover said. Inside were the basketball schedules for four schools: Greenfield Central, New Palestine, Mount Vernon and Eastern Hancock.

The brochure had that lovely local feel to it that all small-town sports schedules do. The Super Bowl may be a huge national event, and the World Series may make headlines around the world. In Hancock County, though, Greenfield Central (varsity and reserves) will be playing Pendleton Heights on February 19; the New Palestine girls' team will be playing in the sectionals the first week of February; Mount Vernon will be playing Lapel on February 5.

Even the advertisements in the brochure make you want to stick around to see these games. At Chicago's Pizza on State Street in Greenfield, fans can sit in on WOOO radio's (AM 1520) "Cougar Court" broadcast every Monday at 6:00 P.M. Type Style Full Service Printers on Main Street in New Palestine offers commercial and quick-print service, typesetting, newsletters and brochures (and I have a good guess about who printed the basketball brochure); Padgett Chevrolet Geo is "a friendly place to trade," and Fred Applegate runs the Applegate Insurance Agency.

I carry that basketball schedule with me, and it makes me wish I could sit in the stands and watch some of the contests. The other document I'm carrying around . . .

Well, I don't want to make too much of this. It was sent to me by the father of a six-year-old boy in the Chicago suburbs. The boy had mailed a letter last September to his favorite player on the Chicago Cubs. The name of the player is not really important here—he's not necessarily a villain, no more so than so many other contemporary big-league athletes. The father sent me a photocopy of the letter.

In the boy's handwritten letter—the handwriting shows the pride that boys and girls demonstrate when they are learning to spell and put words together for the first time—he tells the athlete: "You are my favorite player." He says to the athlete: "I hope you never leave the Cubs." He says: "I hope your knee feels better." He asks: "Do you think I could be a Cubs player?" Instead of "Sincerely" or "Best wishes," he ends his letter: "Your Best Fan."

In the letter, the boy asks for an autograph. According to the father, an envelope was sent to the boy within days.

There was no autograph inside, no picture of the baseball player. Rather, according to the father, there was a printed price list. If the boy would make a financial contribution to the athlete's foundation, he would receive an autograph in return. For $7, he would get an autographed baseball card. For $25, he would get an autographed baseball. There was an entire price range, the father said.

Now, this is nothing especially new. Many athletes have been charging money for their autographs for a number of years now. The father believes this particular athlete is a good role model for youngsters, and also believes that the foundation in the athlete's name does good things for underprivileged boys and girls. It's not as if the baseball player cursed at the boy.

Except the boy, at six, is a little less excited about his favorite baseball player now. His favorite player no longer seems like someone he would like to get to know. As the father says: "Going to sleep listening to your team on the radio, imagining what it must be like to wear the uniform, to throw a runner out at the plate from right field, is what keeps baseball's legacy alive. It is in this spirit that a first-grader writes his hero."

The son assumes that the baseball player was never given his letter. "He probably never did see it, Dad," the son told the father.

No tragedy here; no international injustice. It's just the way of the world, and the boy understands.

Although if he's interested, and if his dad wants to make the drive, Mount Vernon plays Noblesville on February 12. It sounds like a nice evening of sports, and I bet he could snag an autograph or two after the game. I just might see him there.

THIRTY-SEVEN

Treat

They'd lived in an apartment for a long time.

"Halloween was always very quiet in the apartment building," she said. She is thirty-one, a wife and mother; she works as a waitress at a country club. "We hardly ever got any trick-or-treaters. I think that children were reluctant to go into an apartment building."

This fall, though, she and her husband and daughter moved to a house. "It's not a big house, but it's very nice, and it's on a quiet street," she said. The family lives in Lombard, Illinois.

"We were looking forward to Halloween," she said. "For all the neighborhood children to come around."

Her husband works in a factory that manufactures food products—among them, corn chips. "At Halloween," she said, "the company gives employees cases of the corn chips to give out to trick-or-treaters. Those little lunchbox-sized packs of the chips."

So they were well stocked on Halloween. The weather was lousy on Halloween this year, but it didn't stop the children of the neighborhood from coming around.

"It was great," she said. "We must have had more than a hundred children come to the house. A lot of the girls were dressed as princesses, or as Disney characters. A lot of the boys were dressed as athletes."

There were seven adults in the house on the afternoon the trick-or-treaters came around. "Family members," she said. "Spending the day with us and seeing our new house." The adults took turns greeting the children and giving out the corn chips.

"There was this one boy," she said, "and he was dressed as a football player. He must have been around eight, maybe a little older. He came to the door all alone. My husband said to him, 'Haven't you already been here?' The boy shook his head no. So we gave him a bag of the chips."

The adults in the house talked about the boy; some of them agreed that, yes, he had been to the house more than once. "It was no big deal," she said. "But we figured out that he had come back several times."

About half an hour later, she said, the boy was there again. "He walked up the short flight of steps to our front door," she said. "His father was waiting for him down on the lawn.

"The boy handed us five packs of the corn chips. He said that he was sorry, and that his father had told him to bring them back. Apparently he had been to our house a number of times, and every time one of us had given him a pack of the chips.

"We thanked him for bringing them back, and we tried to hand him one of the bags of chips that he had just handed to us. But he wouldn't accept it. He said that he still had one pack of our chips at home.

"When the boy left, we laughed about the whole thing. But then my brother Bobby pointed out that this really wasn't the story of a kid who made off with more Halloween treats than he was supposed to. It was really the story of a great dad."

The father, she said, had evidently noticed that when his boy came home from trick-or-treating, something wasn't quite right. A lot of parents, in our sad contemporary times, feel the need to go through their children's Halloween bags to make sure there is no candy that has been tampered with or tainted. But this boy's father, it seemed clear, had noticed something else. He had noticed that his child had gone back to houses—or at least to one house—again and again.

"It would have been easy for the father to blow the whole thing off, or just to scold the boy," she said. "A lot of dads might even have congratulated their sons for getting so much stuff. For figuring out a way to come home with extra goods. You never know what goes on in people's houses.

"But this dad cared. He made his boy do the right thing— the hard thing. We don't know the boy or his father, but it made us feel great that the dad was teaching his son right from wrong in even the littlest situations. I hope the boy knows how lucky he is to have a dad like that. After they left, my brother said, 'You know, I bet you that boy really grows up to be somebody.' "

You can never be sure about that, of course. Who knows what factors help make one child turn into a success in life, and another child turn into a failure?

But on this Halloween—the first Halloween in their new house—the family in Lombard saw a lot of children, a lot of costumes. Only one of the sights will stick in their minds: a boy in a football uniform. And his father, waiting for him on the front lawn.

THIRTY-EIGHT

Words of Love

The wedding of Bob Love and Rachel Dixon brought smiles to a lot of faces. Chances are, some of the smiles may have been there for the wrong reasons.

Love—who, before the arrival of Michael Jordan, was the highest scorer in the history of the Chicago Bulls—got married the other night during halftime of a game between the Bulls and the San Antonio Spurs. The ceremony, performed on the basketball court and presided over by sportswriter Lacy J. Banks, who is also a Baptist minister, was, on the surface, the ultimate National Basketball Association promotion. A wedding at the United Center? With more than 20,000 "guests" in the seats? That's what most of the smiles were for—for the offbeat feeling of the idea.

Yet, for those people who have known Bob Love over the years, the smiles were mixed with genuine tears of emotion. Because as Love stood on the court and repeated the wedding vows—and then said "I do"—he was achieving a victory that, for so long, seemed beyond the realm of possibility. Love could always do remarkable things on a basketball court. Saying a few simple words was not one of them.

It is no secret that Love's horrendous speech impediments—"stuttering" and "stammering" do not do justice to the severity of what went wrong with his voice early in his life—were a problem for him during his basketball career. People have read about it and heard about it. But unless you knew Love during his days in the NBA, you can't really understand the depth of his torment.

It broke your heart to sit with him and try to converse—and it came very close to breaking his heart, and his spirit.

He was an NBA all-star on three separate occasions; thousands of people shouted appreciation for his athletic skills every game night. But then he would leave the arena, and he would be locked in this terrible, solitary world he could not find his way out of. He just couldn't talk—he couldn't get the words out.

He would sit for a minute, two minutes, trying to form a single word. Nothing would happen. His mouth would move, his face would contort—he tried so hard. Nothing. Finally the word would come from his throat—and then the struggle would start all over again. This man who moved up and down the basketball court with such grace could not master the skill of speaking a sentence.

I remember once, twenty years ago, sitting with Love in the house in which he was living at the time. This was on the day of a game. He was attempting so fiercely to have a conversation; he would manage to get a word out, and then everything would shut down. He would work on the next word he wanted to say, and the tears would well up in his eyes, the tears of frustration and shame. He was a big, proud man who, every day of his life, was made to feel small and insignificant.

After his basketball career was over, Love ended up working as a busboy in a restaurant. It was the equivalent of one of today's NBA all-stars—a Scottie Pippen or a John Stockton or a Patrick Ewing—clearing tables and washing dishes for some of the same customers who, only a few years before, had applauded their every basket.

Love was saved because some kind and caring people noticed what had happened to him, and arranged for him to at last receive the kind of expert speech therapy that eventually unlocked his private prison. He worked extraordinarily hard, and the people who were assisting him worked extraordinarily hard; first he was able to speak in one-on-one situations, and then he was able to speak with several people in a room, and finally he was able to speak before groups.

Which he does all the time now. He works as a community relations official for the Bulls, and on a regular basis speaks at schools and at neighborhood gatherings. Many people who hear him have a difficult time believing that this was a man who, not so long ago, could barely talk.

Which is why—with 20,000 people in attendance—it was such an extraordinary moment in Bob Love's life last weekend when he took his wedding vows. All of those eyes on him, all of those people watching. "I do," he said. Made you want to stand up and cheer. "I do."

THIRTY-NINE

Flood of Memories

DES MOINES—There was this moment the other night at the Iowa State Fair, a moment that stood out like a gorgeous scene on a vividly colored picture postcard: Lou Christie, the old-time rock-and-roll singer who had a string of hits in the 1960s—"Two Faces Have I," "Lightnin' Strikes," "Rhapsody in the Rain"—had come back onto the stage in front of the massive grandstand for an encore. He was at the fair as part of a rock-and-roll revival show; he had already sung all of his most famous songs, so for the encore he borrowed a ballad from another sixties group, the Association.

It was the sweet, gentle "Never My Love." There were almost 8,000 people in the grandstand on a warm and beauteous night, and most of them were on their feet, swaying to the music. In front of the grandstand, below the stage and off to the side, though, was the sight that was so pretty.

Twenty or thirty couples—people in their thirties and forties and fifties—had come down to dance. They were waltzing, really; there's no word that describes it better. The husbands and wives held each other, and it was August of this terrible Iowa summer, and at least for this one moment the terrible part was over, pushed aside. Lou Christie, microphone in hand, sang "Never My Love," and the people waltzed, and the troubles were gone.

It was an illusion, of course; the troubles in Iowa are still very much with the citizens, and no one knows how long it will take to recover from the horrors of the floods—some of the worst floods in the nation's history. More bad weather seems always just a few hours away, and the tears of summer remain fresh. Now, however, on this balmy and perfect evening the love song echoed throughout the fairgrounds, and the couples held each other tightly and danced in the night, and there was peace and a measure of contentment.

"Iowans did not have a summer this year," said Kathie Swift, spokeswoman for the fair. "This is our chance to have a summer."

Apparently so. A state fair is always symbolic in the Midwest, but this year in Iowa the eleven-day fair seems to mean something exceedingly special. "Iowa's celebration is a welcome break from fighting floods," the Des Moines *Register* editorialized; the crowds for the opening days of the fair have been large, and when you wander the fairgrounds and observe the patrons jamming the various booths and shows and exhibits, it is hard to conceive that for nineteen full days in July, the people of Des Moines had no drinking water.

"The fair is always a reunion for the people of Iowa," Swift said. "It is always Iowa's largest event, where we gather once a year to celebrate the best about our state. This year, though, it means more than usual."

From the big stage in front of the grandstand you could see

the nighttime panorama of the fairgrounds: the garishly lighted rides on the ten-acre midway cranking high into the air, then swooping down toward ground level; the people heading toward the twenty acres of farm machinery on display; the farm families who had come for the enormous livestock exhibits, bringing sheep and cattle and swine and horses, almost 14,000 animals in all.

When the fair ends, the reminders of the disastrous summer will remain behind, and the work will go on. President Clinton, when he visited Des Moines during the height of the flooding, said: "I've never seen anything on this scale before—to my knowledge there's never been an American city without water that was this large for this long a period of time." Kathie Swift, of the state fair: "Some people were predicting that this was the year we would have to cancel the fair, but we knew that wasn't going to happen. The fair is too important to the people of Iowa."

Almost 8,000 of those Iowans were in the grandstand tonight. They were eating corn dogs and drinking beer and soda pop; they had arrived early for the entertainment, watching Fabian open the show with his old hits, and then dancing to Little Eva as she sang "The Loco-Motion," and clapping while Bobby Lewis sang his Number One hit from 1961, "Tossin' and Turnin'."

Rock-and-roll revival shows like this one are always popular, because people love the music so much, but tonight was something especially fine, tonight there was something exceptional in the air. The evening's headliners, Jan and Dean, would be taking the stage in a few minutes to sing their good-time surf music, but right now Lou Christie was still in the midst of his encore.

"Never my love," he sang. "Never my love." And in front of him the couples waltzed, full of happiness, full of life. Full of summer, dancing in the starlight.

FORTY

Against the Wind

Four miles in the air, Frank Sinatra was dancing with Gene Kelly.

This was on a screen aboard an American Airlines flight heading east. An older man seated to my left—if I had to guess, I would say he was in his seventies—had an expression of gentle appreciation on his face as he watched Sinatra and Kelly. Both entertainers were wearing tuxedos; both were smiling and gesturing with the please-the-audience showmanship that was a hallmark of their generation.

The older man was listening to the Sinatra-Kelly audio track through an airline-provided headset; through my airline earphones I was hearing something else. There was a special presentation on one of the in-flight audio channels, and I had sought it out. I was seeing Sinatra and Kelly, but I was listening to the voice of Bob Seger.

We all have our own memories. The older fellow had a look of pure contentment as Sinatra and Kelly did an exaggerated buck-and-wing, and in my ears Bob Seger and his band hit the opening chords of "Ramblin' Gamblin' Man," and my neighbor and I had nothing in common and we had everything in common. I drank a beer in the sky and thought about drinking beer in another place, and listening to Seger for free.

He used to play at a bar in the town where I grew up; this was before he hit it big, there was no cover charge, Seger's band was the night's entertainment, and we were just at the age when we were allowed into bars for the first time. Buy a beer, walk the eight steps over to where the microphones were set up, and there was Bob Seger, having driven down I-71 from Michigan.

He wants his home and security; he wants to live like a sailor at sea. . . .

Tonight the airline magazine had noted this program on Audio Channel 8, spanning Seger's career. I listened to his music— "Travelin' Man," "Beautiful Loser," "Night Moves"—and I realized how many years it's been that his words and his voice have added something to my life. That kid on the bandstand, no cover, no minimum; that kid in the crowd, savoring the music.

I remember standing on the corner at midnight, trying to get my courage up. . . .

If you'd told Seger back then that, twenty-five years later, American Airlines would be piping his catalog of music into the ears of business travelers on their way to distant meetings, he might have thought you were making fun of him. Making fun, or drunk. If you'd told us back then that someday we would be the business travelers, and that we'd be listening to the same singer we were hearing near midnight at the Sugar Shack on Fourth Street . . .

Sinatra and Kelly danced. My neighbor to my left, hearing some banter from Sinatra and Kelly, banter I was not hearing, broke into a happy grin. We are all touched by different voices. Seger in my ears:

I found myself further and further from my home. . . .

We've gotten to know each other a little bit over the years; Seger is a nice man and a fine person to spend time with, but before I knew that, I knew how much his songs touched me, how comforting his voice and his words could be, and that is all that any of us should require of our music makers. There was bad weather up ahead, and the pilot's voice interrupted Seger's to say that we would be circling for a while.

Movin' eight miles a minute for most of the time . . .

Comfort then, comfort now. It is more likely that we have heard our fathers' music than that they have heard ours; my neighbor over in that seat to the left was listening to Frank Sinatra belt out a song—of course he was belting it out, I didn't have to hear a word to know that, Sinatra was punching at the air as if the air were Max Schmeling—and I have heard and loved Sinatra, but I doubted my neighbor had heard Bob Seger. A shame, really; memories, and memory makers, should be shared, not hoarded.

The pilot apologized and said that it would be at least another twenty minutes until we could begin our descent. Maybe more.

Seger's voice was on a loop of tape somewhere in the airplane: *Wish I didn't know now what I didn't know then.* . . .

I had an urge to tap my neighbor's shoulder, to ask how he was enjoying Sinatra and Kelly. I didn't; he seemed lost in his thoughts, and, besides, I knew from his face how he was enjoying his music.

Against the wind, I'm still running against the wind. . . .

The weather lifted and we descended through heavy clouds and the music stopped, and we passengers walked into the bright terminal. Down in baggage claim I looked around for the older fellow who had been sitting to my left, but I didn't see him. We'd already gone our separate ways.

FORTY-ONE

A Soul Is Always There

The saddening possibility exists that we will run out of names before we come up with an answer.

Joseph, Lattie, Robert, Delenna, Eric, Sarah, Richard, Shavon, Terrell . . . using the first names of the children, often in headlines, has become a signal that we realize children deserve to be treated gently, even in death, and even when the most unspeakable things are done to them by other people, or by agencies or judges entrusted to protect them.

So that's what we do. When something so horrid that it makes us ache is done to a child, something so horrid that it rises above the other daily horrors and makes the news, we refer to the child by his or her first name. Joseph, Lattie, Robert, Delenna, Eric, Sarah, Richard, Shavon, Terrell . . .

But it doesn't work. If the headline use of the first names is meant to humanize—humanize not only the children, but us, too—it fails. There are too many children and too many stories of terror and of failure, and too many names. A week, two weeks, a month after a child's name has become a headline name, the name becomes little more than a question mark. Let's see—was that the child who . . . no, that can't be right, he was the one who . . .

At this rate we will use up all the names. The death of Eric Morse last week would seem to be a landmark—would seem to be the one case that defines heartbreak once and for all, the one case with the power to crush us—but the truly crushing thing is that Eric's name will be supplanted by another name within a month or three, the list of first names growing longer even as we helplessly wonder what to do.

Five years old, thrown out of a fourteenth-floor window of a public-housing high-rise in Chicago, as punishment, police say, for refusing to steal. Five years old and—if the early reports of a motive are accurate—sentenced to death for wanting not to commit a crime. In the hours after the news of his death began to spread, an automatic question was posed: Was this a gang incident? It took a moment for the questioners to reconsider. Wait a minute. A gang incident? This child was five.

Five. The instinct to talk in terms of gangs is an effort to explain the unexplainable, to create a distance, a barrier. You could do away with all the gangs, you could even do away with all the guns, and you wouldn't begin to answer the most difficult question. Which is: Where do we now turn in a world where an eleven-year-old boy and a ten-year-old boy are accused of forcing an eight-year-old boy to loosen his grip on his five-year-old brother, thus dropping the child fourteen stories to his death? Where do we turn to extinguish the meanness and to fill the utter, screaming emptiness?

If there is even a whisper of an answer, perhaps it is, against all odds, to be found in the very circumstance of Eric's murder. For—if the official version of why Eric was killed is, indeed, correct—a rather amazing thing happened.

Which is that this little boy—this little boy who reportedly was born with heroin in his veins, this little boy who was beaten up before he died, this little boy who went looking for a clubhouse that other boys promised him was there, and then was lured to the window from which he was tossed—this little boy somehow learned, somehow understood, that it was wrong to steal. This little boy, who, we are told, was ordered to steal candy for the older boys, and was executed when he said no, knew the difference between right and wrong.

He was killed for it; he received the death penalty for choosing right over wrong. And his death proves something. We sometimes talk about the soullessness of today's lost children. There is no soullessness. That is what Eric has taught us. A soul is always there, at least at the beginning; a soul is there, when a child is young enough, when no one has stolen it or slain it. A soul is there, if we can arrive in time to save it.

The worst thought, the thought that makes you lie awake, is the thought of Eric's eight-year-old brother desperately holding onto his hand, trying to pull him back into the window—and of the other boys biting and scratching at the older brother's hand until he is forced to let go. The worst thought is the anguish of Eric's brother, for the rest of his life, knowing that he did everything he could possibly do to hold on, to rescue, and that he couldn't. That's our anguish, too, all of us, as we see the list of first names grow longer, and don't know what to do. That's our nightmare: that we want to hold on, want to help, want to rescue, and that we can't, that we have failed.

FORTY-TWO

Most Likely to Succeed

In the Connecticut town of New London last month, a judge died. His name was Thomas P. Condon. He was seventy-one, judge of the town's probate court. I never knew him, but I was very interested in an editorial that his local paper, the *Day*, wrote about his passing.

Judge Condon, the editorial said, "gave to each person the dignity that a human being deserves"—which is about as impressive a statement as you can possibly make about anyone. But the editorial made another point, too.

It said that Judge Condon, who was born in New London, lived there virtually all his life and died there, never yearned to move to a bigger city—specifically, never yearned to work for one of the giant, prestigious law firms in New York. Once, the editorial said, a New York lawyer visited probate court in New London, and asked Judge Condon why he was stuck in such a small town, using his obvious legal talent and knowledge in a place with only 30,000 residents.

Judge Condon, by way of an answer, asked the New York attorney how far he lived from work, and how long it took him each day to get into the big city.

The New York attorney said he lived a long way from work, and had to commute for ninety minutes each morning.

Judge Condon said that it took him seven minutes to get from his home to his office.

Both the New York lawyer and Judge Condon enjoyed playing golf. Judge Condon asked the New York lawyer how far he lived from his golf course, and how long was the average waiting time on a weekend.

It took the lawyer a half-hour to get to the golf course, and there was usually a forty-five-minute to one-hour delay before teeing off.

Judge Condon said his golf course was eight minutes from his house, and that there were usually no delays in teeing off.

The judge said that, in New London, it took him two minutes to walk to the place where he ate lunch each day—if he didn't run into someone on the street he wanted to talk to. He said it took him five minutes to get to the beach. And he said he lived in New London because he liked it.

That's what the editorial in the *Day* said. Judge Condon's life sounded like a pretty meaningful one. I called his son, Tom, who is a columnist in Connecticut for the *Hartford Courant*, and asked him what he thought.

"My father made the dean's list in college, and was voted most likely to succeed," Tom Condon said. "He finished number one in his class in Army Officers Candidate School. He would have done very well wherever he went, at whatever he wanted.

"What he wanted was New London. He liked where he lived. New London is a very small town—it's only seven square miles or so. In monetary terms he never became a very wealthy man, and he probably could have.

"Was he lacking in ambition? Absolutely not. A desire for material gain was not the driving force in his life. His ambition was to raise his family in a nice town that he loved, and to do the things he truly loved to do.

"My father loved to paint. He was a very accomplished amateur painter. Oils—he painted pictures of abandoned mills, and of barns, and of people and sailboats and lighthouses. All of it was real. All of it he saw around New London."

Did his son think Judge Condon had any regrets? "It's hard to say. I guess, to some degree, everyone does. There are things I think he would have liked to get around to. He wanted to write a novel, but never did."

The important things, though, Judge Condon accomplished. Maybe that was what was so heartening about the editorial his hometown paper published on the occasion of his death. It was a signal of what truly matters in this world of ours.

"Ambition?" his son said. "The question is how you define it. If ambition is to have all the toys when the game is over, all the dough, then he wasn't ambitious. If ambition is to have a life you can define and understand, to find a true community . . .

"My father's wake was on a terrible, snowy night. An awful night. There were more than four hundred people there.

"He was friends with all of his children, and he lived in a town he loved. Four hundred people at his wake. On such an awful night. Yeah, I think my father's life was successful."

FORTY-THREE

"The Way She Smiles"

He's a high school kid in the Midwest. He wasn't trying to make any profound social statements about the direction that life in our country has taken. All he was trying to do was get in touch with a movie star.

Actually, I'm taking his word for it that she's a movie star.

The actress's name, according to the high school student, is Reese Witherspoon. He saw her in a movie called *The Man in the Moon*, and . . .

We might as well back up here for a moment. The high school student wrote a letter and mailed it to the newspaper. He had seen this Reese Witherspoon in the aforementioned movie —it's out on videotape, he said—and he thought that we at the newspaper might have some way to get her address to him, or at least to forward a note to her. Here is part of what he said:

"Something happened as I watched her in this movie. I feel so stupid because, realistically, I'm sure this could never happen. But part of me is idealistic and, for better or for worse, hopelessly romantic. I want to write her a letter.

"I don't even know what I would expect out of this if somehow I could get an address to which I could send a letter. I want to know her. I've seen beautiful people before, in the movies and in my life. Maybe it was something about her smile, her expressions, her voice, or the way she walked. I don't know. . . . I can't stop thinking about her. And I desperately want to write her a letter. . . . Believe me, this has never happened to me before. I don't know what to do. But I have to do something."

Then came the key passage in his letter:

"I'm really a regular person. I get good grades. I play soccer, and I have a sense of humor. I hope you don't think I'm a sick person or some kind of stalker. . . ."

Which, of course, is a thought that may have already occurred to you. Today we all are aware of the reality of fanatical devotion to faraway stars.

And that's the sad thing here. I called the young man up; he's seventeen, and a varsity soccer player, and he says he's simply smitten with this actress from the movie. He summed up the plot of *The Man in the Moon* for me: "There's this girl and her sister, and they both fall in love with the same guy who moves in next door. The younger girl sees him first, but the guy falls for the older sister instead. . . ."

Ever since there have been movies—ever since there have been stars—people have developed crushes on the stars. That's what stars are for: to make people who will never meet them fall in love with them. When I was a kid, my sister used to write letters to Kirk Douglas (who, like all of us, was once very young himself) in distant Hollywood. I am quite sure that my sister never thought it necessary to assure anyone that she was not a deranged stalker.

But today there's that need. Here's the student in the suburbs, and even as he's writing a letter trying to get information about this actress he's fallen for, he's savvy enough to anticipate that the stalker issue is going to come up, and to address it in advance. Recent social history makes this necessary; he knows it and we know it.

"I don't know what I would say to her even if I could get a letter to her," he said on the phone. "I just want her to know that I'm alive. It's hard to explain what's so special about her—it's not just the way she looks, it's everything. The way she talks, the way she smiles . . ."

Yep, we're in pretty somber times. If you're a kid who falls for a movie star, you know right away that you'd better be able to convince people that you don't mean to track her down and harm her. Not much fun. It must not be that much fun to be the movie star, either. Your goal is to make people like you, yet when they do, and they make their affection evident, you'd better be well-protected behind strong barriers. Those are the new rules.

I pulled some clips on Reese Witherspoon. Apparently she's a very talented young actress. She has received good notices not only for *The Man in the Moon*, but for a movie called *A Far Off Place* as well. "I know I'll never get a chance to meet her," her high school admirer said, and he's probably right.

My sister never got a chance to meet Kirk Douglas, either, but neither did she have to feel weird for wanting to. I told the guy that I'd be glad to forward a letter for him, to Reese Witherspoon's movie studio in Hollywood—a town that used to indeed feel like a far-off place, until the world got uncomfortably close, for the stars and for the rest of us, too.

FORTY-FOUR

The Children's Voices

Every school day, around 3:00 P.M., the calls will start.

"The voices?" said Monica Glaser, who is quite familiar with the sound of those voices. "It depends on how the children are feeling that day. Sometimes the voices will sound lonely. Sometimes the voices will sound scared. Sometimes the voices will sound like they just want someone to talk to. The calls are like check-in calls. It's as if the children are saying, 'I just want you to know I'm okay.' Even though the children don't know the people they are talking to."

The program goes by the name of Grandma, Please. It is sponsored and administered by the Uptown Center Hull House Association, in Chicago. Children—most of them children who come home from school to empty houses, so-called latchkey children—call a telephone number. They know the number because it is distributed on flyers to elementary schools.

The phones are answered by senior citizens who volunteer for this. The calls are forwarded from a central receiving station to the homes of the individual volunteers. "Our volunteers receive an average of eight hundred calls each month," said Glaser, who is the director of the seniors program. "The volunteers don't tell their last names to the children, and don't ask the children's last names."

The purpose of this?

"There are so many children who come home to an empty house every day after school because Mom or Dad are at work," Glaser said. "They have a key, they let themselves in, and they're alone. The routine is usually that they call their parent at work, to say they got home safely. And typically the mother or father will instruct the child not to leave the house until they get home from work."

So the children sit there. "They call us because they want to hear another human voice," Glaser said. "Usually a boy or girl will be nine years old when he or she first calls the Grandma, Please line. They may have heard a noise outside that scares them. Or they may just want to share some news with an interested voice.

"A child may say, 'Grandma, I got a hundred on my spelling test.' Or a child may say, 'My basketball team lost today.' Or, 'I got a bad grade in school.' They just want to share what happened to them during the day with someone who sounds interested."

Glaser is proud of the professionalism of the program: The senior volunteers are screened, trained and supervised. There is a resident social worker. But as pleased as she is with the way the program is administered, she wishes it didn't have to exist.

"We certainly wish it weren't necessary," she said. "We wish every child had a place to go after school where there was a parent waiting to welcome them."

One girl, Glaser said, calls three or four times a day, using a different name every time: "She just wants to keep talking to someone until her mother comes home." Others don't pretend to be different people—"They just call constantly, saying, 'I heard a noise, I heard a noise.' "

The thing that affects Glaser the most? "The ordinariness of it," she said. "The ordinariness of children coming home to no one."

The volunteers who take the calls are moved and haunted by them.

"You talk to the children and you wonder, 'What is this child like?' " said Clydie Martin, eighty-five. "You wonder, 'What is going on in this child's life and in this child's mind?'

"Some of the children are very remote and withdrawn, and you have to pull them out. Some are outgoing. But they're all calling because there is no one there when they get home, and they don't like being alone. The human voice makes a difference. To have human contact when there's no one around makes a world of difference. You hang up, and before you know it, it's ringing again. Another child."

Delphine Wolsko, seventy-nine, said, "I will tell them a riddle or a joke to draw them out. I think it's awful that these children have to come home to no one, I really do. Sometimes I feel angry at the parents, even though the parents have no choice but to work. The way the children talk, they feel very downcast walking into an empty house. Our service stops at six P.M. each night. I think about the children often after six o'clock. I feel so bad that I can't do more."

Estelle Brownstein, sixty-nine, has been a Grandma, Please volunteer for six years. "I have heard happiness, sadness, fear, anxiety," she said. "The children will say, 'Oh, Grandma, it's so nice talking to you.'

"We are supposed to limit the calls to about ten minutes. So when it's time to hang up, a child will say, 'I love you, Grandma. What is your name?' "

FORTY-FIVE

Requiem for the Glass Blowers

SARASOTA, Florida—I went to look for the Glass Blowers, but the Glass Blowers were gone.

There was a time when, if you wanted to attract enough tourists to put food on the table for you and your family, all you needed was a quirky idea and a storefront. This was especially true in Florida. The tourists were down here anyway, looking for the sun, and on rainy days they were yours to lure inside.

The Glass Blowers did a good job of it. I know that in the 1950s, when my father would take our family to Sarasota for spring vacation, we spent many a rainy morning at the Glass Blowers, watching them blow glass.

If memory serves, it was a no-frills operation. The Glass Blowers worked out of a structure on North Tamiami Trail. There was a man who blew glass and a woman who blew glass. It cost nothing to watch them. They made their money by selling the products of their glass blowing. Tiny reindeer and tiny birds, as I recall—blown from molten colored glass, with protruding glass eyeballs and button glass noses, yours to take home for a couple of bucks.

This spring, on a rainy morning, I decided to find out what the Glass Blowers were up to. I wondered whether—in a Florida-tourism age that is dominated by the ever-expanding Walt Disney World empire over in Orlando—there was still a place for the Glass Blowers. How do you convince a kid that an acceptable way to kill the morning is to watch the Glass Blowers blow glass, when all kids know that Space Mountain and the Big Thunder Mountain Railroad await them elsewhere?

The answer, apparently, is that you don't. Because at the site of the Glass Blowers—5230 North Tamiami Trail—a chic little restaurant called the Cafe of the Arts is now in business. They serve their food in the Glass Blowers' old building, and they say they have no idea what ever happened to the Glass Blowers.

Who might know? You would think that the owners of Cars of Yesterday might know. Cars of Yesterday, which is still in business, was another rainy-day Sarasota attraction in pre-Disney Florida, just up the street from the Glass Blowers. But the proprietors could offer no clue as to the fate of their former neighbors who blew glass.

Sarasota County's Department of Historical Resources was able to provide some Glass Blowers artifacts. Historian Ann Shank had an old Glass Blowers brochure, circa 1959. "The Glass Blowers Invite You to Visit Our Studio and Gift Shop," the pamphlet proclaimed. "No Charge. No Obligation. We Are Open 9–6 Year Round—Closed Sunday. The Center of the Attraction Area."

That was the problem, right there. The center of the attraction area? The Glass Blowers? Tell that to Mickey Mouse. More to the point, tell it to the marketing executives at the Walt Disney Company. There was a photo in the brochure of the Glass Blowers themselves: "Mr. and Mrs. John Deakin—Master Craftsmen. Owners and Operators." In the photo, Mr. and Mrs. Deakin were blowing glass—or, to be precise, they were heating the glass in preparation for blowing it. "A Fascinating and Educational Exhibition By Professionals Operating An Independent Attraction in Sarasota Since 1948—A Totally Different Experience!—Glass Actually Blown Into Shape By Mouth—True 'Made in Florida' Souvenirs."

According to county records, the Glass Blowers were first

registered as a Sarasota business in the late 1940s, by John L. Deakin. They stuck around until the 1980s—when they abruptly disappeared. An April 1961 edition of "What to Do and See in Sarasota" said of the Glass Blowers that it was "one of the most unusual attractions in Sarasota . . . attracts more than 40,000 visitors each year. . . . Only five families in America practice the Bohemian glasswork." There was a picture of two of those miniature glass reindeer, with pert glass eyes.

Rainy days in spring may be eternal, but the center of the attraction area is ever shifting. Could something as elementary as the Glass Blowers ever draw 40,000 visitors a year in our current world? Would tens of thousands of people drop in just to watch tiny birds being born from hot glass?

In any event, the rain in Sarasota this day eventually lifted, doing away with the urge to seek indoor amusement. Maybe the Glass Blowers are dead. Maybe they are simply over at Walt Disney World, waiting in line at Splash Mountain.

FORTY-SIX

Son of the Glass Blowers

"I'm their son."

You're whose son?

"The Glass Blowers'."

You never know. The recent column about the Glass Blowers wondered what had happened to them. No one in Sarasota seemed to know the answer.

Then their son called.

He is John R. Deakin, fifty-four, a pilot who flies 747s for Japan Airlines. He was phoning from Seattle.

"I blew glass too," he said. "My parents had me start blowing glass when I was twelve years old. I hated it. I cannot tell you how intensely I despised blowing glass. Every minute I put in at the Glass Blowers was against my will."

He said both of his parents are dead; his father died in 1980, his mother in 1982. He holds nothing against them for making him blow glass: "Dad learned to blow glass during the Depression. In those days, having a trade was a valued thing, honorable work. We never had much money, but blowing glass gave us everything we had."

He left home as soon as he graduated from high school—to get away from the Glass Blowers and learn to be a pilot—but he can still describe, in detail, blowing the glass:

"Sometimes there would be people standing thirty and forty deep in the shop, looking at us. We worked at two elevated fire benches, with two sets of fires. Dad worked the one closest to the center, Mother the one closest to the wall.

"You would take a glass tube—the smaller ones were one-quarter inch in diameter, the larger ones an inch—and you would pick a point near the end and you would heat perhaps two inches of it, always rolling it. Roll it, roll it, roll it . . . if you stop rolling it for even an instant, it sags and it drips.

"We made all kinds of little items. The one I remember the most is these little glass nests. Little glass birds' nests. Making those nests was a process like knitting, but with glass. Green glass in the bottom of the nest to look like grass, and three little white glass eggs. I must have made a hundred thousand of those glass nests. How I hated it. . . ."

He said that the assumption in the column—that the Walt Disney World era did away with the Glass Blowers and other simple Florida tourist attractions—is correct. "Oh, how Dad hated Disney," he said. "He considered Walt Disney World to be a giant sinkhole in the middle of the state, taking all of our business. We would be driving in the family car, and when Dad would see a State of Florida sign that mentioned Disney, he would go into orbit."

Deakin realizes that his parents' business may have been destined to failure even if Walt Disney World had not come along. "When they died, I was shocked to find out just how little money they had," he said. "They owned the Glass Blowers building— we lived in the same building—but they had been able to save virtually nothing.

"My younger sister Kathrine took over the business after my mother died. Kathrine did not blow glass—she just ran the place as a store. My father, before his death, had blown enough glass to leave a considerable amount of goods to sell. But fewer and fewer people were coming in, and when they found out there was no one actually blowing glass, they lost interest.

"I felt very bad for my sister. Toward the end, literally days at a time would go by without a single customer coming in."

In the late 1980s, the Glass Blowers was sold and converted to a restaurant. Deakin said he was surprised to read the story about the Glass Blowers in the paper, and was happy to be able to answer the questions. He never goes back to the place, he said, but he can never forget it.

"You could easily cut your mouth blowing glass," he said. "You had to be careful, putting that thing in your mouth. I tell you, words cannot describe how much I hated it. . . ."

FORTY-SEVEN

The Lesson by Interstate 29

PLATTE CITY, Missouri—The restaurant by the side of Interstate Highway 29 was not at all crowded on a Sunday morning. The service was slow; the waitress had explained to the customers that a new cook was at work in the kitchen, and was having some trouble learning the routine.

At one table sat a woman who appeared to be in her late forties or early fifties, chain-smoking. With her were a younger man, his wife and their son, around two years old. They all appeared to be related. They were talking loudly enough, and the restaurant was small enough, that it became evident they were on their way to church.

The older woman asked the waitress where the food was, and the waitress repeated her statement about the new cook.

"Well, tell her to get her ass in gear," the woman said. Her tone was impatient.

The waitress said she didn't know whether she wanted to relay that message.

"If you don't, I'll be glad to," the woman at the table said. "I'll go back there and tell her to get her ass in gear."

She did not seem to think there was anything improper about loudly using that particular phrase in public, and in front of the young boy at her table. She said to the child: "Ain't you going to drink any of your juice? Ain't you?" The boy looked at her with a smile. "Ain't you, honey?" she said.

At a table across the way, another family was sitting. Father, mother, son of around six or seven. The waitress had not had a chance to take their order.

The father and son didn't seem to be bothered by the delay, but the mother clearly was. She stood up and, with surprising anger, said to the waitress: "I don't have to take this kind of abuse." She stormed out of the restaurant, her husband and son following within a few seconds.

What were we seeing and hearing here by the side of I-29, with trucks and cars whizzing by just a few feet from the restaurant's windows? Everything and nothing, really; matters of import, or nothing earth-shattering, depending on your view of our world.

The woman with the message for the cook—the language she chose to use was nowhere near as offensive as some things you hear on America's streets and in America's malls. She was doubtless a product of the slow disintegration of our society, and not the cause of it. But there were other people in the restaurant, and there was the little boy. "I'll go back there and tell her to get her ass in gear." Children learn, and rather quickly. "Ain't you going to drink any of your juice?" Children learn.

And the other woman, the mother in the other family. "I don't have to take this kind of abuse." Whatever the problems in the operation of this modest restaurant, no one was being "abused." Once again, the downward slide of the culture: In a talk-show America where everyone is a victim, where everyone is quick to announce that he or she has been unjustly singled out, an overworked waitress in an understaffed diner is branded as a dispenser of abuse. The woman's husband following her out, and the woman's son, appearing confused and a little embarrassed: Children learn.

The numb sloppiness that has taken over the fabric of American life is doing more lasting harm to us than was done by any past superpower that once threatened to bury us. Before I had come over to the restaurant, back in my motel room across the parking lot, I had done the try-not-to-find-the-gun drill on my

TV set. If you have a television set with sixty or so cable channels, you might want to give it a whirl.

Start on the first channel. Using the remote control, zap up through the channels, pausing for a second or so on each one. See if you can get all the way to the highest channel without seeing a gun on the screen.

You can do it—sometimes there will be no guns at a given instant on any channel. But so many times you will quickly find the gun, and have to start over. We know that ours is a tragically violent country—but nowhere is the violence of America more cynically, almost cavalierly, marketed than on our television channels. Try to get through those channels and escape the waiting guns. See if you can get lucky.

Children learn. In the restaurant, the three adults and one child in the first family were served their breakfast, and then went to their car, on their way to church. They said they thought they'd make it on time. Hope they said a prayer for us all.

FORTY-EIGHT

A Whole New Ball Game

With all the hand-wringing about how athletics plays too large a role in our culture, about how major colleges place greater value on sports championships than on academic excellence, no one ever comes up with a plan that might change things.

Until now.

Scott Brennan, thirty-eight, is an insurance agent in South Bend, Indiana. An avid sports fan, he knows there is merit to the charge that many universities say they want to recruit student-athletes, but really want only the best athletes they can find.

"I was at a college basketball game last winter," Brennan said, "and the teams were getting ready for the tipoff at the beginning of the game. I was thinking that, as far as jump balls go, the referees haven't gotten taller in the last thirty years, but the players have. Most jump balls at the beginning of games are pretty clumsy looking."

And then came his inspiration:

"What if we did away with the opening tipoff in college basketball games, and with the coin toss before college football games? What if the school with the highest graduation rate among its varsity athletes got to take first possession of the ball in basketball, or got to choose whether to kick off or receive in football?"

In other words . . .

"The rules should reward the schools that are doing the best job of educating their athletes. In football, a flip of the coin is just a matter of chance—why not get rid of the coin toss and let the school that graduates the most athletes have that first advantage? The opening tip in basketball doesn't really affect the outcome of the game all that much—why not give the ball out of bounds to the school that has more of its athletes earn diplomas?"

But that would, by Brennan's own admission, give an advantage, of one size or another, to one of the teams.

"They would deserve it," he said. "All these schools say that they favor academic excellence first, and athletic excellence second. Most of them don't really mean it—but here would be a way to demonstrate it, at every game."

Does he think college coaches would go for it?

"They'd have to," he said. "If you're a coach, and you find out that all of a sudden you get a little edge on the field of play if you graduate more of your athletes than your opponent does, that's something that's going to get your attention."

But would not some college coaches and athletic directors oppose the rule before it even went into effect?

"They wouldn't look very good if they did oppose it," Brennan said. "How would a coach explain why he favored a flip of a coin—a matter of chance—over a method that recognizes a university's academic excellence? If a coach took that position, he would be admitting that his school never cared much about academics for its athletes in the first place."

In addition, Brennan said, giving the jump ball or coin-flip advantage to the school that graduated the most athletes would send a message to viewers watching at home: "They could be proud of their alma mater even if the team ended up losing the game. At every football and basketball game, the superiority of one school's commitment to educating its athletes over the other school's commitment would be there for all to see."

Of course, you could always take this a step further.

Instead of merely comparing graduation rates, you could ask each team's captain a question at center court, or on the fifty-yard line.

Who were the combatants in the Peloponnesian War?

Whom did Charles VIII succeed to become king of France?

What was the position being advocated in William Jennings Bryan's "Cross of Gold" speech?

According to the Second Law of Motion, the change in motion of a body as a result of a force is directly proportional to what?

"That might work, too," Brennan said. "The captains would meet on the field before the game, the referee would ask the questions, and the first captain to answer correctly would win the right for his team to have first possession of the ball."

Of course, there would always be the chance that the game would never start.

FORTY-NINE

Historic Change

"What do you think you're doing?" my father said.

"I'm sitting down," I said.

"Not in my seat, you aren't," he said.

"This isn't your seat," I said. "Your seat's at the other end."

"No, my seat is not at the other end," he said. "My seat is this seat. You may sit at the other end."

"Wait a minute," I said. "Is this a joke?"

"You're beginning to annoy me," he said.

We were at the dinner table. The dinner table in his house. He is almost eighty years old. For my entire life, at the dinner table he has always sat with his back to the window, looking into the room. No one was ever allowed to sit in his chair.

Now he was telling me that his chair is the one facing the window—the one at the other end of the table.

"When did this happen?" I said.

"When did *what* happen?" he said.

"When did you change chairs?" I said.

"About two years ago, if it's any concern of yours," he said.

"That's not true," I said. "I was here visiting you last Fourth of July, and you still were sitting in the regular chair."

"I am not going to have this conversation," he said.

Some people think that the upheaval in the Congress was the biggest change in the last year. Some people think that various political revolutions around the world were the biggest change.

To me, those are minor. A big change is when your father, after a lifetime of dinners, decides to change his chair at the table.

"Why did you change your chair?" I said.

"I don't have to answer that," he said.

"Please," I said. "I have to know."

"I changed because I wanted a change," he said.

"You wanted a change," I said. "For your entire life you refuse to sit anywhere but in the chair looking away from the window. And then one day you decide you don't like that chair."

"Do I have to listen to this?" he said to my mother.

Before she could answer, I noticed that she was sitting in a different place at the table, too—on the same side she always sat, but closer to his new chair.

"So you had to move, too?" I said to her.

"I didn't have to move," she said. "I chose to move."

"You're on the same side as always," I said. "But you're farther down the table."

"That's so we can talk to each other," she said.

"You realize something, don't you?" I said to my father. "Your whole adult life you have turned your head to the right to talk to her. Now you have to turn your head to the left."

"I'm ending this conversation," he said.

"Seriously," I said. "For all these years at dinner you've talked to her left profile. Now all of a sudden you want to get used to talking to her right profile?"

"Just eat your meal," he said.

"What's behind you?" I said. "Don't turn around—just tell me what's behind you."

"The Toby jugs," he said.

The Toby jugs are porcelain figurines in the shape of people's faces. They're actually pretty ugly. My father and mother have had them in the dining rooms of the houses where they've lived all of their adult lives. My father could always look at them at dinner. Now they were behind him.

"How do you know they're there if you can't see them?" I said.

"Stop asking questions," he said.

"Why would you not want to look at the Toby jugs?" I said.

"I've seen the Toby jugs," he said. "That white one, of Winston Churchill—that was the first one we bought. During the war."

I looked behind him. The Winston Churchill Toby jug was, indeed, on the bottom shelf of the cabinet.

"Even on Bryden Road," I said. "Even in the old house. You sat with your back to the window, and you could see the Toby jugs. It was a different window—but you never let anyone sit in your chair, just so you could look away from the window."

"So?" he said.

"So?" I said. "*So?* So you want me to just sit here and not wonder about this?"

"No, I don't want you to sit here," he said. "I want you to sit *there.*"

There. Down at the other end of the dinner table. With my back to the window.

"Why have you done this?" I said.

"I decided to look out the window," he said.

FIFTY

You Can Always Pay Forward

Woody Hayes used to have a saying. He would drop it into his conversations all the time.

"You can never pay back," he would say. "So you should always try to pay forward."

I never understood precisely what he meant—the words sounded good, but I wasn't certain of their meaning.

But in the years since Hayes's death I have come to learn that the "paying forward" line was not some empty slogan for him. It was the credo by which he lived his life—and now the dividends of his having paid forward are becoming ever more evident.

It happened again the other day. I heard from a man named Robert Ryan, who lives in Hilton Head, South Carolina. Like so many other people, Ryan was well aware of Hayes's reputation as a belligerent, angry-tempered football coach. That's the reputation Hayes lived with through twenty-eight years as head coach at Ohio State University—through 205 victories, thirteen Big Ten championships, eight trips to the Rose Bowl. Right up until the day he was dismissed after the 1978 season for slugging a Clemson player during the Gator Bowl, Hayes was considered a one-dimensional man by millions who knew him only through his much-publicized outbursts.

Whatever flaws he may have had, though, Woody Hayes was paying forward virtually every day of his life. Which is where Robert Ryan's story comes in.

"During the Vietnam War, my brother-in-law was in the infantry," Ryan said. "His name was Paul Allen Ballard. He was seriously wounded twice—and then, a few days before he was due to come home to Ohio, he was killed by a land mine.

"Anyway, in 1968, after his second wounding, he was in the hospital over there. And several weeks later, on a Saturday morning, there was a ring at his mother's front door in Grandview, Ohio.

"The way she described it, a portly, graying man in a suit was standing at her door. He tipped his hat and introduced himself as Woody Hayes."

Now, it should be noted that in 1968, Woody Hayes was perhaps the most famous man in Ohio. But there were still some Ohioans who did not follow sports—and who did not immediately know who Hayes was. Marie Ballard, the soldier's mother, evidently was one of these people: "She knew the man had a name she should recognize, but she couldn't place it," Robert Ryan said.

Hayes told Mrs. Ballard that he had just visited her son in the hospital in Vietnam, and had promised the young man he would let his family know he was all right. Hayes had come to the house to do just that—and to bring photos of Paul Allen Ballard.

So Mrs. Ballard invited him in—she still didn't know who he was—and she asked him what he did for a living. "I'm a football coach up at the university," Hayes said.

He spent fifteen minutes filling Mrs. Ballard in on her son, and left the pictures with her. It turned out that Hayes had been in Vietnam under the auspices of the State Department, and had visited Ohio boys, especially those in hospitals, so that he could serve as a courier to their families back home. He had wanted no publicity about this; volunteer student drivers from Ohio State took him all around Ohio so that he could call on the families.

"I find this story to be a towering measure of the real Woody Hayes," Robert Ryan said. "I'll tell you this—there's at least one family who will never forget what he did."

I hear stories like that about Hayes all the time. Since his death in 1987, I have run into dozens of people who were touched by his private acts of kindness—acts of kindness that were never reported.

On Christmas Eve I was in Columbus, and I called Anne Hayes, Woody's widow, to wish her the best of the season. I told her the story that Robert Ryan had told me.

"Yes, I know," she said. "It was very important to Woody to visit those families. He said that the boys were making such a sacrifice, it was the least he could do."

I reminded her of the "paying forward" line. "He wouldn't want to take credit for that," she said. "One of his favorite essayists was Ralph Waldo Emerson—it was from Emerson's writings that he learned the concept of paying forward. Woody wouldn't want to claim it as his own."

Wherever he learned it, he learned it well. So many people try in vain to determine and control their own legacy. Woody Hayes seemed to have figured it out: Pay forward, and everything else will take care of itself.

FIFTY-ONE

Who Will Say, "You Have a Home"?

In a thirtieth-floor corridor of the Daley Center in Chicago one morning last week, outside the room where the Illinois Appellate Court was about to meet, a large man wearing a blue sport coat shook with sobs.

That morning, he said, his adopted son—referred to as Jacob in court papers—had awakened in the house where the man and his wife live. The boy, who is three and a half years old, and who has lived with the family since he was four days old, came downstairs wearing pajamas with pictures of cars on them. As he often does, he asked his dad to go out and get doughnuts for them.

So, the father said, he did. The family sat at the kitchen table eating the doughnuts and drinking milk. Then an aunt arrived; the son sensed something was wrong. Usually when the father goes to work, the mother stays home with him. Today, though, the father said, "Mommy and Daddy have to go somewhere for a little while."

And now the father stood outside of court, trying to choke back his sobs.

In a few minutes, three judges would begin hearing arguments that could take Jacob out of his home—that could send him to live with a man he has never met.

The boy was born to a woman who gave him up for adoption. She had obtained an order of protection against a man with whom she had been having sexual relations; she was having sexual relations with another man during the same period of time. She believed that the second man was the father of the child.

The first man believed he had made the woman pregnant. The baby was born, the woman placed him for adoption, and he found what by all accounts is a happy, loving home.

Later, the first man initiated a legal action. Blood tests were performed, and it was determined that he was the biological father.

And now he was asking the appellate panel to help him gain custody of the boy—the three-and-a-half-year-old boy, who has a home and a family and a future, and who did not know where the only people who have ever been his mother and father had gone this morning.

In the courtroom, the three appellate judges—Mel R. Jiganti, Robert Cahill and Thomas E. Hoffman—asked pointed and intelligent questions. They were being put in a terrible position. Anyone with any sense knows that the child has a home, and he has parents, and he is where he belongs. But the judges were being asked not to consider what is good for the boy, but to weigh legal niceties. Was a certain petition filed within the required thirty-day period? If not, were there extenuating circumstances?

Meanwhile the child waited at home for his parents. They have bathed him all his life, and nursed him when he has been sick; they have watched him take his first steps, and listened to his first words. They are his mother and father; he is their son.

They left the courtroom with wet eyes. I noticed something that would not be considered germane as evidence, but that I found rather striking:

The man who is trying to take the boy from his parents was not at the hearing. He had not bothered to come.

I asked his lawyer why he was not there.

"He lives in De Kalb," the lawyer said. "He probably thought it was too expensive to fork over the train fare."

Just out of curiosity, I called the man in De Kalb, which is about an hour away from Chicago. He was home; he is unemployed, sitting around the apartment at 1:00 P.M.

"I'm a little low on money, and I didn't want to spend what I have on gas to get to the train station," he said. He said he lives with two roommates, and this is where Jacob will come live should he gain custody.

One of these days our legal system is going to figure out— or be forced to figure out—that having intercourse does not make a man or woman a parent; that having intercourse does not give a man or woman the right to tear apart a child's life. One night four years ago this man had intercourse with a woman; now, depending upon the decision that judges Jiganti, Cahill and Hoffman are deliberating, the future of a boy will be inalterably changed, one way or the other. There was a legend on the wall of the courtroom: "In God We Trust."

The mother and father went home to their son. Their life savings are gone; they have used it all to pay for lawyers to defend themselves in this action. The money, they say, could have been used toward the boy's college education.

At home that night, they said, he greeted them at the door. The family had dinner together. The boy watched one of his favorite videos, *The Velveteen Rabbit*.

Then the boy, as he does every evening before bed, brushed his teeth. His parents joined him in his bedroom, and said with him the prayer he recites every night:

"Now I lay me down to sleep . . ."

FIFTY-TWO

Adults Only

It's one of the great untruths of our times, and it is so common that it passes without notice.

You see it—or some variation of it—on television screens, in movie advertisements, on the labels of recorded music. The wording goes something like this:

"Adult content." Or: "Contains adult language."

Few people ever stop to think about what this means. What, exactly, is adult content? What words constitute adult language?

In our contemporary culture, adult content usually means that people are shown attacking each other with guns, hatchets and blowtorches; that half-naked people are assaulting other people, ripping their clothes off, treating humans like garbage; that people are detonating other people's cars and houses, setting fire to property, bludgeoning and disemboweling and pumping holes in one another. That's adult content; that's how adults behave.

Adult language? Adult language, by our current definition, consists of the foulest synonyms for excrement, for sexual activity, for deviant conduct. Adult language usually consists of four letters; adult language is the kind of language that civilized people are never supposed to use.

It makes you wonder what lesson we are sending—not only to children, but to ourselves. If a TV show or a motion picture concerned itself with responsible adults treating each other and the people around them with kindness, with consideration, with thoughtfulness, that TV show or movie would never be labeled as containing adult content. If a TV show or movie dealt quietly and responsibly with the many choices of conscience and generosity that adults face every day in the world, it would not warrant an "adult content" rating.

Similarly, if a movie featured adults talking with each other civilly, never resorting to gutter language or obscenities, choosing their words with care and precision, no one would ever think to describe the dialogue as "adult." A cable TV show or a music CD in which every word spoken or sung was selected to convey a thought or emotion without resorting to cheap and offensive vulgarities—that TV show or that CD would never be labeled as containing adult language.

We seem to be so sheepish about what our culture has become—so reluctant to concede the debasement of society— that we have decided to declare that darkness is light, that down is up, that wrong is right. We are sending a clear signal to young people: The things in our world that are violent, that are crude, that are dull and mean-spirited are the things that are considered "adult." The words that children are taught not to say because they are ugly and foul are "adult language." As if they are something to strive for, to grow into.

What is the solution? Truth in packaging might be a good idea, although it will never happen. No movie studio that has hired a top-money action star to headline in a film that consists of explosions, bloodshed and gore would ever agree to describe the movie truthfully. The lie of "adult content" is acceptable to Hollywood; the true label of "pathetic, moronic content, suitable for imbeciles" will never see the light of day.

Language? The movie studios, cable channels and record labels can live with the inaccurate euphemism of "adult language." To phrase it honestly—"infantile, ignorant, pitiful language"— would remove a certain sheen from a big-budget entertainment project.

Ours is becoming a society in which the best ideals of childhood—innocence, kindness, lack of spitefulness, rejection of violence—are qualities toward which adults ought to strive. A paradoxical society in which the things labeled "adult"—lack of restraint, conscienceless mayhem, vulgarity, raw and cynical carnality—are the things that children should be warned against growing up to embrace.

So perhaps we should learn to read the current "adult" warning labels in a different way. "Adult content" on a movie or television show should be read as a warning against becoming the kind of adult who welcomes such things into his or her life. The "adult language" label on a TV show or CD should be read as a genuine kind of warning, a warning to children against becoming the sort of adult who chooses to speak that way.

Then there is "For Mature Audiences Only," but that will have to wait for another day. . . .

FIFTY-THREE

What Lies Beyond the Highest Rung?

NEW YORK—Life's lessons sometimes are slow in arriving. When they finally do set in, you wonder why you hadn't figured them out for yourself much earlier.

The nature of ambition and of dreams, the scale of our aspirations . . .

Yankee Stadium, to me—to a lot of us, I imagine—has always stood as the pinnacle, the symbol of achievement. If the world is, indeed, a stage, then Yankee Stadium has long represented the biggest stage of all. If you grew up in this country, the thought of Yankee Stadium carried a weight that is almost beyond description. What's that line from the song "New York, New

York"? "If I can make it there, I'll make it anywhere. . . ."? Not quite: You can make it in New York—millions do—and not make it in Yankee Stadium. Only a few do that.

I had never been in Yankee Stadium. My whole life, every stadium I ever walked into, no matter how pleasing or impressive, the thought was: This is nice, this is big—but it's not Yankee Stadium. This is grand. But it's not Yankee Stadium.

Yankee Stadium was the place that was always out there in the distance—the best place, the finish line. It didn't matter where you went—Yankee Stadium was the top of the mountain. It was so wondrous in concept that it might as well not have existed. Yankee Stadium, in the American mind, has been our national monument—our rung beyond which there are no more rungs.

The other week, I had some business that was supposed to take me to Yankee Stadium. It was a trip I could have skipped; taking the trip would disrupt other plans I had. But this was like an invitation from the president, or a command from the queen. Although the White House or Buckingham Palace would not be quite as intimidating. Yankee Stadium.

The New York Yankees were not in town on this day. Arrangements had been made for the people who run Yankee Stadium to open the place for my colleagues and me. Which made the prospect of the trip all the more irresistible: You fly to New York, ride over to the Bronx, and they're going to open up Yankee Stadium for you.

So I got on the plane, and I rode to the Bronx, and the people who were supposed to let me in were at the gate where they were supposed to be. They pointed me in the right direction—even that seemed odd, it seemed that you would need an escort in that place, you shouldn't be allowed to just wander around as if you were in some strip shopping center—and I walked into the stands and it was a bright and sunny summer day and I was in Yankee Stadium.

And I looked around and I thought:

This is nice. This is big.

But it's not Yankee Stadium.

The street address was correct, the seats were configured properly. This was, objectively, Yankee Stadium.

Yet it wasn't Yankee Stadium. It was a big ballpark with seats made of some blue plastic-like material, and advertising signs wherever they could be sold, and solid railings. I looked at the pitcher's mound and tried to see Don Larsen throwing the final pitch of his perfect game, tried to see Yogi Berra ready to run into his arms, and I realized that the Yankee Stadium that came out of the radios of our childhoods back in the Midwest was more real than the real thing. I tried to imagine where the boxing ring had stood when Floyd Patterson had fought Ingemar Johansson for the heavyweight championship of the world—the fight "in the ballpark," that phrase always uttered so casually, as if this were just any ballpark—and I looked around, and this was, indeed, just any ballpark. Good ballpark. But it's not Yankee Stadium.

For Yankee Stadium—Yankee Stadium as an allegory—is supposed to exist only in your mind. That's the secret, right there. If there is, indeed, a top rung of the ladder—if there is a finish line—then you're never supposed to see it. If you see the finish line, it's not really the finish line. If you reach the top, then the top cannot exist. This is the top? Nah. There's got to be more.

Which isn't a bad bit of knowledge to have. For all the people who spend their lives trying to make it to the metaphorical Yankee Stadium, it's not so bad to find out that, when you get there, it's not there after all.

I walked out to right field. I stood on the grass, looking toward home plate, trying to see what Babe Ruth must have seen on all his New York afternoons in right. I wondered if he felt like he was ever here.

FIFTY-FOUR

The Heroes of a Certain Spring

SARASOTA, Florida—It has been a spring without heroes. At least that is what the baseball aficionados have decreed about this year's spring training, which the major-league players refused to participate in for weeks as a part of their strike. And if you judge life only by what transpires upon the fields of play, that evaluation is probably correct.

The big-league millionaires couldn't even be bothered to form picket lines in support of their own strike. The multimillionaire owners saw grace and beauty only in their closely guarded ledger books. The men who were persuaded by the owners to play in the replacement games were nice-enough fellows, trying their best, but certainly not heroes.

So if you were looking for heroes at spring training this year, you were probably destined to go home empty. Once in a while, though, if you look around you, you realize that you have been focusing in the wrong direction.

The hotel where I stayed during spring training is on the Gulf of Mexico—a lovely place with tennis courts and a wide beach and balconies overlooking the water. I would come back from the ballpark to this place, and write my stories about the baseball players and the baseball owners.

The place was full of families with children. Every day there were boys and girls splashing in the pool, pushing rafts out into the Gulf, zipping through the parking lots on skateboards and Roller Blades.

I was down here a long time. And twice during my stay, families arrived with sons who could not take part in any of this.

In each of these two families, the boy was seriously and permanently infirm, unable to get around without the use of a special wheelchair. It's difficult for a nonphysician to make a medical diagnosis, and it would have been impolite to ask, but my guess is that one of the boys had cerebral palsy; he twitched almost constantly, and made guttural sounds when he spoke. These two families came and left during separate parts of my stay here; they did not see each other.

But I saw them both. And what I noticed—what I could not help but notice—was how the fathers in both families treated their sons.

Which was with total devotion and love. You have to understand—this hotel was filled with the sights and sounds of youthful energy and athleticism every day of every week. Children full of life and vigor raced around the tennis courts, cannonballed into the pool, played volleyball on the beach. Every moment of it must have sent an unending message not only to those two boys, but to the fathers, too. Every moment of it was a reminder of what these two families cannot have, ever.

But the families were on vacation; it was a vacation for their boys the same way it was a vacation for all the other boys and girls at the hotel. The boys appeared to just be entering their teenage years. And not for a moment did either of their fathers leave their sides, or let them down.

While the other children and teenagers frolicked in the pool, these fathers would sit with their sons on the pool deck and play hands of cards. When the other children and teenagers tossed rubber footballs around, these fathers would show their sons around the grounds. One thing that struck me especially: There was a sharp drop in the sand right before the beach touched the Gulf. I would see the father of one of these boys cradle him in his arms—the boy was reaching the age and the weight at which this was not easy—and carry him down the slope in the sand until they were at the water's edge. Then they would sit in two chairs, side by side, next to the water, just talking quietly, for hours.

This cannot be easy; it may be fueled by love, but that does not make it easy. If the fathers work all year to provide a vacation like this for their sons, perhaps it is not much of a vacation for the fathers. They might never say it—but if a vacation is supposed to be a time to rest and forget, for these fathers the vacation is yet to come. They didn't seem to mind at all.

So I would come back from the ballpark, the place of no heroes, and I was lucky enough to see these two fathers and these two sons, and to be reminded of certain things. This summer there will be sportscast highlights of home-run hitters and curveball whizzes. I have no interest in watching. I found my heroes at spring training. Sitting by the water, sitting in the shade, spending their days and nights with the sons who so need them. Never walking away.

FIFTY-FIVE

Music Police

Ted Strawser, fifty-five, owns an establishment called the Patterson Furniture Store, in Wolcottville, Indiana. There are only 890 or so residents in Wolcottville, so Ted Strawser was surprised to get an official-looking letter from BMI on the East Coast.

If the truth be told, Ted Strawser had never heard of BMI. BMI stands for Broadcast Music Inc.; along with ASCAP, BMI is one of the two giant organizations representing music composers.

Strawser's furniture store, on Main Street in Wolcottville, would seem to have nothing to do with the music business. But as Strawser read the letter, he realized that he could be in big trouble.

The letter from BMI informed Strawser that he was in violation of the law. The letter said that Strawser was illegally withholding money from the men and women who composed songs under the jurisdiction of BMI. There were several references to attorneys in the BMI letter, and a deadline by which Strawser was advised to comply with BMI's demands.

Confused, Strawser called BMI headquarters in New Jersey. He found out what he was doing wrong:

Strawser was playing a radio in his furniture store.

That's right. He was playing a radio in the store, and it was audible to the customers. He had always played a radio in the store; the music on the radio kept him company. There were seldom more than six customers in the store at a time; when we spoke with Strawser, there were no customers. He just liked the sound of music in the store.

"I had no idea I was doing anything wrong," Strawser said. "This wasn't special music being piped in or anything. We don't even have a radio station here in Wolcottville. I just have always kept the radio tuned to an easy-listening station over in South Bend. The radio played all day, commercials and all."

BMI informed Strawser that if he wished to keep playing his radio in his store—at least loud enough for other people to hear it—he must sign a contract with BMI, and pay BMI an annual fee.

"It came out to about six hundred dollars a year," Strawser said. "I had never heard of this particular music society, but they said that if I wanted to keep my radio on, it would cost me six hundred dollars a year."

Strawser didn't know what to do. The references to attorneys frightened him. He got in touch with the Better Business Bureau, over in Fort Wayne, and he also wrote a letter to Paul Harvey, the famous radio commentator.

"I didn't know where else to turn for advice," he said. "Both the Better Business Bureau and Paul Harvey could hardly believe this could be true."

Strawser said that, after doing some research, the Better Business Bureau told him that BMI could collect enormous damages if it was determined that music was being played illegally in Strawser's furniture store.

"I was told that I could be fined up to a hundred thousand dollars for every BMI song that came out of that radio," Strawser said.

We called BMI to see if this could all be a big mistake. We were told that it was no mistake.

"When music is used as a tool to enhance the atmosphere of a business, it is considered commercial usage," said James Popik, a BMI licensing representative in New Jersey. "If the radio can be heard throughout this man's store, then it is necessary for him to sign a contract with us, and to pay us a fee."

Even if the music is just a radio playing in a store on Main Street in small-town Indiana?

"That's right," Popik said.

Strawser had been concerned about an additional matter: Who had turned him in? Had one of his friends or customers notified BMI that he was playing the radio?

"I'm sure that was not the case," said BMI's Popik. "BMI has a number of companies that we buy information from."

So, under threat of legal action, Strawser turned off the radio in his furniture store. He signed up with Muzak, which now supplies him with piped-in music. He doesn't even particularly like the Muzak music, although it's costing him $38 a month.

"But I was told that Muzak was licensed by BMI, so that I didn't have to worry about being sued," Strawser said. "If I turned my radio on in the store and I got caught, and they sued me for a hundred thousand dollars, it would wipe me out."

Strawser has promised not to play his radio again.

"I can't afford to take the chance," he said.

And then he added:

"Sometimes I really don't know what's going on in this country."

FIFTY-SIX

The Night a Miracle Came to Town

To see a performance on the Broadway stage is something that most Americans will never experience; economics and geography argue against it. And with television and the movies solidifying their positions as the dominant avenues of entertainment, it's a safe bet that Broadway will eventually mean even less to the mass culture than it does now.

A ticket to a Broadway show will run you about $60 these days. There is a weaker and weaker impulse in people from the rest of the country to travel to New York for carefree pleasure; a weekend in New York conjures up quite a different mental picture than it did a generation ago.

Even back then, however, there was an alternative. You might never make it to Broadway, but on occasion Broadway would come to you. That's what I found myself thinking about when I heard that Ralph Bellamy died the other day.

Bellamy performed in more than a hundred movies in his life, including *Forbidden* with Barbara Stanwyck, *The Awful Truth* with Irene Dunne, and *His Girl Friday* with Rosalind Russell. He was also frequently seen on television.

In the late 1950s, though, Bellamy performed the role of

Franklin Delano Roosevelt in the Broadway play *Sunrise at Campobello*. The play, for which Bellamy won a Tony Award, was a moving drama based on Roosevelt's battle with polio.

Sunrise at Campobello was one of the Broadway shows that went on the road after becoming a success in New York. It toured the country—the actors, support crews, scenery and costumes moved from city to city, sometimes for as little as one night, by train and by plane. One of the towns where *Sunrise at Campobello* stopped was the town where I lived in Ohio.

My parents took me to see it, in the Hartman Theater downtown. It may have been the first play I ever saw. The curtain rose, and the actors were there.

I'm sure, in his various movie, TV and radio roles, Ralph Bellamy reached millions upon millions of people during his career. On that one night, though, for one boy sitting in the audience of a theater in a city far from Broadway both in miles and in attitude, it seemed as if the performance was the only one of Bellamy's life.

That, of course, is the secret of live theater; writers far more cultured than I have pointed that out far more eloquently. Big-budget movies and network TV shows, for all their craft and artistry, are exactly the same for every person who ever sees them. The nuances and inflections are locked in. Nothing is open to the slightest change.

The beauty of the live theater is that on a given night, when you are in the audience, a great actor or actress is giving a performance that he or she will never give again. In small but important ways, the performance is different than it was the night before, and different than it will be the night after. The performance is being granted by the human beings on the stage to the human beings who are in the seats on that night and that night only.

That's the essential thrill. It was on that Ohio night. The climactic scene in *Sunrise at Campobello* centered on Roosevelt's angry defiance of the polio that had crippled him. Needing to get to the rostrum at a political convention to address the delegates, the Roosevelt character, slowly and painfully and under his own power, makes the long walk. Not a word is spoken as he struggles along the runway; you can hear amplified cheers, but there is no dialogue at all.

It was a world-famous scene, and Ralph Bellamy made it so, and for one boy in one audience on one night it seemed almost a miracle that Bellamy had come to town to bestow the gift of that performance. People in the audience were weeping as Bellamy made the walk, and for that moment it didn't matter that he had made the walk in a different city the night before and would make the walk in some other city the next night. He had come to town and the performance was magnificent and no TV show or movie can stay in your mind the way a performance like that, by a man in the same room with you, can.

Bellamy was eighty-seven when he died the other day. Undoubtedly he had forgotten that particular performance; maybe he had forgotten that he ever visited the town.

I went to the public library the day after I saw the play, and I checked out a bound volume of the script and took it home, just to try to relive the night. But you can't relive something like that; that's the point. You can't rewind it or fast-forward it or try to capture it again. It's there for one night and one night only, and then it's gone, and maybe the boy in the audience wasn't so wrong when he sat there and thought he was seeing a miracle.

FIFTY-SEVEN

Her Life Was Not a Joke

I heard a comedian tell yet another Helen Keller joke the other night. He got the expected laugh; the comics usually do. When he mentioned Helen Keller's name, he rolled his eyes up into their sockets and flailed his arms about in a spastic motion.

That's how the jokes usually go. Helen Keller, in death, has become an easy target for dim-witted comics on cable stand-up shows and for kids who don't yet know they're being cruel. In our supposedly enlightened era, jokes about disabled people in general are frowned upon, but jokes about Helen Keller get told all the time. Sometimes it seems that this is destined to be Helen Keller's legacy—to be a punch line.

She doesn't need defending; she's been dead for more than twenty-five years now, and no one can hurt her feelings. But the staying power of Helen Keller jokes is more than just another depressing testament to the rampant stupidity of our know-nothing age; it is an insult to one of the most remarkable people who ever lived. Helen Keller was and is a hero to me, and her memory deserves better.

So at the risk of driving readers away—I doubt that there's much of an audience for a biography of a woman people no longer care about—I'd like to explain who she was.

Helen Keller was born on June 27, 1880, in the Alabama town of Tuscumbia. A serious illness when she was nineteen months old took away her sight and hearing. She could not speak, either; the world as we know it was lost to her. Or so it was assumed.

For the next five years, she grew up seeing nothing, hearing nothing, making only guttural sounds. Helen's father, in desperation, sought the advice of Dr. Alexander Graham Bell. Bell referred the Keller family to the Perkins Institution for the Blind in Boston. Through the Perkins Institution, Anne Mansfield Sullivan was sent to Alabama to try to free Helen from her self-contained prison.

Sullivan, twenty years old, had been blind herself, but had been partially cured. She arrived at the Kellers' home just before Helen's seventh birthday. Within one month she had begun to teach Helen the manual alphabet by spelling out words on her hand. Helen quickly learned the names of objects.

Helen learned to read Braille, and to write using a specially designed typewriter. At the Horace Mann School for the Deaf in Boston, she, at the age of ten, learned to speak.

Helen enrolled at the Cambridge (Massachusetts) School for Young Ladies; Anne Sullivan accompanied her to classes, and conveyed the lectures to her by touch. Helen passed the entrance exams for Radcliffe College, one of the nation's most prestigious. There, too, Sullivan went to classes with her to help her understand the lectures. In 1904 Helen graduated from Radcliffe with honors.

After graduation Helen devoted herself to the causes of blind and deaf people. With Sullivan's help, she wrote the classic autobiography *The Story of My Life*. It was the first of many books she was to write, including *Optimism*, *The World I Live In*, *The Song of the Stone Wall*, *My Religion*, and *Teacher*. Her books were translated into more than fifty languages.

Her high-pitched voice was not easily understood, but she toured the world as a distinguished lecturer, advocating the rights of the disabled. Anne Sullivan, whose own blindness had recurred, died in 1936. Helen continued to lecture and travel, helped by her secretary Polly Thompson. She was an ardent opponent of fascism prior to World War II, and worked with soldiers who were blinded after that war broke out. She spoke before legislatures and governments in more than twenty-five countries. Among her many awards was the Chevalier's ribbon of the French Legion of Honor.

She died in Westport, Connecticut, on June 1, 1968, at the age of eighty-seven. From an early childhood that had seemed destined to cage her forever inside a sightless and soundless despair, she had become one of the most admired people in the world.

So pardon me if I have to object to the easy stand-up jokes, the relegation of her to a reeling, buffoonish presence on comedy stages. In these days especially, with so many people endlessly complaining that their birthright in society makes them "victims," with so many people telling the rest of society how "disadvantaged" they are, the life of Helen Keller is not a bad reminder of what one person with courage can overcome.

If only more people in this lazy, sloppy-thinking age of ours would show that courage and that intellect. To those who would continue to use her memory as a source of ridicule, the best suggestion may be that they compare their own goals and accomplishments with hers, and then evaluate their time on Earth so far. To borrow a phrase that is overused these days, but seems applicable here: Get a life.

FIFTY-EIGHT

Rough Takeoff

There are two kinds of dumb business decisions.

The first kind of dumb business decision is the kind that is so empty-headed, you wonder about the qualifications of the executives who made the decision. The best example: Coca-Cola's disastrous introduction of New Coke in 1985.

The second kind of dumb business decision is the kind that is so gloriously goofy that, in a perverse way, you are filled with admiration for the executives who thought it up. The business decision may be dumb, but it's dumb in a grand, inspired way. It will never work, but you sort of love it.

Such a decision was the one made by Continental Express— the commuter-flight arm of Continental Airlines—that resulted in stand-up comedians performing on Continental Express flights last week.

The stand-up comics were booked on Continental Express flights between Cleveland and Detroit. The comedians were hired to perform on late-afternoon and early-evening flights.

"People want to relax in the afternoon," explained Joel Feldstein, a Continental Express spokesman. "People want to hear a joke or two."

So the stand-up comics were hired. The Continental Express flights between Detroit and Cleveland are small, propeller-driven airplanes. They seat only thirty people. So you had thirty people crammed into a plane that is sometimes referred to as a puddle-jumper—and you had a comedian performing in the front of the plane.

"The comedians we hired knew they would have to keep their routines short," Feldstein said. "That's a quick trip between Cleveland and Detroit. The plane is only in the air for seventeen minutes."

Commuter flights, by their very nature, sometimes make travelers a little nervous. With small planes flying through all kinds of weather, commuter flights would not seem to be the obvious place to have a comedian trying for laughs. Many passengers on commuter flights prefer to close their eyes, grit their teeth and count down the minutes until landing.

"We think it is a great idea," said Steven Mason, a Continental Express executive. "A little bit of added value for our customers."

The logistics turned out to be somewhat awkward. The stand-up comics were not allowed to use the planes' public address systems, because those systems are reserved for announcements by the pilots and flight attendants.

"That was no problem," Mason said. "We provided the comedians with over-the-shoulder amplifiers. They were really quite lightweight—the speakers were mounted on straps that the comedians wore on their shoulders. The power was self-contained, and the microphones were attached."

One of the comedians assigned to the Continental Express flights was Al Aprill, fifty, a veteran stand-up comic.

"I performed on four flights," Aprill said. "It wasn't like performing in a nightclub. When I stood up, I saw a variety of emotions in the eyes of the passengers. The most common reaction, if I were to read it from their eyes, was, 'What is this guy doing here?' "

Aprill said the term "stand-up" was not entirely accurate in this context.

"Of the four flights, I was only able to stand up and perform on one of them," he said. "The other three, there was enough turbulence that I was directed to stay in my seat. It's very hard to perform for an audience when you have to sit in the first row of seats and then loosen your seat belt and swivel around to face the people. When you're sitting down, you can only see the people with aisle seats.

"And even when I stood up, I wasn't really standing up. That's a low ceiling in the cabin. I was sort of bent over. It was like crouching for a golf swing."

And the reaction of the audiences?

"It was all right," Aprill said. "On the last of the four flights, I don't think I got a laugh. We hit some really rainy, nasty weather. The plane was bouncing all over the place. I mean, we were up and down. We hit some air pockets. I don't think the passengers were in the mood for jokes. But I tried."

Continental Express has completed its trial run of the stand-up comic flights. The airline is uncertain about whether it will continue the experiment—and if it does continue, what markets to include.

Al Aprill said he is ready to perform whenever Continental Express asks.

"It has to get easier," he said. "This time, I started all my routines by asking the passengers if they were ready for some comedy. They didn't say a word. They just stared at me, dumbstruck."

FIFTY-NINE

The Rules

Kim Everett, who is an executive with a hospital corporation and who lives in Macon, Georgia, could not quite believe what she was seeing.

Everett was on a business trip to Washington. She had a few hours before her flight back to Georgia, so she stopped off to look at the Lincoln Memorial.

"I was looking at the statue of Lincoln when a group of twenty or thirty children came running up the steps," Everett said. "They looked as if they were on a school trip. There were some parents with them, and I heard one of the parents say to the boys and girls, 'Wait till you see this!' The children seemed thrilled to be at the Lincoln Memorial."

After a few minutes, Everett said, the children began singing "The Star-Spangled Banner." The sound of their voices echoing off the marble walls was beautiful, she said: "It seemed totally spontaneous. It seemed that they saw the statue of Lincoln and wanted to sing the national anthem."

Just as the children got to the line about "whose broad stripes and bright stars," Everett said, a uniformed security guard approached one of the men who seemed to be accompanying the children. After listening to the guard for a moment, the man raised his hand as a signal for the children to stop singing. They did.

"The children looked puzzled," Everett said. "The other adults moved closer to the guard. Then the man to whom the guard had been speaking told the children that they would not be allowed to sing any more of 'The Star-Spangled Banner.' And then the children left.

"As the children were leaving, I asked one of the parents what had happened. The parent said that the guard had informed them that no one is allowed to sing at the Lincoln Memorial without a permit."

As the children walked down the steps from the Lincoln Memorial, Everett noticed that on the backs of some of their jackets was the name of a school: Springhurst Elementary School, in Dobbs Ferry, New York.

"I can't believe this can be true," Everett told me when we spoke the other day. "Here were these children standing in the monument to the man who was instrumental in saving the Union. Not far away was the Vietnam Memorial, with the names of more than fifty thousand Americans who died under our flag. Could these schoolchildren really have been told to stop singing the national anthem?"

I called Dobbs Ferry, and got in touch with the Springhurst Elementary School. George Swietlicki, the school's music teacher, said he had been the man the guard had approached.

"There were thirty-one children," Swietlicki said. "They were members of our choral group, the Harmonaires. We had ridden a bus for our school trip to Washington—a six-hour bus ride. The children were fourth- and fifth-graders; they're nine-year-olds and ten-year-olds. They started to sing 'The Star-Spangled Banner' because they were so moved by the Lincoln Memorial.

"The guard simply told me that the children would have to stop singing immediately unless they had a permit. When I told the guard that I didn't understand, he said, 'You can't sing here. Period.'

"I am a naturalized citizen of the United States; my parents were born in Poland. I have always taught the children that you should respect authority, so I didn't put up a fight. I told the children that they couldn't sing, and we just went to the bus and left."

I called the headquarters of the National Parks Service in Washington, which has authority for the Lincoln Memorial. A spokesman told me that, while he was unfamiliar with the incident, "You do, indeed, need a permit to perform at the Lincoln Memorial." I said that, as far as I knew, this was not a performance or a concert; this was a group of children spontaneously singing the national anthem in front of Abraham Lincoln's statue. "The rule is that if there is a public gathering that is done with the propensity to attract attention or draw a crowd, you must have a permit," he said. "We have carefully worked out these rules."

So the children from Springhurst Elementary School rode the bus home for six hours, all the way back to Dobbs Ferry. "I didn't tell them much about why they had to stop singing," George Swietlicki, the music teacher, said. "I just don't know how I would have been able to explain such a thing."

SIXTY

A Blessing from Devereaux

So this interoffice envelope lands on my desk, and it's kind of thick, and when I open it up there's a cassette tape inside, the kind you buy in a record store. The tape is a gospel tape, called *Frontrunner,* and it features what is usually referred to as Christian music.

The album is by a singer named Devereaux, and I can't quite figure out who has sent it to me, and why it has come in one of those brown *Tribune* office-to-office envelopes. Then I notice there's a note attached; Devereaux, the gospel singer who has sent the tape, directed it to the paper's mailroom, asking if the guys down there would make sure I got it. And they did.

This still doesn't explain why Devereaux has sent me his tape, for I have no abiding interest in gospel music. But I look through the note Devereaux has sent, and once again, for about the millionth time, I think about how weird life is, because Devereaux, it turns out, is Chet Weld.

Several years ago I wrote a book based upon a diary I had kept when I was seventeen years old. The diary was my attempt to learn to be a reporter by writing down my observations every day. One of the unhappy things that happened to me that year was getting knocked off the varsity tennis team after having earned a letter the year before; losing a varsity letter after having won one is in many ways worse than never having lettered at all, and a crucial factor in my downfall was getting beaten by Chet Weld.

Chet Weld was a tough little wiseguy, or so I thought; maybe this was just a reaction to his having lowered me in the social strata of the community. Here's the gospel tape by Devereaux, who used to be Chet Weld, and in his note he says he wants to let me know what has become of him. "I'm sorry I beat you in tennis," he writes, and the tone isn't sarcastic at all; he's a pastor now in Arizona, and has devoted his life to God: "I love pastoring and I am quite fulfilled."

Part of this is sweetly absurd—the idea of Chet Weld beating me at something in 1964 and now writing me that he feels bad that I felt bad—and part of it is merely sweet. "I think life is so exciting," he writes, referring to his church work, "and I want to give you back a blessing through this music."

As I read his note, I'm still trying to figure out why he's calling himself Devereaux. Chet Weld was the ideal Ohio name for a wise, cocky kid who's poised to knock another kid off the varsity; Chet Weld sounds like a wiry little athlete who's never had a moment of self-doubt. Maybe, I figure, he's made Devereaux up because Chet Weld doesn't sound like a churchman or a gospel singer; maybe Devereaux is an invention, a softer name for a softer period in his life.

The answer is further down in the note. He moved to our town when he was in the sixth grade, Chet Weld writes; his real first name was Devereaux, but in our town he found that hard to live with. People would introduce him as Dev, or Devvie, he writes; the new boys and girls he was meeting thought it sounded like Debbie. "Too embarrassing for a kid," he writes, understating.

So he went with Chet, which was a shortened version of his middle name. That's what he writes in his note: He writes that he was Devereaux Chester Weld, and that Chet Weld sounded better in the new town. A kid who's determined to knock someone else off the varsity is probably better off as Chet Weld than Devereaux Weld, not to mention Devvie. Or Debbie.

"But I like Devereaux now," he writes in his note. He's forty-three, he writes; he likes a lot of things about his life.

I stuff the Devereaux tape into my shirt pocket; I'll play it when I get home. We all go through changes big and small in our lives; some of us get knocked off the varsity when we're seventeen and feel bad about it, and some of us knock someone else off the varsity and feel bad about our real first name. I look in the diary book, to see what Chet Weld had said after he had beaten me. "The way I figure it, that puts you at fourth doubles now"—that is what he had said. Meaning: I've beaten you and now you're so low on the team, you're never coming back.

"I felt like smacking him." That's what I wrote in the diary that day, about Chet Weld. I didn't know then that he was Devereaux; if he feared people would make fun of him because they thought his name was Debbie, he should have known how nervous the guy he beat was that someone might find out he was keeping a diary. Cocky little athletes didn't want the world to know that they were really Devvie—or that they poured their thoughts into diaries at night.

Things tend to work out, though. I'm still keeping diaries, home-delivered in the morning paper, and Chet Weld is back to Devereaux, singing gospel songs. I get ready to leave for the day, Chet Weld's music in my pocket, ready for the listening. Things tend to work out.

SIXTY-ONE

Bird-watching

MINNEAPOLIS—In the Blue Concourse, they are like wood-peckers.

There are no trees in the Blue Concourse. Just telephones. Fog in Minneapolis, fog in Chicago, and in the Blue Concourse the travelers wait.

As frustrating as a fog-bound airport day can be for a traveler, after a while it becomes instructive, like a little education into what our world has become. We are so accustomed to getting just about anywhere as quickly as we can. New York to Los Angeles, and if we're twenty minutes delayed across the continent, we feel late.

On a fog day, when the planes aren't flying until they're good and ready, the American business traveler doesn't exactly revert to a pioneer, but he remembers that it wasn't always simple to get from one place to another. Minneapolis to Chicago wasn't always an easy hop. Minneapolis to Chicago, conceivably, was once a trip that families might plan for a year in advance.

"Ground conditions in Chicago." That's what the public address announcements coming out of the ceiling of the Blue Concourse are saying. It's Minneapolis's fault as much as it's Chicago's fault, though; there's not much you can see through the fog out the picture windows of the Blue Concourse.

Hence the woodpeckers.

In a forest, the woodpeckers might be tapping at tree trunks with their beaks. In the Blue Concourse, the woodpeckers are in business suits and dresses, and they use their fingers. They're pecking at the silver-colored buttons of the pay telephones, pecking so rapidly their fingers blur.

Not many of the woodpeckers are dropping coins into the phones. The Blue Concourse woodpeckers are credit-card woodpeckers, their calls paid for by their companies. A visitor from another planet, observing, might be alarmed. The woodpeckers appear as if they might be harming the tips of their fingers, so hard and so devotedly do they tap.

Some of the woodpeckers are clearly reaching machines on the other end. You can tell this because the woodpeckers, when they are connected, talk in the same tones they would use if they were speaking to a live person—but they don't pause. They may speak three or four paragraphs, a minute's worth or more, but they don't stop to take a breath or to listen. There's no one on the other end. Just an answering-machine tape running.

Not everyone in the Blue Concourse is a woodpecker. Some fog-day travelers resist the pay phones. They read.

Which is a lesson in itself. On most days, you would not pay much attention to the reading matter favored by your fellow journeyers. On a fog day in the Blue Concourse, though, you notice what they pull out of their purses and briefcases. It's as if they're hanging signs around their necks.

Those two women over there, for example, waiting for the fog-delayed American Airlines flight. Before they take out their reading matter, they seem at least demographically similar. Same approximate age, same style of clothing.

Now both of them are ready to read.

One reaches into her purse and pulls out a magazine: *Muscle & Fitness,* it is called.

The other reaches into her purse and pulls out a paperback book: *The Subtle Power of Spiritual Abuse*, it is called.

Oh.

Yikes.

And the man over there. He had seemed so content, absent-mindedly looking at the television screens that list the fog-delayed flights. But now he reaches into his briefcase, and he, too, pulls out a book.

What's that title?

Healing the Shame That Binds You.

Oh, my.

The woodpeckers aren't reading. The woodpeckers are pecking. If you asked the woodpeckers to stop and to say out loud the numbers they had just pecked—the telephone numbers, the credit card authorization numbers—they might not be able to. The pecking is a craft of its own, and the fingers know what the mind may not.

A long, long day in the Blue Concourse. One of the travelers—a woodpecker who writes a newspaper column for a living —had rejected another means of transportation today. He had been tempted to book passage on the Empire Builder, but the Empire Builder is only a train, and the woodpecker-columnist thought it might take too long to get to Chicago on a busy workday.

But the Empire Builder will beat him to Chicago. On the Empire Builder, he would have been sleeping now. In the Blue Concourse, he is pecking at the phone, standing beside all the other woodpeckers, all of them pecking as if they somehow believe that if they peck fast enough and frantically enough, the fog day may be salvaged.

SIXTY-TWO

John Unitas Jr.

The event was the annual convention of a lawyers' association, and present were hundreds of attorneys, their clients and business associates. At a large cocktail party, men and women were introducing themselves to one another. As is usually the case at such parties, many names floated into the air never to be really picked up on by their intended recipients. The old "didn't-catch-the-name" syndrome.

One pleasant-looking fellow in a business suit, though, didn't have much trouble when he introduced himself to people.

"Hi," he would say in a friendly manner. "I'm John Unitas Jr."

Talk about cutting through the clutter.

I didn't want to bug him about it at the party—it was too crowded and noisy—but later on we spoke at length about what it is like to go through life bearing the name of perhaps the greatest quarterback ever to play football.

"When I was very young, it wasn't so much the name that made me realize that my father was different," Unitas said. He is thirty-three, he lives in Baltimore and he publishes a commercial law directory and does some real-estate work.

"As a child I would go out in public with my father, and strangers would surround him, and I would have to step back," Unitas said. "I didn't think of him as being a celebrity—as being John Unitas of the Baltimore Colts. I thought of him as being my father. It would bother me, having to step back for people I didn't know. But at that point the fact that my name was John Unitas Jr. wasn't a big factor."

That came later. In high school, he played football. Mostly he was a defensive back, but occasionally he was called on to step in for the starting quarterback.

"I wasn't all that good a quarterback," he said. "If I would throw an interception, I could hear the people in the crowd yelling angrily: 'Oh, Unitas!' " To his ears, those words had a different ring than if the people had been yelling, "Oh, Smith!" or "Oh, Jones!"

As a college student, he realized that people reacted immediately when they heard his name. Male students wanted to talk to him; female students were more interested than they might otherwise have been. Or so it seemed to him.

"For a while, I thought about using a different first name—a nickname or something," he said. "But I never did."

Now, in the world of business, he understands that the mention of his name opens doors for him. "If I make a call on the phone to a person I've never met, the person probably will take the call, if only out of curiosity," he said. "The first question will usually be if I'm really related to John Unitas. When I say, 'Yes, sir, I'm his son,' sometimes the person will talk about all the facts and figures of my father's football career. The number of completed passes he threw, and stuff like that. Which is kind of interesting, I guess, but I don't know any of that stuff. I've never been into that."

Sometimes, he said, there will be awkward moments: "I met one man, and I shook his hand and I said, 'I'm John Unitas Jr.' And he said, 'Right. And I'm Joe Namath Jr.' He thought I was trying to be funny. You don't know what to do in a situation like that." And of course there are the predictable remarks every time he pulls out a credit card with his name on it.

He said that he loves his father and remains close to him. His father, he said, is fifty-six now, lives in Baltimore and owns a printed-circuit-board company.

John Unitas Jr. may have complicated feelings about going through life with that name. But he and his wife have a twenty-three-month-old son, and the son's name is John Unitas III.

"When I told my dad what we were going to name our baby, my dad said, 'Son, you don't want to do that,' " John Unitas Jr. said. "It's hard to tell when he's kidding. My father is not a guy who shows a lot of emotion.

"But I said to him, 'I'm sorry. You did it to me and I had no say in it, so now it's my turn to do it.' He knew that I was kidding. I'm proud of the name. My dad is John Constantine Unitas, and I'm John Constantine Unitas Jr., and my son is John Constantine Unitas III.

"Although we're going to call him J.C. instead of John. I just think it will be easier for him."

SIXTY-THREE

It's No Time to Be a Kid

If you needed any more evidence that this is a pretty cruddy time to be a kid growing up, here is the story of what happened when the Evanston, Illinois, police responded to a 911 call about a rape in progress.

Kenneth Palmer, who lives in Wilmette, a suburb near Evanston, has a part-time job on Friday nights. He's fourteen; he and two of his friends—one of them is named Carlos and is fifteen, one of them is named German, and is Carlos's brother and is twelve—stuff Sunday newspapers.

"See, on Friday nights, they bring up a lot of the sections that make the Sunday paper so fat," Kenneth explained to me. "The real estate section, the home section, all those sections. We stuff them all together."

They do this stuffing at the North End News Agency, 1926 Harrison Street, in Evanston. "Our scoutmaster got us the jobs," Kenneth said. Kenneth, Carlos and German are Boy Scouts; their scoutmaster, Bryce Taylor, also is a youth adviser at their church, and is the manager of the news agency.

So on a recent Friday night, Kenneth, Carlos and German showed up to stuff the papers. But the preprinted Sunday sections hadn't arrived yet.

"My friends and I got this really great idea," Kenneth said. "We'd have a rubber band fight."

The three were the only people at the news agency; they had let themselves in with their key. "I guess we all were bored," Kenneth said. "We got some rubber bands from a desk, and we started firing them at each other and running around.

"Then Carlos said, 'Why don't we all take our shirts off so the rubber bands will hurt more?' " A perfectly logical idea, which you will understand if you were ever a kid.

So the three boys, shirtless, were shooting rubber bands at each other. "Carlos said he saw a guy who was watching through the window," Kenneth said. "But I didn't think too much about it."

They kept running around, waiting for the papers. "German has a real high-pitched voice, and I guess he was screaming a lot," Kenneth said. "We went to get some more ammo"—more rubber bands—"and we heard this banging at the door.

"These voices were yelling, 'Let us in! Let us in!' We got real scared. We thought it might be a gang or something, coming to beat us up.

"We've been taught to call 911 when we're in trouble. So we went into a back room, and Carlos called 911. But the lady who answered said it was the police outside. The 911 lady said to let them in.

"Carlos went to the door and said, 'Officer, this is a big mistake.' But the police ran in and made us lie on the floor and pointed their guns at us. They kept saying, 'Where's the girl? Where's the girl?' "

Here is what had happened:

The man outside on the street, seeing the shirtless figures running around and hearing the screams, had feared there was a rape in progress. He had called 911. The police team had been dispatched to the building.

There was no rape, of course; there was a rubber band fight among a bunch of kids.

Evanston Police Chief Ernest Jacobi told me: "You surmise correctly. The citizen thought he was witnessing a rape. He saw some people with their shirts off chasing someone else with no shirt, and he heard screams. He called 911. When our officers arrived, the boys called 911, too. They were having a rubber band fight, apparently."

When I spoke with Kenneth about this, he was accompanied by his mother. He wasn't angry at anyone—not at the police, not at the man on the street who'd called 911—no one. He was embarrassed that anyone would accuse him of the crime in question; this kid is Huckleberry Finn. "I don't even go on dates yet," he said.

So what's the lesson here?

The citizen who thought he saw the crime in progress and called 911 did the right thing; that's what a citizen should do, no question about it. The police who responded quickly did the right thing; think of the criticism they'd face if they hadn't taken the call seriously (the drawn guns you can argue about). The three boys who thought a gang was coming in did the right thing by calling the police; that's what their parents had told them to do if they ever needed help.

The lesson, then, is that it's a pretty lousy time to be a kid. You want to have a little rubber band fight, and all of a sudden rape and street gangs and 911 calls are thrown into the equation. When you're a kid today, you're forced to know about those kinds of things. A simple little rubber band fight among friends, screwed up because these days a kid can't be a kid anymore.

"The lesson?" Police Chief Jacobi said. "I guess the lesson might be, 'All's well that ends well.' "

Except for this stupid world of ours.

SIXTY-FOUR

Christmas Story

More than fifty Christmases ago—in December of 1936—a young woman and a young man worked at a now defunct firm called the Stecom Boiler Company, located on North Avenue in Chicago.

The woman—Helene Coan, called Susie by her friends—was a secretary at Stecom Boiler. The man—Bill Graham—was the company's chief engineer.

Graham had been born in Scotland. That Christmas of '36, Susie Coan sent him a "reusable" Christmas card that had an eraser attached. The card was designed to elicit a smile at the supposed Scottish trait of frugality.

"We were not romantically involved," Bill Graham said the other night. "We were friends. We lived on the South Side, and I would give her rides to work and back, and we were members of an archery club in Ogden Park."

The next year—the Christmas of '37—Bill surprised his friend Susie by sending the card back to her with his signature on it. She saved it for another year, and in 1938 she sent it back to him.

They have sent the card back and forth every Christmas from

then to now. They have never missed. Either Bill or Susie will receive the card one December, will keep it for a year, and then will remember to send it back the following December. Bill Graham is eighty-two years old now; Susie Coan—she married and became Susie Kopp—says that she is in her seventies.

"I keep it in a safety deposit box at the bank during the years I have it," she said the other night.

"I keep it in a locked box in my home during the years that I have it," he said the other night.

Bill Graham is married and the father of two daughters; he and his wife live in Sun City, Arizona. Helene Kopp is a widow and lives in a suburb of Chicago.

"We have only seen each other half a dozen times in all these years," Mrs. Kopp said. "But we are friends who know each other so well."

To read the card—even for a stranger to read the card—is a moving experience. Bill and Susie have added pages to it over the years; each year the person sending the card writes a short note about what has happened during the last twelve months. To see the faded handwriting, to read the words, makes one think about the history of two people, and the history of a country.

During World War II, Bill Graham signed the card "Pvt. Graham" in 1941; "Capt. Graham" in 1943; "Maj. Graham" in 1945. In 1944 Susie sent Bill the card in Burma.

In 1948 Susie wrote, "How old can a Christmas card get?" She could not have known that, almost fifty years later, the old Christmas card would still be being mailed.

In 1949 Bill wrote, "Hi Susie. This has the OK of the new Mrs. G., so it will still go on." In 1950 Susie wrote, "A husband, two babies, a house in the suburbs and a few gray hairs later."

By 1956 Susie was writing, "Cub Scouts, Girl Scouts, and music lessons . . . Whatever happened to wine, women and song?" By 1959 Bill was writing, "Almost forgot this rare old card." But he didn't.

Susie in 1962: "Our firstborn has left the nest and gone away to college. She's getting almost as old as I am." Bill in 1963: "Had the old bow and arrow from Ogden Park out last month. Brought back memories."

In 1970 Susie wrote: "We're both in college . . . working at the local community college, that is. Our family increased this year as Greg married Carolyn last May. I love this card. It answers the question, 'Where have the years gone?' " In 1975 Bill wrote: "I retire Dec. 31 and have a couple of jobs to go to, but may decide on just retiring to play golf. . . . We toured Europe this year. I've seen it and can think of other places I'd rather see before I go back."

Susie, 1976: "Almost forgot to get this out of the safe deposit box . . ." Bill, 1977: "We have our house up for sale and will move to Sun City, Arizona . . ."

As the years go by, the notes grow longer. Sometimes there has been pain. Susie's daughter and then her son died young, and then her husband; she told Bill in the Christmas card. Bill had some bad news, too, and began one note: "Dear friend, this has been a tough year." Susie, in 1990: "I keep remembering that gorgeous ring you were making. So fragile! I'm glad our friendship was stronger, and lasting."

Last week, Susie mailed the old card again.

"You cry a little, reading it every year," she said the other night. "I read it all again, every time. What it tells me is that I've had a pretty good life."

Bill was waiting to receive it.

"I always wonder what she will say in the card," he said the other night. "But the most important thing is that when the card arrives, I know she's still there."

SIXTY-FIVE

"Please . . . Don't Send Me Away"

"Please, Mommy, don't make me go alone. Please go with me, Mommy."

The four-year-old child known as Richard was sobbing so convulsively he seemed barely able to breathe. His adoptive mother was holding him, inside the home in Schaumburg, Illinois, where Richard had lived his whole life. This was just before 3:00 P.M. Sunday.

"I don't want to go." The boy tried to scream through his sobs, but the words were choking him. "Don't make me leave."

There was no way for the woman he has always known as his mother to answer him. She was sobbing, too. "We'll love you forever," she managed to say.

"But don't make me go," he begged. "Please. Please. Don't send me away."

Minutes away, a van carrying Richard's biological father and mother—she is the woman who willingly placed him for adoption at birth and sent word to the biological father that the boy was dead—was heading toward the house. The van, driven by the biological father's attorney, was on its way to pick Richard up and drive him to the biological parents' home. Richard had never seen them. This would be their first meeting.

Richard's clothes had been packed. His belongings—the belongings of a child's life—were ready to be carried onto the front lawn so that they could be loaded into the van once it arrived.

The boy's head rolled back and his voice was the sound of utter terror, of grief and mourning.

"Mommy, please don't leave me," he cried.

Not getting an answer from her—seeing that she was unable to get the words out, that she was as devastated as he—he turned to his adoptive father, a foot away.

"You, Daddy," he called, stopping the crying for a moment, allowing himself a few seconds of hope. "You can come with me."

His adoptive father, a firefighter, dissolved into tears.

Richard's older brother—seven years old—stood, weeping, looking up at this.

Richard reached his arm toward his brother. "Come with me," Richard called down to him. "I don't want to go on the sleepover alone."

Richard's brother's face was a mask of pure agony. He took Richard's hand in his, and Richard tried to pull the older boy off the floor and up to him. "Come to the sleepover with me," Richard begged his brother. "I don't want to go to the sleep-over."

Apparently this was what, in his panic and confusion, Richard was partially able to process—that he was going to a sleepover of uncertain duration at a house where he had never been. The thought appeared to terrify him. "Why do I have to have a sleep-over by myself?" he said to his brother.

Richard was packed and ready to be taken because five prevailing justices of the Illinois Supreme Court had so ordered. Those five justices decreed that he should not be permitted to have a hearing to determine—with witnesses testifying under oath—the truth about his life. The five justices had ordered that Richard be turned over to the biological father and thus to the woman who had said that he was dead—turned over to a household the justices know nothing about—"forthwith." They ruled that he was not entitled to a best-interests hearing—that the rights of the biological father were absolute.

"I'll be good," Richard sobbed to his adoptive mother. "Don't make me leave. I'll be good."

The five prevailing justices had been asked, in a motion last month, to at least appoint a qualified psychiatrist, independent and with allegiance to neither set of adults, to help make the transfer of Richard less painful for the boy. Whatever the failings of the adults in Richard's life, the fact that is absolutely unarguable is that Richard never lied to anyone, never deceived anyone, never did anything deserving of this kind of punishment.

With that in mind, the Illinois Supreme Court had been asked to at least try to help in making the agony as bearable as possible. At least to order that, as this was done to Richard, he have someone to attempt to ease the pain.

The Illinois Supreme Court said no. The court was not required to explain its ruling, and did not.

Outside the house, Richard's neighbors and friends had gathered to say goodbye to the child. As difficult as this was going to be to watch, they wanted him to know, as he was carried out, that they had not abandoned him.

The five prevailing Illinois Supreme Court justices—James D. Heiple, Michael Bilandic, Charles Freeman, John Nickels and Moses Harrison II—were not present. They were not there to look into Richard's eyes and to explain to him why they were so certain that he deserved this. To tell him why they were sure this was fair.

The carrying of Richard to the van, though, would come later. Right now the van had yet to arrive. Richard was calling out one word, over and over:

"Why? Why? Why?"

I had never met Richard before. This was the first time I had ever seen him. When I had arrived at the house Sunday afternoon, a relative on the front lawn invited me to come inside for a few minutes. I do not know the adoptive parents, either, other than to say hello in courtroom hallways. In all of the columns about Richard, I have done my best to look only at what has been done to this child by the courts. The adults are not the issue here. This child, and what has been done to him in the name of all of us, is the only issue.

He wasn't an issue, or a controversy, or a court case on Sunday afternoon. His expression becoming numb, his face slick with tears, he dug his fingers into his mother's neck so deeply I thought he was going to tear her flesh. "Oh, Mommy," he sobbed.

The van driven by the biological father's lawyer pulled slowly up to the house. It was time for me to leave. The sounds of the four of them—father, mother, Richard, brother—were like nothing I ever want to hear again. "Oh, Mommy," he cried, begging for an answer.

SIXTY-SIX

You've Got to Trust Your Milkman

BEXLEY, Ohio—At first I thought it had to be a mirage.

After all, it's no secret that I tend to idealize my hometown. Friends who still live in Bexley chastise me for this; they tell me that, in the quarter-century since I moved away, Bexley has proved no more immune to the troubles of the real world than any other American town has. They tell me that what I'm really in love with is a place that existed in 1964.

So as I walked west on Bryden Road on a bright and sunny summer morning, the vision that suddenly loomed into sight struck me as unreal, impossible. Like an oasis on a parched desert, it defied reality.

It was a truck. A squat little white truck with orange and yellow stripes. On the side of the truck was one word:

"Milk."

Could this be? Could this apparition on the streets of Bexley be genuine?

As if in answer to my question, from the sidewalk door of the truck emerged a man in dark shorts, carrying a supply of milk toward a house a few feet away.

I stood close to him, thinking him a ghost. But the expression he flashed at me—"Why are you staring at me?" the expression said—was proof that he was no ghost.

He was a milkman.

Mark Lehmer, by name.

"Yes, there are still milkmen," he said. "There aren't many of us, but we're out here. Our customers seem to like us."

He handed me an order sheet imprinted with the name of his employer: Foster Dairy. The sheet contained a lengthy list of products the Foster milkmen were available to deliver: milk, half-and-half, apple juice, eggs, hot dog buns, Popsicles, ham salad . . .

At the bottom was a notation: "We Appreciate Your Business! Dear Faithful and Valued Customer: If there is anyone you think might be interested in my service, please list their name. . . . Thank you! Your milkman."

Milkmen, I knew, were an endangered species in the United States; they used to be a constant part of the American scene, but in the last twenty-five years, with the growth of supermarkets, most families have become accustomed to picking up their milk at the grocery. I could not recall the last time I had seen a milkman with his truck on any street, anywhere.

But here was Mark Lehmer, on Bryden Road. When I was growing up on Bryden Road, our milkman—his name was Bill Quinn, and he drove for Borden Dairy—had a key to our back door; he would let himself in before dawn, go through our refrigerator, determine what dairy products we needed, leave them for us, and be gone by the time our family awakened.

Now, I assumed, in a crime-spooked America, no family would allow a milkman such free access to their home.

"Oh, sure they do," Lehmer said. "They trust us. The only difference is, now a lot of families give us their keys, but they also give us the code numbers to their security systems, so that we don't set off the alarm when we come in."

He said he was in sort of a hurry; we shook hands and he carried the milk up to the house. Later, still thinking about this, I called Foster Dairy.

"We have five trucks and about three thousand customers," the proprietor, Steve Foster, said. "All we have to sell is service —we're more expensive than the supermarkets. I think the day of the milkman may be coming back. There's something personal about having a milkman. If we see your newspaper on your lawn, we carry it on up to the house. If you leave us a note saying you need some bread, the bread is there for you. Supermarkets are great in their own way, but they're a part of a big, confusing new world. A milkman . . . a milkman makes the world seem a whole lot smaller."

And people's loyalty to their milkman is intense: "I became a milkman many years ago, before I owned this company. I worked for a company called Meadowgold. I went around Bexley trying to get customers. But the people were very loyal to their old milkman, and they didn't want to leave him. He was a fellow who drove for Borden's. I believe his name was Bill."

Bill Quinn?

"That was it," Foster said. "Bill Quinn."

I said I thought so. Borden's doesn't deliver milk anymore, and Bill Quinn is long gone, and I told Foster that when I had seen the truck on Bryden Road, I had doubted my own eyes.

"Oh, we're out here," he said. "Sometimes I think we're a part of an America that used to be. But then I think that maybe we're a part of an America that people would like to see come back. You've got to trust your milkman."

SIXTY-SEVEN

The Shoulder Season

EBENSBURG, Pennsylvania—Travel writer Jim Buerger refers to this as "the shoulder season," which is probably much more elegant a term than Thumper Silvasky would choose to use.

The shoulder season, by Buerger's definition, is "those two or three weeks that cannot be categorized as either summer or autumn, but which constitute a transition period with some of the best characteristics of each season." That name—the shoulder season—refers to the uncertainty of people in September about whether they should expose their shoulders or cover them, not knowing what the weather may be.

I'd not heard the term before, and I wasn't going to mention it to Thumper. He's nineteen, and he is what used to be referred to as a carny; from spring to October he travels to carnivals and county fairs all around the country, serving as barker and proprietor for a particular attraction that has been around ever since the invention of fairs.

He sits on a stepladder in front of one of those he-man machines—the carnival devices that propel an object upward when someone smacks the target at the bottom with a wooden mallet. Popeye did it a million times in a million cartoons. You pay a dollar, you get two swings, and the world—or at least the world that has gathered at a specific moment on a specific fairground—judges how strong you are.

"Come on, man, I need a bell-ringer!" Thumper calls out, but right now he has no takers. Sitting on that stepladder in cut-off jeans and a red Budweiser cap, he looks out across the dusty floor of the Cambria County Fair. Autumn is coming to western Pennsylvania, the trees are already beginning to turn, and there won't be many fairs after this one.

"School's started," Thumper says, those two words explaining everything. "The kids can't come in the daytime. Not on a weekday. We'll start getting people at seven, seven-thirty."

It isn't quite chilly now, a few minutes after 6:00 P.M., but you know it isn't July, either. The shoulder season. "The first week of October, I go home," Thumper says, then, returning to his barker's caw, turns toward the midway again and brays: "I need a bell-ringer!" and, getting no response, adds loudly: "Give you a free bandanna just for trying!"

There's something about summer that makes you want to hang on. When fall turns to winter, it happens overnight, like a piece of amber changing suddenly to something opaque. Spring emerges softly out of winter, and is so welcome that you're eager to forget what came before. The border from spring to summer is often seamless.

This, though, this right now, this shoulder season in September, is built in as if by nature's design. It's a time for getting ready, and a time for saying goodbye. They know this feeling in fancy places, and they know it in modest places; they know it at the Cambria County Fair, which always rolls around during the shoulder season, and which eases into its weekday nights slowly, because school is in.

The words from an old hit song bleed out of a loudspeaker somewhere on the fairgrounds: "You were mine, at the time . . ." It seems a perfect sound for a September evening. All fourteen chairs—thirteen metal, one wooden—at Red's Lunch stand on the midway sit empty right now, waiting for the nighttime diners who may or may not arrive. "You were mine, at the time, and the feeling was divine . . ."

The evening's business on the fairgrounds is beginning to pick up already; over there, at the Berry-Go-Round ride, a line has formed. The ride—it is for the youngest fairgoers; they twirl slowly in cars painted to look like strawberries—has drawn a crowd. The parents will take their toddlers on this ride and then will head for home, in Johnstown or Altoona or here in Ebensburg, before the night's temperatures start to drop, in plenty of time to get plenty of sleep for school tomorrow, for work tomorrow.

"You were mine, at the time . . ." Not much business right now over at Deedy's Dime Pitch. The easiest rule at the fair, now and always: Take a dime out of your pocket, toss it and try to make it stick inside a glass tumbler or a shot glass or an ashtray, take your prize home if you do. Tonight you toss, and your dime doesn't have a chance. It skips harmlessly into the dust, from where the proprietor retrieves it and banks it. "Getting chilly," she says.

So it is, in the inevitable shoulder season. Hang on to summer; hang on as long as you can. It was yours, at the time. Thumper Silvasky, across the way, is still at it. "I need a bell-ringer," he calls to someone who does not stop. "You're the man for the job," he calls to the figure in retreat.

SIXTY-EIGHT

Traffic Jam

DAYTONA BEACH, Florida—I didn't think it was such a stupid question.

"That's a stupid question," the fellow in the Pontiac Grand Am said to me for the second time.

I'd heard him the first time around. No need for him to repeat it. I'd merely presented him with a very simple query:

"Why do you do this?"

He was behind the wheel of his car. Nothing so out of the ordinary about that. Stuck in traffic. Nothing so out of the ordinary about that, either.

Except that he was just a few feet away from the Atlantic Ocean. Driving on the beach. There were long lines of cars heading in both directions, like on an expressway at rush hour. Dodge Ram pickup trucks behind him, Toyota Corollas in front of him, Jeep Wranglers visible down the beach. Gorgeous Florida day, traffic jam on the sand, and I'm the one standing barefoot by the water's edge and being called stupid.

"I'm serious, sir," I said. "Why do people drive their cars on the beach?"

"You're allowed to do it here," he said, somewhat defensively.

I wasn't questioning that. It is, indeed, perfectly legal in Daytona Beach. Drive your car onto the sand, steer between the sunbathers and volleyball players, pull into traffic and gun your engine. You're allowed to do it—but why would you choose to?

"There's not many beaches in the world with sand hard enough for this," he said.

Which is also a fact. Earlier in the century, there were actually auto races on the beaches here in Volusia County. In one of them, a racer named Fred Marriott powered his car to a speed of 197 m.p.h. when, in the middle of the race, he hit soft sand and crashed into the surf. You can do it—no argument over that.

A beach, though—especially a beach with a spectacular view of one of the world's great oceans—seems like such an inappropriate place for bumper-to-bumper traffic. The lush expanse of sand, the diamond-blue sky, the fresh sea air . . .

Here comes a Nissan Maxima. There's a Honda Accord.

Right next to the water, by the way—the cars here are assigned to more desirable sections of the beach than the people are. You can get to the ocean, as long as you're willing to snake your way past the Ford Taurus that's blocking your path, and quick enough to dash in front of the Olds 88 out for a Sunday drive.

"Please adhere to the speed limit of 10 m.p.h. as posted." That's an actual line from the printed beach regulations, handed to visitors. "Park only in designated areas as posted." I forgot to mention that little fact—that you are allowed to park your car on the beach.

"No double parking." "Please do not sit or lie in any traffic lane or in the area directly to the side of a parked vehicle." "Please do not throw any Frisbees, balls or other objects through any line of traffic." "Sunbathing is permitted only directly to the west of parked vehicles or east of the driving lanes."

Granted, every tourist area needs at least one factor that makes it unique and separates it from competing cities. And Daytona has long been one of the most famous beaches in the world, precisely because of its association with cars. But is the storied motor speedway not sufficient? Would even auto enthusiasts not prefer to see the high-powered cars over at the speedway, and give themselves freedom from exhaust fumes and growling engines when they go for a peaceful day at the beach?

Oops. Apparently not. Sorry . . . lost my train of thought there. Almost got dinged by an Acura Integra.

I attempted to speak with one couple who were cruising along the beach—they were in a Ford Aerostar—but they had their windows rolled up. It was a warm day, and they appeared to have turned their air conditioner on. Now, for a flash of a moment, that makes sense—if the day is hot, you go with your air conditioning.

But why would you go to the beach on a bright and sunny day if all you want to do is drive in your minivan with the windows up and the air conditioner on? It's the motor-vehicle version of the woman I saw coming out of the ocean in her bathing suit.

Lovely day, sparkling water, delicious sea air . . . and she's got a cigarette dangling from her mouth.

Oh, well. There are certain advantages to this, I suppose. I've been strolling on the sand for quite a distance now, and it's a good half-hour walk back to my hotel.

Think I'll step to the edge of the surf and try to hitch a ride with that Buick Park Avenue.

SIXTY-NINE

With Honors

When Lori Rader was a junior at Big Walnut High School in Sunbury, Ohio—this was in 1974, and she was sixteen—she became pregnant.

She found out in March of that year. "I went to a doctor by myself," she said. "I found out I was pregnant and I was scared and I didn't know what to do."

She and her boyfriend decided to get married. They waited until April to tell Lori's parents that she was pregnant. "It was April 10," she said the other afternoon. "I will never forget that terrible, terrible day. We were a very close family. My parents were so upset. The tears . . . I just felt I had hurt them so badly. They didn't want me to get married. My father was furious. My boyfriend had come to the house with me, and my father said to him, 'Get out, and don't come back.'"

Lori and her boyfriend, Mark, did get married. When school let out that summer, she was four months pregnant. She took some summer courses that year, but in the fall the baby—a boy named B.J.—was born, and she did not return to school.

"Pregnant girls, and girls with babies, didn't really go to high school," she said. "My world seemed very different from the world I had shared with my friends."

She and Mark had another son, Mike, two years later. Her husband and her father made up—her father hired Mark to work with him in his construction company—and over the years Mark and Lori and the boys became a good family. Lori worked in a warehouse at the Limited, the clothing company, putting price tags on merchandise.

"I always felt I had missed something important by not finishing high school," she said. "Especially every September, when my boys would start the new school year, I thought about it."

Last year she telephoned her old high school to see if there was a way she could be tutored, so that she could get her diploma. "The woman I called turned out to be the same guidance counselor who was there when I got pregnant," she said. "She said that I could get an equivalency degree by being tutored, but that the only way for me to get a real diploma would be to return to high school."

At first Lori didn't even consider that to be in the realm of possibility. But then the guidance counselor called back and said she had spoken to the principal at Big Walnut. If Lori—at age thirty-five—wanted to come back to her old school, she would be welcome.

"I thought, 'No, no, no,'" Lori said. "It just didn't seem like something a person could do. My own two boys were students at the high school."

She talked with her family about it. She talked with the principal.

And last September she returned to the same hallways she had left when she became pregnant in 1974.

"Oh, my gosh, I was terribly scared at first," she said. "The bell would ring, and the hallways would be filled with all the young people, and I would feel claustrophobic."

She got up at 6:00 A.M. each day, and she and her sons headed off to school. "We drove separately," she said. She took five classes. "At the beginning I didn't have many friends. At the beginning the only people in the school I really talked to were my own sons, and their friends I had known over the years."

At night she did homework. When she was ill or had to miss a day of school, she wrote her own absence notes—"it was required, so I wrote the notes and gave them to the teachers when I got back." She was afraid that she would embarrass B.J., a junior at the school, or Mike, a freshman. "But when I saw one of them in the halls, I just felt glad to see a friendly face."

B.J.—he was the baby who was in her womb when she quit Big Walnut in '74—explained his mother's presence in school to any students who asked. "I'm proud of her," he said the other day. "I just told everyone that she'd had to quit to have me, and she had always wanted to come back."

In January an election was held for winter homecoming queen. The students voted Lori onto the homecoming court. "I declined, and I asked that the girl with the next-highest number of votes be given my spot," she said. "But I was so touched and so honored."

Last month, at the end of the semester, she earned her diploma. She had a 4.0 average for the term.

She told her parents. She remembered that day—April 10, 1974—when she had told them she was pregnant. "It was a very sad day. Telling them was a hard, hard thing to do."

Last month she told them she was going to graduate at last. "They were so proud," she said. "They gave me a gold bracelet as a graduation gift. I did it. I did it."

SEVENTY

A Stolen Life

In San Jose, California, last month, burglars who intended to steal items from a house found that a resident of the house was unexpectedly at home that day.

Instead of fleeing from the house, or leaving the resident unharmed, the burglars, according to police, beat the resident, hacked at him with a butcher knife and a meat cleaver, marched him from room to room, stuffed a sock into his mouth, wrapped tape around his face and left him in the house to die slowly.

The resident of the house did, indeed, die.

It is hard to make a case that he presented much of a danger to the burglars.

For the resident of the house was an eight-year-old boy, a third-grader who was staying home from elementary school that day because he had a cold and a fever.

And the killers, according to police, were neighbors, friends of the family. The killers, according to police, were three teenagers who butchered Melvin Ancheta, an eight-year-old who knew them and who let them into the house because he trusted them. The items they stole while Melvin Ancheta lay dying had a market value of less than $100.

Our nation grows increasingly violent, and children are being killed in heartbreaking numbers by teenagers who seem to have no concept of the value of life. We can try to fix the economy, we can strive for a strong military, we can endeavor to help people in need around the world. But if we cannot solve the terrifying numbness of the soul that we are seeing among murderous young criminals from one coast to the other, nothing else will matter. We will be finished.

What happened to Melvin Ancheta defies understanding. He had stayed home from school that day to try to rest and recover from his cold. There was no one with him because both of his parents worked.

According to the San Jose police, the three neighborhood teenagers—one of them was the best friend of Melvin's older brother—had decided to steal items from the Ancheta house that day.

"Our understanding is that they had made the decision that they would kill whoever happened to be home," said Sergeant Dennis Luca. "They expected the mother might be home, but she had left for work."

When the teenagers—eighteen, sixteen and fifteen—knocked on the door, Melvin told them they could not come in.

"He was an eight-year-old boy who had been taught not to let anyone into the house if his parents weren't home," Sergeant Luca said.

But the teenagers returned. Through the door, they reportedly told Melvin that one of his brothers had run away from home, and that they had been sent to pick up some clothes to take to him. Because Melvin knew the teenagers, apparently he decided he should let them in.

Police say that the teenagers took Melvin upstairs to a bedroom and apparently beat him, then stabbed him repeatedly with a butcher knife. He did not die.

"They walked him downstairs," Sergeant Luca said. "At some point they stuffed a sock into his mouth and then wrapped tape around his head. They put him on a couch while they looked for items. They turned on a television set to a cartoon show."

Then, according to the police, one of the teenagers took a

meat cleaver and hacked at Melvin's throat. They left the house with a hand-held video game and a portable telephone.

Melvin lay face down on the carpet all that day. There were slashes on his neck and head, and his chest and back were covered with puncture wounds. His right arm was twisted behind his back, his palm up. His brother Ryan, fourteen, came home from school around 3:30 P.M., let himself into the house and found Melvin. According to police, Melvin's eyes were wide open, the brown plastic tape wrapped over his mouth, a cord twisted around his neck.

"The officers who made the arrests talked to all three of the teenagers who are charged with doing this, and 'remorse' was not a word that came up," Sergeant Luca said.

Melvin's third-grade classmates struggled to understand what had happened. They knew he'd had a cold the day before. The San Jose *Mercury News* reported that some of his schoolmates talked about the movie *Home Alone*. That's what they could relate it to. A friend of Melvin's, the newspaper reported, agonized that perhaps he could have saved Melvin by trapping the intruders, like the boy in the movie.

"You grope for words to explain it," Sergeant Luca said. "But there's no explaining." And meanwhile our society veers ever further out of control. Balance the budget, repair the highways, feed the hungry. But unless we can figure out a way to cure the dying national soul, we might as well just turn out the lights and say a prayer on our way out, because it's over.

SEVENTY-ONE

The Night He Went Inside

It has been a basketball season of many indelible moments at the Chicago Stadium. But for all the thrilling victories, for all the on-court heroics by the Bulls, I believe the memory I will take with me this year is one that never warranted a headline.

On a mean and rainy night during the playoffs—this was a game against the New York Knicks—Louise Harbach of Freeport, Illinois, approached the Stadium with her husband, their nephew and their son. They go as a family to three or four games a year, Mrs. Harbach said.

"My nephew saw something in the gutter, and he knelt to pick it up," Mrs. Harbach said. "We could hardly believe it—it was a ticket, a valid ticket, for that night's game."

The ticket was for standing room—that area at the very top of the highest balcony. This was the same kind of ticket that Mrs. Harbach and her family had.

"I felt terrible for whoever had lost the ticket," she said. "It's so difficult to get tickets to see the Bulls play, and especially in big playoff games. We went to a police officer and asked him if anyone had reported losing a ticket. He said no one had. We really wanted to give it back."

The rain was coming down hard, and game time was approaching, and the Harbach family had this unexpected, precious extra ticket.

Mrs. Harbach's son—Scott Harbach, thirty-four, a security

consultant—spotted a young boy hovering near an entrance to the stadium.

"You see these children from the neighborhood all the time," he said. "Some of them are so little, and they stand there begging spare change. All the wealthy people who come to the games, and these kids from the neighborhood have nothing."

He's right. Sometimes it's shocking to see children as young as five years old standing alone on the sidewalk, hoping someone will give them a quarter or a dollar. The Stadium is located in one of the most economically depressed areas of Chicago. The children, many of them residents of public housing projects, watch the ticketholders come and go on game nights, and in the quietest of voices ask for handouts.

"My mother said she had seen this one little boy before," Scott Harbach said. "She said she had noticed him standing there at other games."

So on this rainy night Scott Harbach approached the child.

"Would you like to go to the game with us?" Harbach said.

He said the boy looked at him disbelievingly. To the boy, the Stadium was only the exterior of an old building, and crowds on a sidewalk, and cars left in a parking lot. The wonders that went on inside the walls were something he knew he would never see.

"Would you like to see the Bulls play?" Harbach said.

"Sure!" the boy said, still not trusting what he was hearing.

According to Harbach, the boy's name was Frederick. He said he lived a block from the Stadium, and that he was in third grade. He was eight years old. He said that his mother knew he was hanging around outside the Stadium.

"We walked up the stairs, and his eyes were so full of life," Harbach said. "Think about it—he lives so close to the Stadium, he knows everything about the Bulls, yet he had accepted the idea that he would never get to go inside."

They reached the top balcony. "We asked him if he was hungry, and he said yes, and we bought him a pretzel and a

Coke," Harbach said. "He stood with us, and when it was time for the starting lineups, he knew every player.

"They were passing out towels or something as a promotion, and Frederick got one, and he was waving it around in the air the whole game, and laughing, and cheering for the Bulls. Way down below us there was Scottie Pippen and Horace Grant, and there was Michael Jordan, and Frederick was looking at the Bulls like he couldn't believe this wasn't a dream."

Harbach said that Frederick yelled for the team during the whole game, and chewed nervously on the towel at tense moments, and laughed aloud when the team made spectacular plays. "We kept looking at each other when the Bulls did well," Harbach said. "It was so loud that we couldn't talk much, because you couldn't hear.

"At the end of the game he just left, all by himself. This little kid. I think about him a lot. I don't know whether this will make any difference in his life. Probably it won't.

"But maybe it's a night that will stick with him. The night he went into the Stadium instead of standing outside. The night he went inside and saw Jordan and Pippen and all of them, the greatest basketball team in the world. And there was Frederick, cheering his heart out, cheering them on. Cheering his team."

SEVENTY-TWO

The Women in Room 811

Mother and child.

Is there ever a stronger love? Is there ever a more precious connection?

In Room 811 of the Westshire Healthcare Centre, a nursing home in Cicero, Illinois, two women live as roommates. To most visitors to the building, they would seem to be just two more elderly people.

The roommates are Della Norwood, who is one hundred and ten years old, and Ella Walker, who is eighty-two—and who is Della's daughter. More than eighty years after Ella's birth, they are still together. Every morning, every night, mother and child.

"We have never really quarreled," said the mother. "And when we have, it has never come to anything."

"We talk with each other a lot," said the daughter. "Sometimes we sit and don't need to say anything."

For many years they lived together on a farm in Mississippi. Both of their husbands are dead; so are Della Norwood's two other children. In the early 1980s, Ella became ill. Her mother wanted to take care of her, but felt she was not able to do so alone.

They moved up to Chicago, to live with Ella's son, Willie Walker, and his wife, Sarah. "They are really blessed with love for each other," said Sarah Walker. "They will read the Bible together, or watch a baseball game on TV, and there is just this love between them in the room."

Last year, though, the Walkers themselves became sick, and could no longer care for the elderly mother and daughter. So Della Norwood and Ella Walker moved into the nursing home, sharing a room.

When they had moved north from Mississippi, it was because of the fierce need of the mother to make sure her daughter was all right. "She saw that her daughter's health was failing, and she had to think of a way to take care of her," Sarah Walker said. But now, with the mother well past one hundred, "sometimes it seems as if the daughter has become the mother," said Mrs. Walker. "I suppose that happens in a lot of families."

Yet this family is quite special. Elleke Hayford, the primary-care nurse for the two women, said, "They each look out for the other. They'll talk about something that has happened here in the building, or they'll talk about what life used to be like back in Mississippi. It must be hard for them, at times—for years they lived in a very rural area, with no noise, and open spaces. Now they're in a place with traffic outside and a lot of people, but they still want to take care of each other."

So in the morning, when they awaken, they look across the room to see each other's faces. "It feels good just to wake up for another day," said Della Norwood. "I thank the Lord for waking us up each day," said Ella Walker. Della, the mother: "I don't think I would change a thing about my life."

Each knows that the duration of a person's time on Earth is most uncertain. Recently, according to Sarah Walker, Ella became ill enough that she had to go to a hospital until her health improved. "Every day, Grandma said, 'When is she coming back?'" Sarah Walker said. "She was very lonesome. She missed her daughter."

They are roommates, they are best friends, they are mother and child. "This is very, very unusual," said Elleke Hayford, the nurse. "All these years, seeing each other through the good times and the bad times." Willie Walker, Ella's son, Della's grandson, said, "When you're around them, you are just around so much devotion."

Their days are not long ones. Before they go to sleep at night in Room 811, each woman prays.

"I say my prayer to myself," Della Norwood said. "I ask the Lord to take care of us as we sleep."

"I thank the Lord for all we have," said Ella Walker. "I thank the Lord for my loving and wonderful mother."

Neither knows what the future may hold. They know that eventually the day will come when one will have to live without the other. But they seldom verbalize that knowledge, and never dwell on it. "What I wish for my daughter is that people will always be good to her," said Della Norwood. Ella Walker said, "I hope my mother will always be happy and have what she needs."

They could not have known that life would bring them here, more than eighty years later, still together. The women in Room 811. The mother and her child.

"She's everything to me," said Della Norwood. "She's all I've got. She's my girl."

SEVENTY-THREE

The Ride of a Lifetime

"Well, once maybe small dinosaurs lived here," the boy said. "Because certain kinds of dinosaurs can stand the cold weather."

His mother, sitting on the aisle, looked over to see what he was talking about. The boy was on his knees, looking out the window.

"They could survive the frozen winters," the boy said. "The dinosaurs could."

That's what he was seeing—a place where dinosaurs might once have lived. At least that's what he was imagining he saw. The rest of us, if we looked out the windows at all, were seeing a commuter route. A Metra train making the long and routine haul from the outlying counties of northern Illinois en route to downtown Chicago.

"You really think the dinosaurs lived here?" his mother said.

"You know, you can call them gigantic reptiles if you want," the boy said. "Because that's what they are. Gigantic reptiles. That's what dinosaurs really are."

They looked alike, mother and son. Red-haired, both of them. He must have been six or seven. He wore a Cubs jacket over a gray sweatshirt; she wore a raincoat and carried a handbag with illustrations of sailing ships on a map of the world. Same faces, one thirty or so years older than the other.

"You know what I like about construction?" he said, seeing a building going up across a desolate field.

"What do you like?" his mother said.

"I like it that the holes are so deep," he said.

The holes were, upon observation, rather deep. The rest of us had likely long ago stopped noticing such things—stopped noticing much of anything as we looked out the world's windows at life. Harvard, Woodstock, Cary, Fox River Grove, Barrington . . . some of the stops on this commuter line from rural Illinois into the city. Palatine, Mount Prospect, Cumberland, Des Plaines, Dee Road . . . the passengers read their newspapers and paperback books, or simply stared straight ahead. Not the boy. His window was like a wondrous screen, revealing secrets by the minute.

"For sale," he announced to his mother, quoting a sign. He could read; sometime in the last year or two he had learned how.

"Open to the public," he read.

Slowly, imperceptibly, the scenery outside the train shifted; what at the beginning of the ride was mostly farmland and undeveloped acreage turned to houses and towns and streets increasingly congested. There was a highway clogged with motorists who had chosen not to take the train.

"Hey!" he announced to his mother. "The expressway isn't even expressing!"

He wasn't being loud about it; he was simply seeing things and letting his mother know. He reached between the edge of

his seat and the interior wall of the train and pulled something out.

"Look," he said. "A candy wrapper."

"Don't touch that," his mother said. "It's dirty."

He gave the piece of paper a quick once-over, examining
every inch of it, as if it contained some sort of secret.

"Put it down," his mother said.

He did not drop it to the floor; instead he jammed it right
back where he had found it.

"Every time I built a track, she would just wreck it and ruin
everything I had set up," he said.

"Well, that's part of being a little sister," his mother said.

"Every time, I'd have to pick her up and carry her away from
the track," he said.

Park Ridge, Jefferson Park, Irving Park, Clybourn . . .

"That's the end of *that* wheel," he pronounced with certainty.

His mother looked out the window. Apparently he had noticed a discarded tire by the side of the tracks.

"Downtown Chicago next," the conductor called.

"Yeah!" the boy said.

He had had the best ride of any of us. Maybe we were all
him at one juncture in our lives; maybe, whatever he had inside
his heart right now, we all once had. Maybe we were all, once
upon a time, lucky enough to be him.

"Last stop for this train," the conductor called.

"Did you know turtles could jump off anything?" the boy
said to his mother. "Even a whole building?"

SEVENTY-FOUR

A Century Ends in T-Shirts

PITTSBURGH—Among the tank tops, cut-off blue jeans and determinedly ragged T-shirts on the streets of downtown here on a
warm Saturday afternoon, you did not, of course, see any men
wearing tuxedos, or women in formal gowns.

What you did see was the stately, austere building that is
Horne's department store. And in its own way, Horne's appeared
as out of place downtown at the beginning of summer in the
1990s as that apocryphal man in the tux or woman in her gown
would have among the free-and-easy crowds.

Horne's, which has graced the corner of Stanwix Street and
Penn Avenue for almost a century, is one of those grand, bigger-
than-life department stores that were once a fixture of big-city
American downtowns. It has been sold; by autumn it will no
longer be Horne's, and no one seems quite sure of its eventual
fate.

As Georgia Sauer, fashion editor of the Pittsburgh *Post-
Gazette*, wrote recently:

"It was a place of marble floors and shimmering chandeliers,
a place with a bustling carriage trade and a doorman and tearoom
to cater to it, a place renowned for its high fashion and intricate
window displays at Christmastime, which would draw shoppers
and lookers from miles around. . . .

"Women in their 40s fondly remember dressing up when they
were little girls to go shopping downtown at Horne's with their

mothers, putting on their patent leather shoes and frilly dresses and their white gloves—always their white gloves. . . ."

White-glove America—an America in which people, regardless of their means, valued the chance to be formal once in a while, to dress up just for the sake of an occasion, to find reasons to make a day seem different and special—was epitomized by the old downtowns, and the old downtowns, as their courtly capitols, had the great department stores.

Cultural historians like to say that, while a democracy has no royal palaces, the United States had people's palaces in the ornate movie theaters that have largely disappeared. But if the movie houses were palaces, so were the legendary department stores—and Americans treated those department stores with, if not reverence, at least a touch of secular awe. It is, indeed, easy to imagine the girls of Pittsburgh, circa 1950—not just the daughters of executives, but the daughters of steelworkers—dressing up for that special and memorable trip to Horne's.

And while many of America's great downtown department stores still exist, many others have disappeared, and still more have changed drastically, both in mission and in mood. We live in a suburban-mall America, not a downtown-department-store America; our commercial vision has been scaled down, and in towns where you will no longer find downtown department stores, you will find city stores devoted entirely to selling party balloons, or chocolate chip cookies, or muffins. It's the new downtown—downtown as a casual corner.

On this day in Pittsburgh, for instance, the reason for the T-shirts-and-cutoffs crowd was the presence of two events: one of those sidewalk-exhibit-and-performance bazaars replete with food booths, and, across the bridge, a six-hour-long oldies rock concert that was drawing 40,000 people into Three Rivers Stadium. America's downtowns once had to offer no special lures to attract people—they *were* the lures, by definition. Now, by necessity, they paint themselves up and put on flashy clothing, trying to catch the eyes of people who need to be persuaded to visit.

It works on occasion; downtown Pittsburgh on this day was bustling. The white-gloves days are gone and will not return, just as the days of men wearing suits and ties to the ballpark will not return. Hard to say when we turned that casual corner—when we figured out that no one had the power to demand formality, that you could board an airplane wearing shorts and rubber sandals, that you could walk into Horne's department store wearing an undershirt—and it would probably do no good to pass judgment on whether we are better off or worse.

On this humid downtown Saturday, street vendors were selling lemonade slushes and meat-on-a-stick, and James Brown, the godfather of soul, pulled up to the baseball stadium for his oldies-concert performance in a white limousine with a hot tub built into the trunk and a license plate that read "I FEEL GOOD." The tearoom at Horne's was closed.

SEVENTY-FIVE

Who Has Won and Who Has Lost

SARASOTA, Florida—Because the world tends to remember in shorthand, Michael Jordan's attempt to make the major leagues down here may be destined to be recalled for only a couple of things. One is that he wasn't good enough. The other thing that may be remembered is the national sports magazine that put him on its cover to make fun of him—the magazine that said Jordan and the Chicago White Sox were embarrassing baseball.

Had Jordan, in his grief in the aftermath of his father's murder, gone out and gotten publicly drunk every evening, had he been seen gambling every night in Las Vegas, it is doubtful that he would have been ridiculed any more mercilessly than he has been ridiculed down here. It is doubtful that a national sports magazine—a magazine that for years has attempted to recruit subscribers by offering videotapes of Jordan playing basketball—would have laughed at him on its cover.

But he committed the most serious crime of all, in the eyes of the sports world: He failed. He tried to do something and he did not succeed. When Jordan was asked by reporters to rebut the magazine story that called him an embarrassment, he would not display anger. What he did say is that everyone should be given a chance: "It should be a game that everyone has an opportunity to play—no matter who, Michael Jordan or Leroy Smith, it doesn't matter."

I did not see any stories in the press that explained the Leroy Smith line. Perhaps everyone thought it was just a name that Jordan was making up, a symbol for Everyman. But there is a Leroy Smith.

When Jordan was fifteen, it was he and his friend Leroy Smith who walked together into a high school gym in North Carolina to see who would make the school's basketball team and who would be cut. Leroy Smith made it; Jordan did not. That was the day he was told that he was not good enough to play basketball. Had he believed the people who judged him then, we would never have heard his name. Even now, many times when Jordan is checking into a hotel on the road and does not wish to be bothered by callers, he registers under the name Leroy Smith. It is a constant and self-imposed reminder to him: The world is always waiting to tell you you are no good.

He has tried his best down here—not just at baseball, but at all the things that go with it. One day at his house I saw him studying a booklet put out by the White Sox, containing pictures of all the players and staff members. He was looking at it for twenty minutes, and finally I figured out what he was doing. He was learning the names—matching the names with the faces. When he went into the clubhouse, he wanted to make sure that no one—ballplayer, locker attendant, equipment man—felt awkward about saying hello to him. He wanted to be able to say their names first.

The first player to arrive each sunrise, on days when things went badly he also insisted on staying late to take more hitting practice. He said there was a reason: "I never want to go home at the end of the day on a failing note. I want to go home feeling I've done something right." Some of the players who have publicly spoken well of him have been devastatingly unkind behind his back. He knows it. He has never responded.

Major league baseball is a sport in which many players are casually rude to fans, refusing to stop to sign autographs or even wave hello. Jordan, at the end of his hitless days, almost always worked his way down the stands, meeting the customers and signing whatever they handed to him. Jerry Reinsdorf, owner of the White Sox, stood in right field of Ed Smith Stadium after one game, observing Jordan with the fans, and said, "I hope the other players are watching him. They might finally learn something."

He has given as much effort as he was capable of, knowing day by day that it was not going to be sufficient, and he has not walked away. He has heard the mockery and the cruel remarks, and he has refused to be discourteous even to those who have belittled him the most. He has demonstrated that there is honor in trying to do something, and that there is no loss of dignity in coming up short. A man of great accomplishment, he has decided to take the risk of appearing ordinary.

An embarrassment? What Jordan has done down here is an embarrassment? If the baseball experts say so. But if you have children, you ought to hope against hope every day of your life that they will some day grow up to embarrass you like this.

SEVENTY-SIX

Mass Surrender

RENSSELAER, Indiana—On the highways leading from Chicago to the rural fields of Indiana, you see the billboards and signs. They're come-ons of the most obvious sort: invitations to gamble.

The invitations are sanctioned by the state governments. That's not unusual these days; governments all over the United States are in the business of teasing their citizens into gambling, and the tease has been going on for so long that it has become part of the backdrop of American life. Your elected officials hope that you are a gambler—or if you're not, that you will become one. They want your money.

The state lotteries are the most common form of government-backed gambling, but casinos—either land-based or on water—are catching up fast. Casino-type gambling exists or has been proposed in thirty-six of the fifty states. The reason is elementary. As Chicago *Tribune* reporters Rob Karwath and George Papajohn noted recently: "Politicians, afraid of raising such everyday taxes as those on real estate and income, [have] embraced gambling as a seemingly painless way to fuel their municipal and state budgets. As a result, governments throughout the U.S. are becoming ever more reliant on taxes and fees from gambling."

True. Gambling, as a way of bringing in money, without question is effective. But in the rush to raise cash by endorsing and sponsoring gambling operations, whether in lotteries or casinos, state governments have trained themselves to close their eyes to two unpleasant realities:

1. It is wrong for a government to lure its citizens into gambling their money.

2. It is yet another sign that we, as a nation, are surrendering—not just in this way, but in many important ways.

Politicians and gambling corporations and some gamblers will dispute that first observation; they will say there's nothing wrong with government being in the gambling business. But of course there is something wrong with it, which is why for centuries most states and cities stayed away from being gambling entrepreneurs. Many people will gamble when given the chance, yes; that does not mean the government should be the bookie. A government that goes into the gambling business cannot claim to be a healthy government.

Which brings us to the second observation. Because so many state and local governments are not healthy—because so many state and local governments are desperate for money—they have embraced gambling as a form of surrender. If taxes based on income, on property, on manufacturing production have been exhausted or increased past the level of acceptability, then weary governments—weary cities, weary states—raise their arms and say: We give up.

And the surrender only begins with gambling. In Fort Worth, Texas, recently, members of the City Council were considering putting six street gang leaders on the municipal payroll. The stated reason is to combat violence.

City and police officials in Fort Worth seem a little nervous about the project, but according to reports they are verging on going ahead with it. Gang-related shootings in the city, as in so many U.S. cities, have become a severe problem. So why not hire gang members, and ask them to persuade other gang members to change their ways?

Maybe it will work, maybe it won't. But it sounds like paying protection money. It sounds like giving up. It sounds like saying: "The government can't stop criminality using methods that have worked in the past, so it's time to give money to the criminals." It sounds like surrender.

As does the current proposal to redesign U.S. paper currency. The U.S. Treasury and Bureau of Engraving are considering making paper money look dramatically different from what it traditionally has. The reason: to stop counterfeiters in the drug trade. Plans are to change the look of hundred-dollar bills first—the bills favored by drug dealers.

The government can't stop the drug traffic; the government can't arrest the drug criminals. Might as well change the money that we all use. Maybe that will work.

Might as well surrender.

Maybe those gang leaders who are about to go on the government payroll in Texas will end up spending some of their leisure time gambling in government-run casinos somewhere, using the new paper currency that will be printed to combat crime. Some people would find that ironic. But it's not irony. It's merely surrender.

SEVENTY-SEVEN

Endless Songs

LONGBOAT KEY, Florida—A moment for a private smile:

In the middle of one recent evening, well after dark, I came up off the beach after a walk next to the Gulf of Mexico. I heard music; a singer with an acoustic guitar was performing for a very small audience at an outdoor café a hundred feet or so from the shoreline.

The singer, who appeared to be in his forties, was just completing his version of an old Crosby, Stills and Nash song. Only one table was occupied: by a man and woman who also, by appearances, were in their forties, and by their son, who looked to be about five.

The father, in that tone of voice that indicates the third beer has just been consumed and that the warm glow of perceived wisdom is just setting in, said to the singer: "I think Stephen Stills was really the driving musical force behind that group."

The singer said: "Not Graham Nash?"

"Not in that group," the father said.

"Yeah, I guess Graham Nash just sort of sang along," the singer said.

And the five-year-old—this was the nice part—yawned an open-mouthed yawn that bespoke the boredom of the truly tedium-beset, and fidgeted as if being forced to sit through a year of Sunday sermons. Stephen Stills? Graham Nash? The benumbed expression on the kid's face could not have been more lacking in interest had his dad and the singer been discussing the relative merits of Mozart and Brahms.

Whatever part of his younger self the dad might have been reaching for in this shoreline conversation with the singer, it wasn't young enough for his own son. Whatever release from the seriousness of his own daily business life the spring-vacationing dad may have been essaying, the release itself was way too serious and old-fashioned-sounding for his son.

It's less than polite to eavesdrop, so I returned to the shoreline to continue my walk. I have been coming here, on and off, since I was a child, and the lesson I leave with is always the same. It is a lesson taught by the Gulf of Mexico, which stretches as far as the eye can see from the sand of the key.

The waves roll in, touching the sand and then dying, to be replaced by more. You can stand by the water for hours at a time, if you choose, and you will see nothing and everything. You can stand by the water at midnight, and you can come back at dawn, and the Gulf doesn't know you're there and doesn't care. It was here for centuries before our own, and will be here for centuries after. It has no worries, no goals, no thoughts. The worriers and the goal-seekers come to visit, so certain of the urgency and importance of what is transpiring in their daily worlds. The Gulf knows there is no such thing as urgent.

Stephen Stills and Graham Nash . . . they are old-time singers now; they had not sung a professional note when I first came to the Gulf. The father talked and his son twitched, and a hundred years from now other fathers will speak of singers and athletes and political men and women who have not today been born. The news comes out of the sky to Longboat Key, as the news comes to everywhere; satellites far above the Gulf transmit the video versions of insistent events into TV sets here on the key and in every town in the land. It all seems so pressing, at least for a moment or two.

Dwight Eisenhower was president in the presatellite days when I first came here, and it was his name that was in the news every sunrise. Bill Clinton has that dubious distinction now; there have been many others in between. They are all a part of history, whatever that is. The Gulf knows nothing of history. The Gulf cannot care.

Which should not, of course, be its lesson. The waters of the Gulf will roll in and then subside regardless of what goes on in the world, and just because the Gulf lives without caring about anything does not give us permission not to care. But the slow song it sings—the song the waters have been singing forever— does have the power to teach us that it's all right to slow down. That regardless of how big a hurry we think we're in, regardless of how insistent our own schedules and timetables may seem to us, we are very small and utterly transient, actors playing bit roles in the longest-running stage play of all.

By the shoreline, I heard the sound of music again. Not the Gulf's song; this was the guitar music of the singer a hundred feet away, playing for the father and the mother and the son. I could not make out the tune. I hoped it pleased the boy.

SEVENTY-EIGHT

Standing Tall

Writing a newspaper column sometimes seems a little like tossing bottles into the ocean. You wonder if they're ever going to surface anywhere.

And then something happens.

More than two years ago I wrote the story of a fifteen-year-old Texas boy named Tucker Church. Tucker, who was born with cerebral palsy, weighed just fifty-six pounds and stood four foot nine. He loved the game of baseball, and tried to play, without very much success. "His feet turn in somewhat severely," his mother, Judi Church, told me. "His knees turn in, also, and he has trouble running. He will often fall down on the basepaths. He knows that, and we know it."

Tucker tried his hardest, anyway. He played in a league with younger boys—boys between the ages of nine and twelve. "I know that I'm not the best player there is," Tucker said. "A lot of times I can't catch the ball." But the coach of the team, Scott Davis, encouraged Tucker's efforts, and let him play in every game.

Near the end of the season, someone—allegedly a coach on a rival team—complained to the league. The complaint was that Tucker was breaking the rules by being in the league with the younger boys. The complainant wanted Tucker's team to be forced to forfeit all its games. Coach Davis was told by the league that he would have to throw Tucker off the team—and that Davis would have to resign as coach for violating the rules.

That is what I wrote about in the column—the meanness toward Tucker, who was trying his best. The column was reprinted widely, including in the *Reader's Digest*.

The *Reader's Digest* may not be the most trendy and fashionable publication in America—it is not snide and it is not sarcastic—but its circulation is massive. Fifty million people read each issue of the *Digest*—far more people than watch the highest-rated series on network television.

And one of the people who read that column in the *Digest* was a Shriner in Houston.

He read about Tucker and took the trouble to refer Tucker to Houston's Shriners Hospital for Crippled Children. Doctors at the hospital took a look at Tucker.

"Tucker had always walked almost as if he were crouched over," his mother said. "His muscles had bunched up so tightly that he literally could not stand up straight. He hated being that way—he would fall down in the hallways at school sometimes."

The doctors, after examining Tucker, said they thought they could change this. They said that there was a form of surgery in which the muscles and soft tissues were released—were, in effect, loosened and relaxed. Surgeons at the hospital specialized in that kind of surgery.

Tucker had three operations; he was in leg casts for months. After that, he went through intensive physical therapy. It did not cost his family one cent; the Shriners Hospital, as is its policy, paid for everything.

And Tucker can walk steadily now. He can stand up straight and he can walk.

"It brings tears to our eyes," his mother said. "He walks through a crowd, and no one stares at him. He fits in with the other boys and girls. He has said to me, 'Mom, no one even thinks there's anything wrong with me.' "

At the Shriners Hospital in Houston, staff member Kathy Gunner said, "Give the credit to Tucker. He's a great kid. It's a painful operation, and the physical therapy is tough. He's brave and he's determined and he's the one who got it done."

And Tucker?

"I think I'm better now," he told me. "I'm not perfect. But my legs and feet are straightened out, and I walk a hundred percent better. I'm almost six inches taller than I was when I was all bent over. I didn't even know there was an operation like this. Please say thank you to all the people who thought about me after that baseball thing happened. It's funny—if I hadn't been thrown off the baseball team, then none of this would have happened. No one would ever have known about me, and I wouldn't have had the operations. So please say thanks to everyone."

The last of the casts is scheduled to come off this week. Tucker is seventeen now, and is looking forward to a life where no one makes fun of him, and no one stares, and no one pushes him around because he is different.

The world is a place that is constantly filled with bad news: tragedy and pettiness and heartbreak. There's no reason to think that will ever change.

Today, though, I'm going to try to forget about the world's bad news, if only for a few hours.

Tucker Church can walk.

SEVENTY–NINE

Ledger

Some of the hottest-selling books today are reports and analyses of the free-spending 1980s. The eighties are already being viewed from a distance as a bizarre and outlandish period of American fiscal history, and people seem fascinated with nonfiction accounts of an era when wealthy people squandered money without compunction.

I've been reading another book in the last few days. This one wasn't published for mass consumption. This one is a little ledger book with dark-green binding, kept by one person during one year.

The book belonged to a man I knew, who died last year after living almost a hundred years. He filled out the ledger book in the school year of 1914–15, when he was a freshman in college. The old ledger book was found in his estate.

Whoever said that dry numbers can't tell a story was wrong. All this ledger book consists of are detailed accountings of how he spent his money in 1914 and 1915. Yet as I look through the ledger, it reads like a novel to me. There's a tale there, a tale that's unexpectedly moving.

The man who was a college freshman in 1914 turned out, later in life, to be a man who was responsible in everything he did, who was careful in his business dealings, who looked out for details. You can see that in the ledger book he kept the first time he was away from home. His parents obviously had told him that he must learn to account for his money, and he did, every week.

The cover of the pocket-sized ledger book identifies it as a Crown Memorandum. A tag inside says it was purchased at a store called Smythe's—"Come, Browse Around." On September 13, 1914, the young man began college with a financial balance of $105.51.

He purchased books on September 16—the books cost him $3.75. That same day he treated himself to some candy—"Milk Chocolate," the notation says. Fifteen cents.

He needed streetcar tickets that first week: twenty-five cents. He bought a notebook—five cents. Apparently young men going away to college in 1914 were in the habit of carrying calling cards. He ordered a box for $2.50.

His total expenditures that first week in college were $49.76, assiduously recorded. He got a shoeshine on September 26, and made note of the ten cents it cost. His haircut that week was twenty-five cents; the necktie he purchased was fifty cents. He went to a fraternity "smoker," and the price of admission was fifty cents. He didn't eat many meals out; an exception was October 13, when lunch cost him twelve cents. He went to a dance on October 16. He took his date in a taxi—$1.50.

As I look through that ledger book I see the story of his first year away from home. He bought a bar of soap one day, and paid eighteen cents for it. He went to the "picture show" at a theater called the Majestic, for ten cents. He got his shoes repaired and it set him back a dollar. He bought something called "Peg of My Heart"—sheet music?—and it cost him a quarter.

Every week, all year, he was diligent in keeping his ledger book. Once a month or so, apparently his parents would send him money. It was always noted in a separate column: "Received 'Dad'—$15." Or: "Received Mom—$1." Although the ledger book listed only dates and not days of the week, I can always tell which days were Sundays, because he would go to church and list his charitable contribution, often five or ten cents, under "Collection."

The prices may seem quaint, and some of the expenditures— "Eats after Purdue game"—bring a smile. I don't think it's stretching the point, though, to regard the little ledger book as a preview of a life. The college freshman who so punctiliously wrote down each transaction grew into a man who was just as precise in his adult dealings. In the ledger book there was a distinction between money that his parents voluntarily sent to him ("Received 'Dad'—$5") and money he had to ask for in a pinch ("Borrowed Mom—$3"). The borrowed money he knew he must pay back.

With all the books available about the financial craziness and profligacies of the eighties, somehow I get real pleasure out of reading this ledger book from 1914–15. It's no surprise to me that the man who kept the ledger book never became the kind of person who would get swept up in the easy-money, go-for-broke financial atmosphere of the eighties; he was conservative in what he did from the first day he stepped onto a college campus, and he stayed that way.

He did very well for himself, too; when he died he was a lot better off than many of the Wall Street speculators who piled up tens of millions in the eighties and then saw it all go away. He played by the rules. On the last page of the ledger book, he makes a note that his total receipts for the school year were $363.80, and his total expenditures were $363.76. His balance at the end of the year was four cents. He came out ahead.

EIGHTY

A Nation Behind Bars

ALLEGAN, Michigan—We're rapidly approaching the point at which we really are two nations: the people who are locked behind bars for the horrors they have committed, and the people who are fearful and free outside, demanding even more locking.

In Allegan County this summer, a woman named Kimberly Lundgren, thirty-three, was lying in bed with her husband, James, forty-two, and their four-year-old daughter. Suddenly, police say, a man burst into the bedroom and shot James with a small-caliber handgun while his wife and daughter lay there.

Dennis Leonard, nineteen, was arrested and charged with the murder. But Kimberly Lundgren was arrested, also, and charged with the same crime.

"They planned it together," said Allegan County Sheriff David Haverdink. "They worked in a factory together and were having an affair, and they wanted to get the husband out of the way so that they could continue their life together. We believe that the plan was for Dennis Leonard to shoot the children, too —the little girl lying in bed, and a two-year-old boy in the other room. The mother wanted her children killed, but the boyfriend couldn't make himself do it."

If convicted, Leonard and Mrs. Lundgren face up to life in prison. Allegan County is a rural area, but it is not immune to the nauseating violence and murderous meanness endemic to so much of America these days. Terry Colley, the father of British tourist Gary Colley, who was murdered at a rural Florida highway rest stop, said, "The United States is a sick country," and it is very hard to dispute him.

The sickness starts young. In Chicago, the parents of three-year-old Antwan Polk try to comprehend what was done to their little boy. Police say he was playing in a sixth-floor hallway of a public housing project when two other boys, ages eleven and thirteen, saw him. According to police, they grabbed the three-year-old, dragged him to a garbage chute, urinated on him, and then threw him down the chute. He was stuck in the cramped chute somewhere between the sixth floor and the basement for an undetermined number of hours, with no one but his assailants knowing where he was; he was rescued after a janitor saw him about to be pulled into a basement garbage compactor.

The thirteen-year-old and eleven-year-old have been charged with attempted murder. If convicted, they will most likely be locked up somewhere. This is what society demands, and what is undoubtedly just. The problem is, as we evolve into a nation of those who are locked and those who do the locking, the United States is becoming something quite different from what it ever was. A sick country, in the words of Mr. Colley.

Commuters on the Parkway expressway in Pittsburgh have become accustomed to a familiar sight on the outskirts of down-town. It appears to be a huge new high-rise apartment going up, but it's not. It is the new Allegheny County Jail, and it will have room for 2,397 prisoners once it opens. The people who will run it expect it to be filled to capacity right from the start.

"It's pretty clear that the public wants criminals taken off the street and locked up," said Edward Urban, assistant deputy warden. "We haven't had enough cells. The number of lawbreakers keeps going up."

The sight of the enormous jail rising in Pittsburgh seems to be an answer to the demand of so many frustrated Americans: "Build more prisons." According to Urban, "This is going on left and right all over the country. Everywhere you look, more prisons and jails are being built."

In Washington, the Justice Department backs up this contention. A spokeswoman said that in the last five years, 142 state and federal prison construction projects have been commenced. The reason, she said, is that there are not nearly enough cells to lock up this nation's criminals.

The number of inmates in state and federal prisons, she said, is 883,593. As recently as 1980, that number was only 329,821. Crime is a growth industry, and so is locking up criminals. The average occupancy in the nation's prisons is well over 100 percent of the available beds—a hotel chain would be overjoyed to have the occupancy rate that U.S. prisons do. In Illinois, the prisons are filled to 129 percent of official capacity; in Ohio 177 percent; in Michigan 144 percent; in California 191 percent.

The streets and rural roads get meaner; in fear and in rational desperation we build more places to lock the wrongdoers. Something is very wrong in the land, and we race to keep up with the criminals, somehow not as reassured as we should be at the sounds of the prison locks closing, again and again and again.

EIGHTY-ONE

The Circus That's Always in Town

SARASOTA, Florida—On the ceiling of the master bedroom of the mansion where John Ringling used to live, there is a painting mounted.

The painting—it is called *Dawn Driving Away the Darkness*—is an oil on canvas by the eighteenth-century Dutch artist Jacob de Wit. The painting is full of shepherds and nymphs among clouds; Ringling could look up from his bed and, as the first thing he saw each morning, observe this scene.

Ringling, of course, was one of the Ringling brothers, whose Ringling Brothers and Barnum & Bailey Circus was one of the greatest successes in the history of this country's mass-consumption culture. The five brothers, born in the Midwest, made a vast fortune from their traveling circus. The Ringling brothers brought the outside world to communities all over the United States, communities that had few other ways to have contact with that outside world; the circus once meant something quite wonderful to America, it inspired dreams as intimate as a child's "I-want-to-run-away-with-the-circus" fantasy, and as outsized as a wide-screen Technicolor epic: *The Greatest Show on Earth*, directed by the master of cinematic grandeur and scope, Cecil B. DeMille.

Like many wealthy men of humble beginnings, John Ringling celebrated his prosperity by reaching for the world of high culture. He built his mansion here and filled it with works of art: The circus may have titillated the lower denominators of the national taste, but the man who ran the circus strove to become something different. Yet that painting on the ceiling of his bedroom—the painting he could gaze upon without lifting his head from his pillow—teaches a separate lesson about how our world has changed in the almost sixty years since Ringling died.

There was no television in the America of John Ringling; that's one of the basic facts that made the enormous success of his circus possible. The citizens of the United States did not have the daily, nightly opportunity to witness the world delivered to them on a screen, did not have the twenty-four-hour visual entertainment-on-demand that today's citizens take for granted. When the circus came to town, there was genuine excitement. It was the one occasion during the year when a dizzying array of fast-changing amusements was there for the sampling.

And John Ringling? The John Ringlings of the world—like the Rockefellers, like the DuPonts, like the other persons of great wealth—might live much better than the people who had made them wealthy, but their options were similarly limited. Ringling and his brothers might own the circus, but the boundaries of their own world were somewhat constricted. They could sail to Europe; they could travel the United States by train, either their own circus train or in private cars on the nation's rails. But they didn't have available to them the ever-changing tapestry of images that is now available to just about every person, rich or poor, in the land.

Which is the quaint, if poignant, unspoken message of the painting on the ceiling above John Ringling's bed. This, he could give himself—an expensive and tranquil oil-painted view of life, something pretty to look at before he was even fully awake. In this way he could separate himself from those who did not possess the kind of money he did. He could open his eyes and see something lovely. See art.

The real democratization of American life extends well beyond the basic freedoms. The amusements of the very wealthy are today available to the very poor; the man in the top percentile of earnings is likely to have watched the same sports event, looked at the same newscast, laughed at the same comedy program last night as the man in the bottom percentile of earnings. This all began with the movies and with network radio, back in John Ringling's era, but television turned it into a phenomenon like nothing we have ever before been a part of—something whose entire meaning and import is not likely to be fully understood for generations to come.

And there's that painting above John Ringling's bed. The man who owned the circus could give himself that. What was it he was seeking? Probably nothing more than the rest of us, if we could. Dawn driving away the darkness.

EIGHTY-TWO

Turning Their Knobs to Bob

MINNEAPOLIS—At 100.3 on the FM radio dial here, it's all Bob all the time.

Which would seem to be a mixed blessing, at best.

A couple of years ago, the owners of a Minnesota radio station were deciding on a new format. The station had been a religion-oriented outlet; its managers had determined to switch to country music.

They called in a hotshot national radio consultant—one of those guys who specialize in formatting stations and giving them memorable names. You've encountered the most popular station names in cities all over the United States—Magic this, Zoo that, Thunder and Star and Power and Rock and Hot and Cool and

Kool and Z and— You get the picture. Radio stations like to identify themselves with nicknames that have pizzazz and style, that sizzle and pop.

So this Minnesota station brought in the consultant, and they were in a day-long meeting, and . . .

"Our consultant was a guy named Randy Michaels," said Kevin McCarthy, vice president and general manager of the station in question. "At the end of a long, long day—this was an eight- or nine-hour meeting—we were still sitting in the conference room, looking at all of our data, going over all of our printouts containing the research. We just didn't have the name yet.

"And then Randy said to us: 'You may think I'm crazy—but what if we named your station Bob?'

"There was a moment of silence. Then we all looked at each other, and one by one we fell onto the floor laughing. We had our name."

Thus, the new country station in the Twin Cities was ordained as Bob 100—sometimes referred to on the air as Bob Radio, sometimes merely as Bob.

Why?

"Bob is just such a friendly name," McCarthy said. "Who wouldn't want to listen to a radio station called Bob?"

Well, there happens to be a body of literature on the subject of the word "Bob"—and those of us burdened with the name know that it may be a friendly one, but that it is hardly majestic or stirring. The definitive work on the name "Bob" is the classic *The Bob Book*, written by David Rensin and Bill Zehme. The subtitle of *The Bob Book* is *A Celebration of the Ultimate OK Guy*, and in the book Rensin and Zehme say that "Bob thinks he is nothing special, and in fact he isn't—which is exactly what makes him so special. Bob is the opposite of fabulous. Bob rarely exclaims unless a car backs over his foot. Bob is the cake so that others may be the icing."

We Bobs know and accept that Bob is a dull and clunky

name. Bob is the plain, boring, sensible shoe of names. Bob has no dash. Bob sounds like a cork dipping up and down in the water.

So of course no radio station had ever named itself Bob. And now here was this country station in Minnesota, and . . .

"We launched a full-scale campaign," Kevin McCarthy said. "Television commercials, billboards, everything we could think of. The same slogan appeared everywhere:

" 'Turn Your Knob to Bob.' "

Against all odds, it appears to have worked. Ratings at the station, he said, have more than doubled since it went on the air. "Turn Your Knob to Bob" has become something of a mantra. "Bob is friendly and easy to remember," McCarthy said. "We say the word 'Bob' all day long. Every time we open our microphone we say 'Bob.' Bobness has become our life."

The station's official call letters are WBOB. "We consider 'Bob' to be a call to action," McCarthy said. He is aware that when listeners contemplate the existence of Bob Radio, they probably smile or even burst out laughing. There is nothing remotely threatening or hip about Bob. "Not in any way, shape or form," McCarthy said.

Bob is not supposed to dazzle; Bob is just there. "It helps in the ratings diaries," McCarthy said. "Radio ratings are determined by listeners who fill in diaries saying what they've listened to. With us, they don't have to struggle to remember a call letter, or a number on the dial. We're just Bob."

There are no disc jockeys named Bob at Bob Radio. McCarthy said that if a Bob were to be hired, he would have to change his name: "No on-air personality here can be Bob. The station is Bob."

Which is perhaps the ultimate indignity—the kind of thing we Bobs have gotten used to.

Bob Radio. No Bobs need apply.

EIGHTY-THREE

A Saturday Night to Remember

LAKE BUENA VISTA, Florida—The fantasies are supposed to be outlandish. A mountain of water that a person can ride down on the crest of a wave. A cruise through a jungle within touching distance of lions and giraffes who will never hurt you. A flight into Peter Pan's night sky, and a submarine journey beneath the sea, and a railway that hurtles its passengers through tunnels cut into solid rock.

That's what they're selling at Walt Disney World, or so the story goes: a visit to a place beyond imagination.

Except the thing that is really for sale—the thing that is seldom spoken about—is something quite simple, something we all used to have. Something we once took for granted in this country, something absolutely free.

Just after nine o'clock on a Saturday night, I sat at a table having a late dinner in the Liberty Tree Tavern. The Colonial-era atmosphere was, like everything else at Disney World, orchestrated to near-perfection, from the pewter decorations to the spinning wheel in the corner to the ladder-backed chairs. The restaurant was meant to take its patrons to another time and place.

I was thinking about another time and place, all right, but it wasn't New England in the 1700s. My table was near a window, and as I looked outside at the Disney-designed town square, I could see hundreds upon hundreds of people moving past, out on a Saturday night.

It was full darkness here, and something seemed vaguely foreign, and of course it was the sight of so many people walking unhurriedly in the nighttime, enjoying the evening. The Magic Kingdom is an amusement park, yes, but no ride toward which the people might be heading could ever be as exotic as where they were at this moment. Which is to say: out together in a citylike setting, in great numbers, at night. It felt like America in 1951, or what I have been told America '51 felt like; it felt like America before fear of the night reached critical mass.

I had brought a newspaper with me. You don't see many newspapers inside Disney World—a Disney property is, by nature, a place of anti-news—but I had the Orlando *Sentinel* with me at dinner, and I was reading a story about downtown Orlando, just up the highway.

The story said that once downtown Orlando was a vibrant place that drew crowds of teenagers, "honking horns and acting silly" as they had fun. Today, according to the story, teenagers are still downtown, "but instead of engaging in harmless antics, they sometimes carry weapons, drink alcohol and leave beaten, unconscious bodies in their wake. Downtown, Orlando police warn, soon could be lost to roving bands of young thugs intent on claiming it as their turf."

On Liberty Square, a Disney dream, families walked hand in hand; there seemed to be strength and security in numbers. That was the trick, right there: By virtue of the numbers of people out together on a Saturday night, a feeling of safety ensued.

All over the country at this very moment—all over the country on Saturday night—you could assume that downtown after downtown sat cold and empty, wary products of our times. Liberty Square might be make-believe, but the people on its streets weren't. Among the Disney dreams they might not have had back in their hometowns—along with the animated cartoon characters they didn't have and the Cinderella's castle they didn't have—was, presumably, this. A street full of people, at ease in the dark. The night reclaimed.

The Disney World monorail that had brought many of the

people to the park—as futuristic as it was meant to seem, it, too, was in spirit something out of 1951: clean and crime-free public transportation, a way to get from here to there in the company of strangers without checking to listen for footsteps, without glancing over one's shoulder to see who the passenger entering that rear door might be. The people in the park, for whatever reason, seemed to be following some unwritten rule of proper comportment and civil behavior; as incongruous as it sounds, in this place filled with transients there was a sense of—I told you it sounds strange—community.

Maybe it was just one more illusion here; maybe it was just one more sleight-of-mind trick pulled off by the Disney imagineers. But as the people strolled down the nighttime Disney streets, this did, in fact, seem like a place remembered. Fantasyland? Not really. Just the United States, a place that used to be. When you wish upon a star, indeed.

EIGHTY-FOUR

Victims

Three murderers were executed by lethal injection in Arkansas last Wednesday night. Before the executions were carried out, Diann Rust-Tierney of the American Civil Liberties Union in Washington said:

"I think what we're about to witness in Arkansas is a shocking spectacle."

She was referring to the fact that all three killers were going to be put to death, one right after the other, on the same evening. Leigh Dingerson, of the National Coalition to Abolish the Death

Penalty, said: "It indicates how desensitized, how numbed we have become about executions."

Well, perhaps. But the number of executions carried out by the states is a tiny fraction of the number of executions carried out by murderers in this country. The truly shocking spectacle is not the state of Arkansas carrying out the court-ordered death penalties against those three killers. The shocking spectacle is documented in America's newspapers every morning of the year—the spectacle of killers in large cities and small towns, devastating the fabric of our nation. Weep, if you will, for the three murderers who were painlessly put to death last Wednesday for their terrible deeds. Some of us will save our tears for the family they destroyed.

The three murderers were Hoyt Clines, thirty-seven; James Holmes, thirty-seven; and Darryl Richley, forty-three. Most of the news coverage of the three men has concentrated on how all of them were put to death on the same evening, and how barbaric some people found that.

Apparently the grieving for the three of them did not extend to the town of Rogers, Arkansas. "There's very little sympathy here for those three guys," said Rusty Turner, editor of the Northwest Arkansas *Morning News*, the paper that serves Rogers. "The people here feel the same pain that the family felt."

The family was the family of Don Lehman, a well-liked businessman in Rogers. The Lehman family has been all but overlooked in the coverage of the executions. Certainly no reporter ever inquired about what Don Lehman was served for his last meal, the way reporters asked what Clines, Holmes and Richley had ordered for supper last Wednesday. Lehman had no chance to beg for his life, the way his killers were given endless chances to let lawyers beg for theirs. He simply opened his front door on a January night in 1981.

According to trial testimony, standing outside the door were Clines, Holmes, Richley and a fourth man—Michael Orndorff, who also would be convicted of Lehman's murder, but who would eventually have his sentence reduced to life in prison. The four of them apparently chose the Lehman house at random. They were simply looking for someplace to rob.

Lehman opened the door. The men burst in. Two of them grabbed him; a third grabbed his young daughter, Vicki. Lehman broke away for a brief moment as his daughter was thrown to the floor. The men chased Lehman into a bedroom.

They beat him with a motorcycle drive chain. The beating was severe enough to damage Lehman's bones and to render him unconscious. An autopsy found abrasions on his face in the shape of a chain, and metal particles embedded in his wounds.

They shot him twice. One of the men picked his daughter off the floor by her hair, and led her to her own bedroom, ordering her to find money for them. She gave them $70. Then they led her back down the hall. In her parents' bedroom, she found her father sprawled and bleeding on the bed, her mother kneeling beside him. Two of the men were going through drawers, looking for cash. The daughter lifted a phone, trying to call for help. One of the men tore the phone from the wall. With Lehman's wife, Virginia, watching, one of the men said, "I'll finish him off this time," and fired a final shot into Lehman.

More than thirteen years have passed since that night. The members of Don Lehman's family have lived with their anguish every day of those thirteen years. His crime was opening his front door. For that he was executed—while his wife and daughter had to watch.

Don Lehman was given a matter of seconds to live. Clines, Holmes and Richley were given thirteen years to live after they murdered Lehman—they were fed, clothed, housed, and, in the end, given their choice of a method of death. Those who do not mourn the executions of the murderers are, according to anti-death penalty activists quoted in one news report, symbolic of a "growing callousness toward human life."

EIGHTY-FIVE

"It's the Best Thing I Can Do"

SOUTH BEND, Indiana—Sometimes you fear that all of the hurtful aspects of contemporary life in our country—the coarseness of language, the celebration of violence, the constant devaluation of civility—will inevitably create new generations of Americans destined to disrespect not only others, but themselves. That's what our care-about-nothing culture often seems to promise.

But then, unexpectedly, you run into something. . . .

There was a charity dinner here, an event attended by some of the most prominent business and civic leaders in this part of Indiana. This was in the course of the school year just past. During the evening—the reception, the cocktail hour, the dinner itself—I noticed the sounds of truly lovely music in the background. I looked around; over in a corner were five young people playing stringed instruments.

I referred to the dinner program, which said that the evening's music was being provided by the Mishawaka High School String Quintet. The boys and girls playing the instruments were going intently at their endeavors; not many people in the big room were looking at them work, but the product of their artistry was elevating the evening, was making the atmosphere more lovely. These were kids with Midwestern faces, dressed all in black and white and looking as if they would be just as at home on a basketball court or in study hall.

They were Jenny Brown, Elizabeth Houghton, Greg Quiroz, Adrienne Stauffer and Andy Josleyn. The songs they were playing—"The Nocturne," "Serenade for String Orchestra," "Harmonious Blacksmiths"—were hardly tunes that are most popular with boys and girls their ages. With all the factors in our culture arguing against young people choosing to do something like this —we hear and read so much about mindless videos and time-eating computer games and weekends of endless mall cruising, what would make a young person choose instead to join a string quintet?—I was interested in finding out what factors had led the five of them to a night like this.

"They are a great bunch," said Jay Miller, Mishawaka High School's director of string instruments. "Somewhere along the way they were successful when they approached their instruments, and the success and satisfaction of playing together is what brings them together."

Jenny Brown, a seventeen-year-old senior, is a violinist. "I love the music, and the challenge of playing more difficult music as we get older," she said. She is also a swimmer; she said she practices her swimming four hours a day, her music two or three hours.

Elizabeth Houghton, also a seventeen-year-old senior and also a violinist, said she has been playing since she was eight: "We got a new orchestra teacher when we were in fourth grade, and she was a very fun lady and played all the instruments. Doing this, I get a sense of accomplishment. I practice my violin two or three hours a day, but it goes quickly because I enjoy it so much."

Greg Quiroz, another seventeen-year-old senior, is a cellist. Why a cello? "I basically like the tone of it," he said. "I loved how it looked when I first saw it. It's just a special feeling I get when I play. It's the best thing that I can do—better than anything I have ever done, so I give it my time and dedication."

Adrienne Stauffer, a fifteen-year-old sophomore, has played the viola since she was in fourth grade. "I joined this group last year, when I was a freshman," she said. "I like the way my instrument sounds better than the violin or cello. I play soccer and

I dance, also. It's hard to juggle everything—I practice my viola two hours a day."

Andy Josleyn, a sixteen-year-old sophomore, plays the bass. "One day Jay Miller came to our elementary school and held up the instrument," he said. "It was the biggest, and in fourth grade you want a challenge and to play something big. You are more nervous when you play in front of a group of people. You tend to worry a little. I haven't played as many events as some of the other people, so I tend to get really nervous and tend to think that I'm playing out of tune."

He wasn't; none of them were. At the charity dinner they played for hours on end, without a break, and then they asked permission to go home because they had school the next morning. There are a lot of things in our country's future that seem destined to go badly, to decline. And then there are certain signs of hope, cloaked in discipline and beauty.

EIGHTY-SIX

Cool

WEST HOLLYWOOD, California—Through some terrible mistake, I found myself booked into a hotel devoted to cool people.

I knew that the hotel was for cool people, and that I should not have been allowed in, because of several factors. One was that the hotel was nestled on a fashionable side street in West Hollywood, near the Sunset Strip but hidden between private residences. One was that the word "Le" was in the name of the hotel. One was that the hotel's dining room was open only to guests—if you weren't staying at the hotel, you couldn't eat there. One was that each room featured a sunken living room, a bed up on a platform and a working fireplace.

Those reasons notwithstanding, though, the reason I knew this hotel was for cool people was that all of the guests other than myself were cool. You could tell by looking at them. They fit into three categories:

1. They looked like motion picture stars trying not to be recognized (boxing trunks, sunglasses, two-day stubble of beard).

2. They looked like contenders for the heavyweight boxing championship of the world (boxing trunks, no sunglasses, satin jackets).

3. They looked like record-industry executives (boxing trunks, sleeveless undershirts).

Embarrassed for being eternally uncool, and wanting to make myself invisible until I could find a nice and unjudgmental Hampton Inn, I carried my suitcase to my room. On the wall of the sunken living room, where the nice hotel-room painting of a New England sunset is supposed to be, was an abstract oil portrait of a naked woman and the word "coke."

Thirsty for a milkshake, yearning for some onion rings, needing to be somewhere as uncool as I, I left the hotel and walked down the block. Within minutes I was on Sunset Boulevard, where I found, much to my dismay, that my neighborhood eatery was the Viper Room.

The Viper Room, I knew from news reports, was the spot outside of which the actor River Phoenix met his unfortunate demise. Rather than making the place unpopular, the death of Mr. Phoenix seemed to elevate the Viper Room's prestige among cool people. Magazines and TV shows were always showing the throngs outside the Viper Room late at night, women wearing lingerie, men on the verge of fisticuffs, lusting to get inside.

Because it was broad daylight, there was no line outside the Viper Room's black-painted door. I pulled at the handle, hoping to get a table for one, a glass of milk and a tuna fish sandwich. But the Viper Room was closed, its owners apparently not savvy enough to cash in on the concept of early-bird specials.

My hunger unfilled, I went back to the cool hotel, passed two no-nonsense women in the lobby wearing boxing trunks and carrying briefcases, and returned to my room. In my sunken living room—I had not noticed this because of the distraction of the painting of the naked "coke" lady—was a copy of a local magazine that apparently specialized in trends. The cover line was "The 100 Coolest People in L.A."

One of the hundred coolest people, I learned, was Bryan Rabin, a "club promoter," who was "the man behind clubs like Prague, Highball and Cherry—at which hard-core rockers mix comfortably with soft-core drag queens." Another of the hundred was Kim Dingle, an artist "best known for her paintings of little girls in frilly dresses and boxing gloves." Also listed was Sal Jenco, identified as the owner of the Viper Room.

It must be exhausting to stay that cool. It can be exhausting enough being not cool; I fell asleep watching an old Gary Cooper movie on the American Movie Classics channel on my polished-steel-pole-mounted swiveling TV set (swivel it toward the sunken living room and the naked "coke" lady, swivel it toward the platform bedroom). I awakened late at night, and walked back to the Sunset Strip, where a Tower Records store had a huge crowd, many wearing boxing trunks, gathered in front.

I thought there might have been an accident, but a sign said that Ozzy Osbourne was due in the store on the stroke of midnight, to sign autographs; the mob was waiting for him. I went inside the store to purchase the same thirty Beach Boys hit songs I've been purchasing since 1965, thoughtfully repackaged by the record company every year or so to give us uncool people the illusion we are getting something new. Be true to your Viper Room.

EIGHTY-SEVEN

The Man in Front of the Movie House

"I'd like to thank you for writing that nice story about my dad," Jim Thorpe's daughter said. "He would have liked it."

I suppose I hadn't been aware that Jim Thorpe had children, at least not children who were still alive. I had written a fanciful column about what Thorpe—considered by many to be the greatest American athlete who ever lived—would have thought had he wandered into the big-money, corporate-drenched sports world of today. Thorpe, an American Indian born in Oklahoma, won two gold medals, for the decathlon and pentathlon, at the 1912 Olympics in Stockholm, and had them taken away from him because it was discovered he had once played semiprofessional baseball for a small salary.

"There were eight of us children," Grace Thorpe, now seventy, said. "Five boys and three girls. My dad had a very sad life in many ways. When he and my mother divorced, I went back and forth between living with the two of them. He was a very quiet man and a very intelligent man, but he had his troubles."

She lives in the small Oklahoma town of Yale now. "Dad was in his middle thirties when I was born," she said. "When I was five or six, he came to the Indian school where I was a student to give an exhibition out on the football field. I remember, the whole stadium was filled with people. Up to then I had been too young to understand that he was a big deal.

"That day he came to the school to give the exhibition, he promised me that he'd take me into town and buy me some candy and ice cream afterward. We all sat in the stands, and Dad stood in the center of the field and drop-kicked the ball, or some other kind of kick, through the center of the goalposts one way, and then he turned around and kicked the ball through the goalposts on the other end. Afterward everyone gathered around him to talk to him. He put me up on his shoulders. I guess I was proud, but I was mostly impatient. I wanted to go get that ice cream in town. It was just my dad and he was just famous, and I wanted to go to town and be alone with him."

The stripping of Jim Thorpe's Olympic gold medals was the defining event of his life. It officially painted him as somehow impure, unworthy. According to his daughter, the salary he had received for playing semipro baseball was $60 a month. For that he was disgraced.

"I think I only asked him about that once," she said. "It was after I was older, and I was living in Pearl River, New York, near the New Jersey line. When Dad would come to the East Coast and had business in New York City—he would appear at boat shows and things like that—he would stay with me, and then take a bus to the city. One time he was staying with me, and I asked him about those medals being taken away.

"He told me that he himself never had written a letter asking to have them returned. Then he clammed up. He didn't like to talk about it. I think he was bitter, but I don't really know, because he didn't talk much about himself, good or bad. The athletic ability, I don't think he thought it was anything great. I think it all came so naturally to him."

After his gold medals were taken away, Thorpe played sports for a living. Later, he had difficulty finding work, and was beset with alcohol-related problems, his daughter said.

"He would drink," she said. "He would be out somewhere drinking, and he would be challenged by someone who wanted to take on Jim Thorpe, and the police would come and put him in jail. They would just keep him overnight, until he sobered up. Grandpa Thorpe, my dad's dad, was that way too. I didn't think any worse of Dad because of that. He was a world-famous athlete, but he was a person too.

"He would never get drunk at home, but sometimes he would come home after he had been drinking, and he wouldn't be physically graceful. He would slur his words and he would walk unsteadily, and it was a sad thing for me to see."

Thorpe's fame came in the days before television, his daughter said, but he was immediately recognized anywhere he went in the country. Especially after his great athletic days were over, this was not something he welcomed.

"It bothered him," she said. "I remember once, he and I were driving from Los Angeles to Oklahoma. We stopped at a diner and ordered sandwiches. The food hadn't even come, and I remember a man walking up to us and saying to my dad, 'Aren't you Jim Thorpe?' And I looked at my dad and I knew that he wanted to say, 'No, I'm not.' "

•   •   •

"When Dad was too old to play sports anymore, he had to make a living. He had no money. There were no pension benefits or anything. He didn't know quite what to do. When he was in his forties, he took a job out in California digging ditches. He didn't say much about that to me. He dug ditches because he had to make a buck.

"Dad was a very quiet man," Grace Thorpe said. "He used to go hunting and fishing. He loved being out there in the woods by himself. I think that if he had made a lot of money, like the athletes do today, the one thing he would have done for himself would have been to buy a hunting and fishing lodge up in the mountains. He always used to talk about that as being his dream. But he didn't have the money for that, so he died without it happening."

Whatever bitterness her dad felt about his life, she said, he hid beneath his silence. "He was pretty calm, and simple in his pleasures. He liked to cook. He would clean the fish he'd caught, and he'd go hunting for jackrabbits and then cook us up some stew. He'd make those fried potatoes, too. He was very good at making those—he'd use hot bacon grease, and he'd brown some onions. . . ."

Her words were probably not dissimilar to the words any grown son or daughter might use to recall a parent long gone. Yet this was Jim Thorpe she was talking about; this was a man most of us know only as a distant legend, a squinting face in a faded old newspaper photograph. We somehow don't think of him as being real. We don't think of Jim Thorpe browning onions and sitting around the house talking to his children. . . .

"He was always so graceful," his daughter said. "When I was very young I didn't understand what a great athlete he was, but I knew what a graceful person he was. He taught me how to ballroom dance. He took me in his arms and taught me how to dance."

When Thorpe died in 1953, he was living in a California trailer park with his third wife. "When Dad passed away, he didn't even have enough money for a burial," his daughter said. "The news of that got out, and all these states started sending wires saying that they'd build a memorial to him if the body would be sent to them. I don't think it was out of the goodness of their hearts. I think they knew that if Jim Thorpe was buried in their state, it would make a good tourist attraction."

One of the last times she saw her father, Grace Thorpe said, was in 1951, when he had come east to visit her at her home in Pearl River.

"Dad stayed with me, and he had to go to New York City for something, and I drove him to the bus stop," she said. "In Pearl River, the bus stop was right underneath the marquee of the movie theater.

"Years before, when he needed money, Dad had sold the rights to make a movie of his life to Warner Brothers. He had only been paid fifteen hundred dollars for it. In 1951 Dad was sixty-three years old, and the movie had finally been made and had just come out. It starred Burt Lancaster, playing my dad. And it was showing at the Pearl River Theater that day.

"So Dad was standing underneath the marquee, and the marquee had the title on it: *Jim Thorpe, All-American.* I dropped him at the bus stop, and I looked back, and there he was. Dad was wearing his old suede jacket and a broad-brimmed hat, and he was carrying the same old suitcase he always carried. He was standing there kind of quiet, just waiting for the bus."

EIGHTY-EIGHT

Was She Really So Different?

NEW YORK—She was sobbing.

One minute she was walking down the airport concourse, one traveler among hundreds. The next moment she was sobbing.

It wasn't a case of her having received bad news over a pay phone in the airport. She hadn't been on the phone. She had been walking in the midst of the rest of us. Twenty-eight years old, maybe, dressed in business clothing, nothing to set her apart from the crowd.

And then she burst into wrenching, shaking tears.

The reaction of the other people heading to their flights was instructive. We—or so we have been told—have been hardened to everything. At least that's the way things are reputed to be. We see grisly scenes of carnage on the evening news, we read about humans doing incomprehensibly cruel things to other humans, we accept the reality of savagery halfway around the world and half a mile away. Nothing is supposed to be able to reach us. We are protected by invisible shells.

Yet this sight—the sight of this woman suddenly dissolving into sobs—stopped people in their tracks. Some tried not to look; others made a point of looking. No one knew quite what to do. If—for example—a dog was being beaten by its owner in a public place, someone most likely would have gone over and told the tormentor to stop. But this was more complicated. Whatever was tormenting this woman was not visible to the eye.

Did people owe it to her to say something? Or would that have been wrong—an intrusion into a place not open to visitors? Was the sobbing—it was getting worse, louder—the product of a real-world affront, something she could define, or was this something she had gone through before, part of a problem without a name? Whatever the case, she stopped for a moment—trembling fiercely as the tears came—and then started again up the corridor.

That was the other thing: Whatever it was that was going wrong with her, it did not physically stop her. She continued to walk, and with some apparent purpose in her step; she was not wandering aimlessly as she wept, but heading for a destination she seemed quite aware of.

Whatever it was that was transpiring in her life is hers to know; for the rest of the people, perhaps, the thing that made this scene so uneasy was not that her condition was so far removed from everyone else's, but that in many ways it was perilously close. Most grown men and women go around wearing masks; the masks depict smiling, contented faces. When you're in kindergarten you are permitted to cry in front of others, but soon after you are taught that it's not a good idea. That's what doors are for—or so the world learns. Doors are to close and lock so that no one else sees this when it happens.

And the surprising thing is not that this woman was sobbing in the airport. The surprising thing—maybe—is that it doesn't happen more often. The surprising thing is that such a scene catches people by surprise. All the people behind those masks of bland contentment—are they, in truth, closer to the placid emotions symbolized by those masks, or are they sometimes secretly a little closer to the woman sobbing in the midst of them? Was that, by any chance, the reason for the sense of discomfort in the concourse—not the feeling that she was so far removed from everyone else, but rather the knowledge that everyone else had the capacity to be her? That she simply had lost, temporarily, the ability to govern it—and that if she was capable of losing that ability in an instant, then who is not?

So perhaps the men and women who were so riveted in the corridor were stunned not because they were seeing a stranger, but because they feared they might be seeing themselves. That the woman looked not notably different from any of them was precisely the point. She had been pierced by invisible arrows—and if it could happen to her . . .

Or maybe not. Maybe she was just a woman crying in an airport. As she made her way up the corridor, and the crying did not stop, the hallway was filled with various sounds and images. Flight announcements coming out of the ceiling. Reports of world crises coming out of concourse TV sets. Headlines beckoning from newspaper vending boxes. There is news and there is news. Everyone kept moving toward their destinations, and one among them cried.

EIGHTY-NINE

His Greatest Move

If you're sick of the direction sports in this country have been taking—from the preening and taunting of Deion Sanders and his many followers, to the tiresome bickering between millionaire professional athletes and the millionaire owners of their teams—then here's a sports story for you.

Chances are, it's unlike any other you may have read recently.

At the end of the high school soccer season in the suburbs of Chicago, there was a big game scheduled between Wheaton Christian and Waubonsie Valley.

Because it was a high school game, it was not destined to make the national sports pages like pro football and basketball, or big-time college sports, do. But to the communities involved, high school games, and their outcomes, are vastly important.

The Wheaton Christian–Waubonsie Valley game turned out to be a close one. Even though Waubonsie Valley is a bigger school, and its team had a better record, Wheaton Christian was holding its own.

Late in the game the score was tied 2–2. Then, with a minute or so left, Waubonsie Valley scored a goal to go ahead 3–2.

As the clock ticked down toward the end of the game, Waubonsie Valley took another shot at the Wheaton Christian goal. The Wheaton Christian goalkeeper stopped the ball, then threw it to Wheaton Christian's star player—Rob Mouw, a senior who is the top scorer in the school's history.

Mouw took the ball and moved it upfield toward the Waubonsie Valley goal. He managed to get past the defenders until the goal was within range. He threw a fake on the goalkeeper, kicked the ball—and it went in, tying the score at 3–3.

The Wheaton Christian crowd erupted in cheers. Mouw's goal had saved the team from defeat.

But Mouw, eighteen, had noticed something.

"The clock was on a scoreboard behind the goal I was shooting at," he said. "There were only two seconds left in the game when I started bringing the ball up the field. It took me more than two seconds to get to the goal and take my shot—and I could clearly see that the clock had ticked down to zero before I kicked the goal."

As many people know from watching World Cup soccer on television, the official clock for soccer games is not always kept on the scoreboard; often the referees keep the official time on stopwatches. In high school games, this can vary.

Mouw, having just made the crucial goal, walked over to the referee.

There was only one referee at this game—there should have been two, but one didn't show up. So the one referee was in charge.

"I asked the referee whether the official clock was on the scoreboard, or whether he was keeping his own time," Mouw said last week. "He said the scoreboard clock was the official time.

"I knew that he hadn't seen the clock at the end of the game, because if he had, he wouldn't have counted my goal. So I knew that the other team deserved to win."

The referee quickly left the field—reportedly there was a great deal of commotion and arguing going on and, as we have read, sometimes referees feel fearful after making close decisions that affect the outcome of games. Rob Mouw walked to the sidelines and talked to his coaches—head coach Wes Dusek and assistant coach Steve Hellier.

Mouw told his coaches that the goal shouldn't count, and that Waubonsie Valley should get the victory.

Which is what happened. Dusek and Hellier told Waubonsie Valley coach Angelo Di Bernardo that the game belonged to his team—that Rob Mouw had not wanted a win if the win was unfairly achieved.

"The referee just wasn't able to see the clock, because he was working by himself," Mouw said the other day. "Look, there was no question about it—I saw the clock was on the zeroes before I kicked the ball. And when I asked if the scoreboard clock was official, and found out it was, there was no way I could allow my goal to count."

He said that he considered the situation not a tough decision—but an opportunity.

"Every time in your life you have an opportunity to do right, you should be thankful," he said. "For a person to know what right is, and then not to do it—that would be a sin. To have won the game—I mean, really, who cares? Doing the right thing is more important. It lets you have peace. In my opinion, every time you are lucky enough to be given the opportunity to do something right, you shouldn't pass it up."

NINETY

The Final Word on "Quarter to Three"

GAITHERSBURG, Maryland—Some men endeavor to find the answers to the great mysteries of the universe. What is life? What is truth? What is the square root of 2?

Others of us have more humble quests. More humble, but no less significant.

"Mr. Bonds?" I said. "May I talk to you for just a moment?"

This was on the dirt infield in front of the grandstand at the Montgomery County Agricultural Fair here in Maryland. Standing on that infield, I had spotted him—Gary U.S. Bonds.

Now, that name—if it means anything to you at all—brings to mind a number of hit songs of the early 1960s. "School Is Out," "New Orleans," "Dear Lady Twist"—the records all made the charts and sold well, if not spectacularly.

But there was one Gary U.S. Bonds record that became an enormous success—the Number One record in the United States, a record that, during the summer of 1961, came out of every jukebox, every car radio, in the country. That record was "Quarter to Three," and if you are of a certain age, you undoubtedly can hear the lyrics in your head right this moment: "Don't you know that I danced, I danced, till a quarter to three . . ."

What I had to know from Gary U.S. Bonds as we stood in the infield of the county fair, though, had nothing to do with the purely musical aspects of "Quarter to Three." Rather, what I felt this gnawing need to know was . . .

"Mr. Bonds, I feel stupid for asking this. But there was this rumor, see, and I don't know whether it was just a central Ohio rumor, or whether it was a national rumor, but—I don't know how to say this—everyone thought that there were these *words* at the beginning of 'Quarter to Three.' . . ."

Gary U.S. Bonds sighed deeply.

"It was a national rumor," he said.

"Then you know what I'm talking about," I said.

"I know what you're talking about," he said.

What I was talking about was a phrase that was supposedly murmured at the very beginning of "Quarter to Three." The song begins with the raucous sounds of a party in progress, and underneath the party noise you allegedly could hear . . . well, I'm not going to even hint at the words here. Suffice it to say that the words were absolutely filthy—and every kid who listened to the record that summer thought that he or she could discern those words.

"It's that phrase at the beginning of the song, right?" I said. "That's what the rumor was, right?"

"Right," Gary U.S. Bonds said.

"What was the phrase people thought was in there?" I said, just wanting to make sure that Gary U.S. Bonds and I were barking up the same tree.

"The phrase they thought was in there was . . ." Bonds said, and then he said a phrase that was every bit as dirty as the one I had in mind—but slightly different. Same idea, small variation in words.

"So was it in there?" I said.

"No," Gary U.S. Bonds said. "Absolutely not. I mean, my *mother* was at the recording session where we did 'Quarter to Three.' Do you think I would say something like that in front of my *mother?*"

He said that he was well aware of what everyone thought they were hearing at the beginning of the song. "I have listened to that record over and over again, for years and years," he said. "I have tried to hear it. I'm telling you—that phrase was never in there."

The great irony, of course, is that the rumor of the filthy phrase had a lot to do with "Quarter to Three" becoming a Number One hit. "Quarter to Three" was a terrific song, yes—but the real reason it made it to the top in that summer of '61 was all those American kids attracted to something forbidden.

Something forbidden that, at least according to Gary U.S. Bonds—a very nice fellow who is now fifty-five years old—was never there. Which makes it parallel to another legendarily dirty song—"Louie Louie"—that, according to Richard Berry, the man who wrote it, was never dirty, either.

Ah, the sweet twists and turns of life. "I swear," said Gary U.S. Bonds. "Those words are not on that record." We're all a little older, and the truth shall make you free, although not necessarily Number One.

NINETY-ONE

In Good Standing

The mother of a high school student called our office, upset for her son. He had been denied membership in one of his school's most prestigious honorary clubs, and was distraught.

"I'm trying to tell him that it's not the end of the world," she said. "But when you're that age, and you're left out of something that means so much to you, it devastates you. He feels so low."

I didn't know what to tell her. But, coincidentally, soon after that I heard from Robert J. Groves, a sixty-four-year-old retired executive who lives in Arizona. And now I pass his story on to the mother and her son.

"I graduated from Senn High School in Chicago in June of 1949," Groves said. "Five years ago we had our fortieth reunion. I was nervous to see everyone again, but it was great—much too short, but absolutely great.

"A year or two later, back in Tucson, I received a call from one of my classmates who had attended the reunion. His name is Bob Armbrust; he said he and his wife, Grace, would be traveling to Arizona, and asked if they could come visit.

"During our high school days, Bob had been a superior athlete—he was a letterman in football, basketball and swimming. If that wasn't enough, he spent his summers as a lifeguard on Chicago's North Side beaches. In contrast to Bob's athletic accomplishments, I possessed none of the skills to play on a varsity team. I never made it."

So more than forty years later, Mr. and Mrs. Armbrust—who live in Bettendorf, Iowa—visited Mr. and Mrs. Groves. One night, after the wives had gone to bed, Groves shared a remembrance with Armbrust.

"Senn had a club called the Green & White Club—the school colors," Groves said. "As stated in the '49 yearbook, the club 'is composed of outstanding senior boys who have shown leadership, participated in various school activities, and proven themselves able to uphold the fine standards of Senn.'

"In my final year at Senn there were forty-seven persons elected to the Green & White. As you might have already surmised, I was not one of the forty-seven.

"My best buddies were elected—Wally Brown, Hartley Hagemann, Carl Newey, and Oscar Lennard all made it. Bob Armbrust made it. Guys I didn't know made it; even guys I didn't like made it.

"I don't recall ever expressing my feelings of hurt to anyone. But, oh, how it hurt. I was just one of the boys who was destined to be passed over. What a hurt that was."

Now, more than forty years later, he spoke about it for the first time—to Bob Armbrust.

"He said he never realized how important membership was," Groves said. "Which, I suppose, makes some sort of sense. When you're included in something important, it probably doesn't mean as much to you as if you had been left out."

The visit in Arizona between the Armbrusts and the Groveses ended; Mr. and Mrs. Armbrust went home to Iowa. And before long, a big envelope with an Iowa postmark arrived in Robert Groves's mailbox.

There was a letter to Robert Groves:

Dear Bob:
The following document was recently discovered in an unused inter-office mail slot. Please accept our sincere

regrets for this undelivered notice and please consider
yourself a member, in good standing, of the Green &
White Club.

> Sincerely,
> The Review Committee

There was a second piece of paper—on the stationery of the
Green & White Club, Senn High School. It was a photocopy,
and it had been dated October 7, 1948:

> To the division teacher of Room 207:
> It is with great pleasure we inform you that after careful
> investigation, Robert Groves of your division has been
> elected to membership in the Green & White Club.
> We would appreciate it if you would inform him of
> this and ask him to report to the meeting, 3rd period,
> Friday, October 8, in room 246.

It was signed by the president and the secretary of the Green
& White Club.

It didn't take an FBI investigator to look at the letter and see
what had happened. Bob Armbrust, after his visit to Tucson, had
whited out his own name on his old Green & White Club membership letter, had written Robert Groves's name in, had photo-
copied it and mailed it to his old friend.

"That he would do this—I couldn't help getting all choked
up," Groves said. "It really meant something to me. A gesture of
friendship like that, all these years later—it was better than if I'd
been selected back in 1948. The good things in life—they always
seem to come around."

NINETY-TWO

A Father's Farewell to His Dearest Friend

Kevin Christopher "K.C." Conlon, three and a half, of Flossmoor, Illinois, died last month of a rare type of brain tumor. Near the end of K.C.'s life, as he lay in his bed at Boston Children's Hospital, his father, Kevin Conlon, wrote a letter to him.

Here is Kevin Conlon's letter to his son.

Dear K.C.,

As I lie in bed holding you, I am so painfully aware that you will be with us for only a few minutes or hours. The hour is late, but my feelings are so strong that I leave you with your beautiful and loving mother to find a place of refuge in the hospital to compose my thoughts in this letter to you.

My heart breaks when I think of the struggles you have endured in the last eight months to get that "rock" out of your head. I would give anything to switch places with you. Nothing would make me happier.

As you close your eyes and decide when you want to go to heaven, please remember how proud I am of you. From the day you were born to today, you have brought me only joy and happiness. You have exceeded my highest expectations of what fatherhood would be like. You have not only been my son, but my dearest friend and constant companion; when I was at work or out of town, I ached to be with you.

K.C., we had so much fun together. Do you remember how you would always pull me out of bed early every morning to watch your kid shows with you on the couch? We loved to read our books together, like *Curious George* and *Barney*. Think back on all the times we played with your toys, the train set, the blocks.

Remember how often we went swimming in the summer at Max's house, Dolphin Lake or Lion's Pool? How many hours did the two of us spend on the swing set or in the sandbox? What about the walks to the park, or to the train station to get Mommy? How many times did we go out for pancakes, or to buy chocolate doughnuts from the Flossmoor Bakery? Did you enjoy the trips to Dairy Queen for ice cream as much as I did? Most of all, I loved to pick you up at school and wait for you to tell me about your day.

My greatest joy was to watch you with your little brother, Cody. You embraced him so beautifully from the first day Mommy and I brought him home from the hospital. As much as I will miss you, my deepest hurt comes from the realization that Cody won't have you every day as his big brother. I cannot imagine a better big brother than you.

What I will especially miss about you are your charming, gregarious ways. I will miss hearing those silly jokes of yours. Somehow, you made everyone feel important. Your capacity to remember people's names was amazing to me. You were truly the life of the party. I don't know how you found the time in three and a half years to make so many friends.

Yes, K.C., I will miss you day to day, on our trips, but also on special days like Christmas. Last year you were too sick to enjoy Christmas, and for the last eight months I have dreamed of making Christmas a special one. I can't imagine the day without you ripping open your presents or playing with Cody and your cousins.

I will miss you terribly. All I have learned from you validates that my life is on the right course and that my values are in the proper place. How else could I have such a wonderful boy as you? For this I thank you.

Since December of last year, your life has been dominated by the struggle to get well. You fought as if you were an army of 10,000 men. You were so brave.

As you prepare to go to heaven, please know that Mommy, Cody, your grandparents, cousins, uncles, aunts, friends and I passionately love you. We will never forget all the joy and happiness you brought us each and every day. I am the luckiest man in the world to be your father and friend. I love you madly.

So, K.C., it is OK to close your eyes and rest peacefully. You do not have to fight anymore. You have won life's greatest battle: You have become a completely full and beautiful person and for this God has invited you to His house in heaven. Thanks for being my son.

Love Always,
Daddy

NINETY-THREE

The Sound of Distant Cheers

Veterans of the military sometimes say they feel underappreciated by the American people. It's not uncommon to hear soldiers who fought in Vietnam and Korea say they often sense that they are forgotten; even veterans of World War II, a war effort that had the support of virtually the entire nation, occasionally express these same sentiments.

But the American veterans who are truly forgotten rarely are heard from. During World War I, 4,734,991 U.S. citizens served in the military. According to the best records available, of the 4.7 million, 19,747 are left.

"I'm not surprised that so few people think about us," said Ray H. Fuller, ninety-eight, a World War I infantry sergeant who is now commander of the Veterans of World War I. "It's not so important that they remember us individually, but it would be nice if they would at least remember what we fought for. If once in a while they'd take the time to think about what our country might be like if we hadn't won the war."

Fuller, of Oshkosh, Wisconsin, sailed off to Europe on a troop ship called the *George Washington* on February 8, 1918, to serve in the Red Arrow Division. He had graduated from Oshkosh High School, had worked several factory jobs ("Oshkosh was a big lumber town"), and went off to war not out of what he considered to be any grand sense of patriotism, but simply because going off to war was what young men in 1918 did.

"My younger brother, Ralph, had already gone," Fuller said,

"and I told my parents, 'If Ralph can go, why can't I?' Well, I went—but Ralph never came home. He was killed in action. My older brother Earl went, and he was wounded—a piece of shrapnel near his heart. But when he came home he served as county treasurer for twenty-nine years."

If that sounds like ancient history, it makes Fuller's point. The World War I veterans among us might as well be invisible—they range in age from 89 to 112, with the average age being 97. It is believed that 85 percent of them live in some sort of care-giving facility—nursing homes, retirement centers—or with relatives who help them out.

There was a time when the Veterans of World War I organization had its own headquarters near Washington, D.C., with a full-time staff of twenty-one. Now the group is administered by one person—Muriel Sue Parkhurst, forty-eight, of Alexandria, Virginia, who runs it from her home, and who is no longer paid for her work.

"I consider it a privilege," she said. "My one regret is that we are having trouble keeping the newspaper going." The newspaper she refers to is called the *Torch*, and it reports news and information about those 19,747 World War I soldiers who are still alive.

"For many of the men, the *Torch* is the only lifeline they have to each other," she said. "It lets them know that they are not alone. The paper reports it when one of the veterans tells us that his great-granddaughter took him to her school for show-and-tell. The paper reports it when a soldier celebrates the seventy-fifth anniversary of earning a Purple Heart.

"But the money that comes in from membership dues isn't what it once was, and the situation is only going to get worse."

The surviving veterans of World War I must contend with the same atmosphere of crime, the same unsafe streets, as other Americans—and often are easy prey because of their age. As their commander, Ray Fuller chooses to remember the country when it was somewhat different.

"When we came home from Europe—what a day," he said. "Those of us who lived in Oshkosh arrived on a train that stopped at the old station on the south side of the Fox River. The station's gone now, but I can still see it.

"We marched across the bridge—in our uniforms we marched across the bridge and over the river, back to our armory on the other side. Right down Main Street, and all the streets were lined with people. Cheering! They cheered us all the way to the armory. Oh, what a day that was."

NINETY-FOUR

One More for the Road

We walked down a cluttered hallway, past a table with a coffeepot on top, and around a corner. A door was ajar, and we walked through it into a small room, and standing there in a tuxedo was Frank Sinatra.

Sinatra turned fully toward us, not expecting any visitors. "Frank, there's someone I wanted to introduce you to," my companion said.

Sinatra looked over with those famous eyes. Not wary, not annoyed, just waiting to see what this was all about. Waiting with those eyes that have seen everything.

He extended his hand, and I shook it, and I said, "May I ask you a really stupid question?"

"Go ahead," Sinatra said.

"Do you practice?" I said.

Maybe it's the word that confused him; maybe "rehearse" would have been the proper word, but it was practice I was interested in. The singer of the century—I just found myself wondering whether, at age seventy-seven, he still feels the drive to practice his craft.

"Practice?" he said.

"Singing," I said.

"Sure," Sinatra said. "Sure I do. I practice all the time."

We talked a little, and I thanked him for taking the time to say hello, and said I'd get out of his way. In a few minutes he'd be going on stage. The man who had taken me to meet Sinatra —Tom Dreesen, the comedian who has opened Sinatra's shows for the last ten years—walked me back down the hallway the same way we'd come.

"He does practice, just about every day," Dreesen said. "He genuinely works at it." I had run into Dreesen a few days earlier, and he had said that he was in Chicago with Sinatra, who was in the midst of a sold-out five-show run at the Civic Opera House. Dreesen had invited me to be his guest at the performance last Saturday night; I had watched Dreesen's act, then during intermission had gone backstage to say thanks, and he had hesitated for a second and that is when he had said, "Come with me for a few minutes." And had led me down a nondescript corridor on an evening that in all other ways could have been nondescript, to a little dressing room where Frank Sinatra waited for his summons to go on stage.

I was back in the audience by the time the lights went down and Sinatra began his first song. Like many people, I had read that his voice, understandably, is not what it was in the 1950s; that he needs the help of TelePrompTers to remember some of his lyrics; that his gait is no longer spry.

None of that mattered. Sinatra's speaking voice as he bantered with the audience between songs was even more strikingly changed than was his singing voice: His speaking voice was a little thin, a little trembly, there was needfulness and vulnerability in it. The ring-a-ding-ding swagger was all but gone, and it didn't make any difference at all, if anything it made Sinatra even more attractive. Who required an embittered tough guy? This Sinatra, grateful and at times almost melancholy, was a man it was a privilege to watch as he worked.

The songs—"I've Got the World on a String," "All or Nothing at All," "Street of Dreams"—were a gift, and there could not have been a person present who wasn't thinking this might be the last time they would ever see Sinatra. You never know. He wiped his brow repeatedly, and put everything he could muster into the music, and at one point offered a toast to his audience: "I hope you live to be six hundred and seventy-five years old, and the last voice you hear is mine."

The Sinatra persona, through much of his career, has been based on the pose that he is a man who doesn't need anybody. That's all gone; he so clearly needs his audiences now, so clearly treasures their presence, that the man on stage has been transformed. I hope Sinatra does not fear this makes him look weak, because the fact is that it only makes him look better.

After his last number, he lingered before leaving the stage. Sinatra used to finish the final song and then bolt, but now he sticks around, saying thanks and letting the evening trail off. I thought of him back in that little room—a complicated man of seventy-seven in a black tuxedo with a red handkerchief, the singer of the century still on the road, still putting out for the customers, still trying. That was the secret he never seemed to want people to know: that in his work he always tried so hard.

When I'd seen him in that little room, he was standing up. Sinatra never sits after putting on his tuxedo in his dressing room, Dreesen told me; he does not want to crease the trousers, because he worries that would make him look sloppy to the men and women in the audience. At seventy-seven he stands until the time he is called to the stage. "Practice? Sure. Sure I do. I practice all the time." Believe it.

NINETY-FIVE

When Big Boys Strode the Land

I'm not sure what the official criteria are for living a happy life, but when I read the obituary for Robert L. Manners it occurred to me that he probably had a pretty great time.

Some men become presidents of massive industrial corporations, and manufacture things. Some men become military leaders, and go to war. Some men become artists, and make the world a more pleasing place to look at.

Robert L. Manners, who was ninety when he died the other day near Cleveland, owned thirty-seven Big Boy restaurants.

Can you think of a better way to spend the 1950s and 1960s than owning thirty-seven Big Boys? That was the Golden Era of the Big Boys—the drive-in restaurants that featured Big Boy sandwiches (two burgers, three-decker bun, melted cheese, pickle, shredded lettuce, Big Boy sauce), onion rings, frosty-freeze shakes, strawberry pie and other gourmet items too fat-soaked to mention.

The obituary said that Manners had sold his Big Boy chain in 1968—probably exactly the right time to dismantle a Big Boy empire—and had retired soon after. From the newspaper story, it seemed that he had lived a full and satisfying life with his family, his church and his civic activities—but it was the Big Boy factor that made the career of Robert Manners seem so alluring to me. Thirty-seven Big Boys. Who could ask for a greater legacy?

I got in touch with Manners's son, J. Christopher Manners,

forty-eight. He said that growing up the son of a Big Boy kingpin was a wonderful experience.

"My dad owned Big Boys all over northeastern Ohio, from Lorain down to Mansfield and all the way to the Pennsylvania line," he said. "A great deal of my younger years consisted of cruising around Big Boy parking lots."

He said that the Big Boy experience should be considered in its historical context, and not just as the act of eating huge multi-decked burgers. "When the Big Boys were becoming so popular, our entire society was beginning to revolve around the freedom that the automobile gave us," he said. "For one of the first times in this country, people were starting to eat out without thinking about it. Before the early fifties, it was unusual, or at least an occasion, to have a meal out. When society started to center around the car, though, you could go out for a meal on an impulse. The Big Boys were just right for the times."

Big Boys weren't exactly health food. . . .

"I'm not sure they were all that bad," he said.

They weren't?

"We used to say that they were a meal-in-one," he said. "You got your starch, your salad, your meat and your protein, all in one Big Boy."

You did?

"Sure you did," he said. "Your starch was the bun. Your salad was the lettuce . . ."

Never mind. We were talking, I realized, about the Big Boy in the past tense, when in fact Big Boys are still around.

"Yes, they are," he said. "There are hundreds of them, all over the country, run by different people. But I think that when my dad owned his thirty-seven Big Boys, that was the great Big Boy era."

You could make that argument. For people too young to remember, it is hard to explain just what a magnet a Big Boy drive-in, with its carhops and squawkboxes and jammed parking lots, was on a summer night. You'd head for that sign with the little red-cheeked guy in striped overalls on it—the little guy on the signs was running, a smile on his face, carrying a Big Boy—and it was a country club on blacktop, a universe of its own with fries on the side.

"A Big Boy cost thirty-five cents in the early fifties," Chris Manners said. "I don't think it ever got over fifty cents even in the sixties—at least the early and mid-sixties."

There was something about that sandwich. . . .

"There was always the great moment of that first bite," Manners said. "The combination of flavors, of course—but there was also the challenge of just trying to get your mouth around it. It wasn't easy. And after you'd accomplished that, you had to think about getting it all down."

But we were talking about his dad. That's why I had called. Had his dad enjoyed owning those thirty-seven Big Boys?

"What do you think?" Manners said. "Dad loved that food. Although I will say, you probably wouldn't want to eat Big Boys three times a day."

NINETY-SIX

Will C. W. Jones Please Report to This Office

ROANOKE, Virginia—There are times when I am convinced that what the world needs now is a little less understanding and a lot more C. W. Jones.

The new school year here in Roanoke, like the new school year all over the United States, has just begun, and the local school board has published its dress regulations.

No caps or hats are allowed in school. Students must wear

shoes at all times. Students may not wear garments "imprinted with obscene, vulgar or suggestive language or pictures," or "promoting an illegal substance or alcohol abuse."

There are no restrictions on jewelry or body piercings, "unless they create a safety hazard for others." Chain belts and spike bracelets and spike necklaces are prohibited, as are tank tops revealing bare midriffs.

The school board is spelling this out so that no one misunderstands. "Dress which disrupts the educational process or which poses a threat to the safety or welfare of the student or others" is forbidden by regulation, but there had been confusion about how various principals interpret those regulations. So the nose-rings-yes, bare-feet-no rules have been instituted.

Which brings us to C. W. Jones, the greatest and most powerful authority figure I have ever known.

C. W. Jones was the principal of the high school which I attended. There was no dress code, either printed or spoken. There was only one code at the school, and it consisted of four words: "Because I said so."

It never occurred to us that there was anything especially unfair about that. If you got kicked out of school for wearing white Levi's, you got kicked out not because you had violated any particular rule, but because C.W. said so. White Levi's were bad; so were regular blue Levi's. C.W., for some reason, didn't seem to mind black Levi's. The class of '65 in central Ohio didn't tend to have their bodies pierced, but if they had, C.W. would undoubtedly have flung them right out the front door, toward Cassingham Road. Why? Because he said so.

Authoritarianism in society at large is often a bad thing, but you can make the argument that in the typical U.S. school, it has its good points. There are times in the lives of young people when they may secretly need an older, more somber person to tell them what to do, whether they like it or not. Egalitarianism and self-determination are fine, but America's schools seemed to be doing a more effective job back when the men and women who ran the schools didn't feel the need to justify every edict they handed down. There's a lot of because-I-said-so in the real world; might as well get used to it when you're young.

Why else, thirty years later, would I keep a photograph of C. W. Jones in my office? At our thirtieth high school class reunion, Tom Hill, a member of the class, came up to me and said, "Look. Wellingtons. Think C.W. will kick me out?"

He lifted his pants cuffs. He didn't need to explain. He was wearing a very conservative pair of black boots. They weren't cowboy boots, they weren't pointy-toed boots, they didn't have stacked heels. They looked like standard black business shoes, but high enough to be called boots.

Wellingtons, to be specific. They were staid and clunky and completely nonthreatening, and C. W. Jones had not liked them. Tom Hill, thirty years before, had been thrown out of school for wearing them, and only now, thirty years later, did he feel confident to put them on again. He assumed C. W. Jones would not be around to expel him.

But C. W. Jones did show up. Now retired and a bona fide senior citizen, he came to a picnic we had at the school. I don't think there was a person present who didn't feel a little intimidated. His first words to me—thirty years down the line, said in that C. W. Jones voice, without a smile—were:

"I see you use my name from time to time in your stories and your books. I haven't seen any money out of it yet."

I could have made a joke; I could have been flippant or sarcastic. What I did was stammer; stammer and say:

"Uh, well, you see, Mr. Jones . . . I mean, I, uh . . . I didn't know, I mean, if you think . . . Uh, uh, I mean . . ."

They could use him in Roanoke, and at schools all over our fast-fraying country. Bare feet? Chain belts? Foul language on T-shirts? T-shirts, period, for that matter?

You don't need a dress code. You just need C. W. Jones. Because he said so.

NINETY-SEVEN

Fall Classic

There are many memorable moments from any World Series—moments that baseball fans talk about for years.

For a father and son who live in Lima, Ohio, though, it will be hard for anything that happened on the playing field to match the World Series moment that unexpectedly came to them.

Don Bruns is forty-three; his son, Aaron, is ten. Aaron loves baseball, and the Cincinnati Reds in particular. He broke his arm in a bicycle accident last summer, and missed the last part of his Little League season. For a birthday present, his dad decided to take Aaron down to Cincinnati for the first game of the World Series. They had no tickets.

"I was hoping that we could find some scalpers who would sell us tickets," the father said. "I explained to Aaron that there was no guarantee we would get into the game. But just being around a World Series, even if we didn't get in, would be exciting."

So they drove the more than two hours from Lima to Cincinnati—Lima is in the northern part of Ohio, Cincinnati is all the way south. For two more hours they walked the streets—Aaron wearing a Reds cap.

"There were a lot of scalpers, all right," the father said. "I didn't realize how much tickets cost. The cheapest ones we were offered were a hundred and seventy-five dollars apiece. The most expensive were three hundred dollars apiece. I couldn't do that, and I explained it to Aaron. He understood."

Then, the father said, they were approached by a man who asked if they were going to the game.

"He told me his name, and he told me that he was staying at the Omni Hotel," the father said. "I explained about our trip to Cincinnati, and I said that I couldn't pay what the scalpers were asking.

"He pulled out two tickets. He said that my son reminded him of himself fifteen years ago. He handed me the tickets.

"I asked him how much he wanted. He said there was no charge. He said the tickets were free.

"I thought that maybe this was part of a scam or something. I kept waiting for something tricky to happen. We were waiting for the guy to play us for fools.

"But he just said that he hoped we would enjoy the game, and he left. We went to the stadium. The tickets were wonderful. I had never been to a World Series game, and of course my son hadn't. The World Series! It feels different than any other baseball game. The intensity, the emotional high, the excitement level . . . and this guy had just handed us the tickets and walked away.

"During the game my son and I must have turned to each other thirty times and said to each other: 'I can't believe this.' "

Here is the story of the man on the street:

His name is Michael Teicher; he works as an account executive for a company called Phoenix Communications Group, in South Hackensack, New Jersey. The company markets TV shows about baseball—the syndicated *This Week in Baseball* and ESPN's *Major League Baseball Magazine,* among others.

Teicher seemed surprised when I tracked him down in Oakland, where he had traveled for the second leg of the World Series. I explained what Don Bruns had told me.

"Here's what happened," Teicher said. "I work for a man named Joe Podesta. He hadn't missed a World Series in sixteen years. A month ago, though, he had a mild heart attack, and he's not at the Series this year.

"I guess like a lot of people who have heart attacks, he felt some kind of new appreciation for the preciousness of life. He told me that he wanted to make some people happy. So he told me that when I was at the World Series I should take two tickets and give them to people I thought would be thrilled by going to the game. That's the only ground rule he gave me—give the tickets to people I thought would be thrilled."

Teicher walked around town for some time before seeing Don and Aaron Bruns.

"I had seen a lot of people on the street who I thought might just take the tickets and sell them," Teicher said. "This guy and his son, though—the father was carrying a sign that said 'I Need Two Tickets.' His son was this nice-looking, skinny kid with glasses, and he looked very disappointed.

"I followed them and I heard the father telling the son about how much the scalpers wanted for tickets. I heard the father say they wouldn't be going to the game.

"I looked at them and they reminded me of my dad and me when I was a kid. I would have died to go to a World Series game with my father. But I never did.

"So I went up and I gave them the tickets and I told them to enjoy themselves."

Because of his work, Teicher has begun to regard going to World Series games as almost routine. "I go to all of them," he said. "That makes you forget how important going to the World Series can be."

How important was it to Don Bruns and his son? Here is what Bruns said:

"This is the most memorable thing that has ever happened to us. My boy and I will never forget that night."

After Michael Teicher had handed the tickets to the father and son, he watched them walking together toward the stadium.

"The little boy," he said, "it was like all of a sudden he had a bounce in his step."

NINETY-EIGHT

Of Baseball and Sincere Friendship

SARASOTA, Florida—The quote you may want to keep in mind, now that the major league ballplayers have ended their strike, was uttered by Lou Whitaker, an infielder for the Detroit Tigers, as he arrived at the Tigers' spring training camp in his Rolls-Royce last week.

Referring to the many baseball fans who felt disappointed about being unable to watch their favorite teams while the players and the owners fought, Whitaker emerged from his Rolls and said:

"It might take fans a little while to get over their crushed feelings. It's just like a man and a woman. Maybe we'll send a few flowers."

So here comes baseball again—major league style, the way we have been conditioned to accept it. Seems like a good time to get out of here. The last story we tell before leaving, though, will not be from the perspective of a player or an owner. Rather, it is from a sixty-six-year-old retired International Harvester worker named Bill Deen. You'll understand his point.

Deen grew up in the small town of Eldorado, in southern Illinois: "Those were Great Depression years, and our recreation was mostly what we could put together in some form of baseball. Very few had gloves, but someone would manage to buy a cheap ball and a bat. I can remember as many as twenty kids coming to my house on Sunday afternoons to play." There was no television, radio coverage of baseball games was erratic in Eldorado, and the big leagues seemed as far away as a foreign country.

But many boys did have a favorite team: the St. Louis Cardinals. Bill Deen—he was Billy Deen back then—fell in love with the Cardinals at the age of eight. He can still recall a magnificent World Series game between the Cardinals and the Boston Red Sox when he was a teenager: "Enos Slaughter led off in the bottom of the eighth with a single and remained at first as the next two hitters were retired. With Harry Walker at bat, the ever-hustling Slaughter took off for second. Walker hit a soft liner to left-center and Slaughter saw an opportunity to score all the way from first . . ."

After the Cardinals won that game—this was in the fall of '46—Billy Deen did something he had never done before. He wrote a letter to a hero: Enos "Country" Slaughter. The letter was in neat, precise handwriting.

> Dear Enos,
> I was very thrilled yesterday as you and the rest of the Cardinals overpowered the overrated Boston Red Sox. I am thoroughly convinced that it was your terrific speed and great throwing arm that was the winning margin.
>
> I am looking forward to next year when I can see you in action again. I hope you have another great year. It was the best World Series I have ever listened to. I was for the Cardinals the whole way through and was confident you would win.
>
> I'm only 18 years of age, but I've been following the Cardinals extensively since 1936. I've never written to a big leaguer yet and I hope that I can receive some kind of an answer.
>
> Sincerely yours,
> Billy Deen

He mailed it to Sportsman's Park in St. Louis, and didn't hear back. He understood—big-leaguers were busy and had millions of fans.

But in 1952—a full six years later—a letter arrived. The return address was Sportsman's Park in St. Louis.

The handwriting was as neat and careful as Billy's had been.

> Dear Bill:
> Recently, going through my 1946 scrapbook, I found this fan letter of yours that I must have failed to answer, and I feel very badly to think that I didn't answer such a nice letter as yours. I've tried never to miss answering all my fan mail.
>
> The old saying "Better late than never" certainly holds true in this case! I'm six years late, but I wish to write and apologize for my neglect. I hope you will forgive me.
>
> > Your sincere friend,
> > Enos Slaughter

Enos Slaughter is in the Baseball Hall of Fame today. Today's big-league stars are willing to play again; soon enough they'll be selling their autographs and walking by young fans without even looking at them. Lou Whitaker: "It might take fans a little while to get over their crushed feelings. . . . Maybe we'll send a few flowers."

Billy Deen—Bill Deen—at age sixty-six still has that letter from Enos Slaughter. " 'Your sincere friend,' " Deen said. "I'll never forget those words, the way he signed it. 'Your sincere friend.' It seems like a long, long time ago."

NINETY-NINE

The Sound of Muzak

Walking through a public building on a recent trip, I was stopped dead in my tracks by the sound of Muzak.

You aren't supposed to notice Muzak. The whole point of Muzak is that it's designed to be the ideal soothing piped-in background music.

But late on this particular afternoon, the Muzak stopped me as effectively as if it had been an electric prod.

Muzak, as everyone knows, has traditionally consisted of lushly orchestrated string arrangements of classic American tunes. Take a song like "The Sound of Music," have a tepid and bland orchestra do a quiet version of it, and you have Muzak.

The song I was hearing was, indeed, soft and lush and filled with string arrangements.

And I was almost sure what the song was:

"Double Shot (Of My Baby's Love)."

I listened some more. This couldn't be.

But yes. "Double Shot (Of My Baby's Love)" was definitely coming out of the ceiling of this building. It was muted and it was gentle and it was Muzak—and it was "Double Shot (Of My Baby's Love)."

You have to understand—"Double Shot (Of My Baby's Love)," briefly popular in the summer of 1966, was a raucous, prototypical bar song recorded by a raucous, prototypical garage band known as the Swingin' Medallions. "Double Shot (Of My

Baby's Love)" was the only hit the Swingin' Medallions ever had—and with good reason. There were only two things you could do while listening to "Double Shot (Of My Baby's Love)": drink beer and throw up. That's what the song was made for.

And here it was. On Muzak.

I listened hard. There are, of course, no vocals on Muzak songs. But I followed the melody that was coming out of the ceiling. The orchestral strings were ever-so-sweetly playing the part of the song in which the Swingin' Medallions had sung: "It wasn't wine that I had too much of . . ."

I couldn't let this go. Maybe I was wrong. In fact, I hoped I was wrong. Listen, I'm a realist. I know that instrumental versions of Beatles songs are now featured on Muzak. I know that instrumental versions of Simon and Garfunkel songs are featured on Muzak. The world changes.

But I'm sorry. The world is not supposed to change so much that "Double Shot (Of My Baby's Love)" is featured on Muzak.

I called Muzak headquarters, in Seattle. I spoke with Bruce Funkhouser, Muzak's vice president of programming.

"I can look in the computer," Funkhouser told me.

"If I'm right," I said to him, " 'Double Shot (Of My Baby's Love)' played on Muzak about ten minutes before six late last Wednesday afternoon, Eastern time."

"Here it is," Funkhouser said. "Yes, yes . . . we do feature that song. To be precise, it played last Wednesday afternoon at fifty-seven minutes and thirty-one seconds after five o'clock."

I asked how this could be. How could "Double Shot (Of My Baby's Love)" have gone from being a drink-and-vomit song to something that was carefully logged in the Muzak master computer?

"We have a rotation of five thousand songs," Funkhouser said. "We used to just have arrangements of old-time numbers such as 'Begin the Beguine' and 'Three Coins in the Fountain.'

People were used to Muzak being just the kinds of songs performed by Mantovani or the Jackie Gleason Orchestra.

"But in recent years we have expanded our repertoire."

Apparently. Funkhouser said that Muzak is piped into 130,000 locations in the United States, and heard by approximately 80 million people each day. "Muzak isn't really intended to be listened to," he said. "It's just supposed to be there, to soothe people and put their minds into a comfort zone."

Thus, every song on Muzak is specially arranged and recorded by Muzak musicians. The lyrics are removed, the sound softened.

"But I always thought that the songs on Muzak were supposed to be the traditional tunes that middle-aged Americans remembered from deep in their pasts," I said.

"Yes?" Funkhouser said.

And I understood. For millions of adult working Americans today, that is exactly what "Double Shot (Of My Baby's Love)" is—a traditional number from deep in the nation's musical past.

"What instruments does Muzak use?" I asked.

"It varies," Funkhouser said. "Flute, saxophone, piano, French horn, oboe, harp . . ."

As a final attempt to explain what was troubling me, I said: "You know, when 'Double Shot (Of My Baby's Love)' first came out, a lot of people enjoyed drinking beer to it. Sometimes they were having such a wonderful time that they threw up."

"That may be," Funkhouser said. "But our purpose here at Muzak is to help people relax."

ONE HUNDRED

A Heart Stops on the Midway

COLUMBUS, Ohio—Along the midway of the Ohio State Fair, the canvas walls of the sideshow are painted with garish come-ons that attest to the seaminess of such enterprises. Among the attractions promoted are the Radium Skin Girl, the Skeleton Girl, the Elephant Skin Boy, Gabora the Gorilla Girl.

In the midst of this queasy milieu, something disturbing and final happened this summer. But the fair will be over soon, and the sideshow will be moving on, and what happened will be quickly forgotten.

One of the sideshow attractions was a person promoted to the crowds as Big Billy Pork Chop, the Rock 'n' Roll Fat Man. The attraction was a young man, only twenty-two years old, who through some misfortune of fate weighed 518 pounds. His job was to sit on a metal chair all day while fairgoers paraded through his tent and asked him questions. The "rock 'n' roll" part of his title derived from the fact that he was required to activate a tape recording of the song "Whole Lot of Shakin' Going On." While the song played, his duty was to stand and shake his body as customers laughed and on occasion touched him to make sure he was real.

The young man's name, of course, was not really Big Billy Pork Chop. His name was David Fleischman, and what the fair-goers did not know was that this was his first week on the job.

Fleischman, by all accounts, had lived an unhappy life that had been forever seared by the death of his mother. After she died he found it hard to find people who wanted him around; Fleischman told friends that every time his father would meet a new woman, the woman would insist that the boy be removed from the house.

Earlier this summer, Fleischman was attending a fair in New Jersey, as a spectator. Tim Deremer, who runs a traveling sideshow, noticed the obese young man.

"We were looking for a new fat guy for the show, and we saw him walking around," Deremer said the other afternoon.

So Deremer decided to send an attractive young woman—sideshow master of ceremonies Maureen Reno—to ask the young man if he would like to be paid for being displayed at fairs.

"I think he thought I was kidding," Maureen Reno said. "But I told him that we really were looking for a fat person, and he said he would think about it."

For whatever reason, young David Fleischman decided to take the job. He was instructed to meet the sideshow in Ohio.

"He took a train from New Jersey," Deremer said. "Apparently there had been no rest room on the train big enough for him to get into. We took him right to a place where he could use the rest room."

He was given a quick course on how to perform his job. There really wasn't much to it. For thirteen hours a day he sat in the tent while the people looked at him, asked him questions, sometimes ridiculed him.

Society is increasingly vigilant about the display and cruel treatment of animals. Sideshows, however, still exist, and humans are displayed for the public's amusement. Some of the attractions are "illusionists"—they are not what they seem to be. David Fleischman, though, was as obese as advertised, and people lined up to look at him.

"He told me that whenever he went to the mall back where he lived, people would point at him and laugh and say things about him," Tim Deremer said. "So as long as people were going to do it, why shouldn't he get paid for it?"

On one of Fleischman's first days on display, Eric Hayot, a summer intern for the Columbus *Dispatch*, stopped by the tent.

"He seemed a little nervous," Hayot said. "He told me that this was the first time he had done anything like this. He said that people asked him rude questions, mostly about if he was able to have sex. He said that some people at the fair traveled in packs and acted like animals."

Indeed, there were reports that some young men at the fair delighted in throwing stones and pieces of food at Fleischman. This was said to upset and frighten him. But he told a friend that he found Ohio clean and pleasant; he said the air was easier for him to breathe. Of people who stared at him, he said: "Whether I'm happy, that has nothing to do with these people here."

Fleischman slept in a trailer with three other sideshow performers. After his sixth day of work he went to sleep. Several hours later, one of the other performers found him on the floor. He had fallen out of bed and was not breathing. Dr. William Adrion, Franklin County coroner, said the cause of death was heart failure due to massive obesity. A sideshow promoter said, "Those kinds of things happen to people like that. They don't live to be too old."

So Fleischman's body and his belongings were shipped back to his home. He had not survived a week as a sideshow attraction. He was replaced in his tent by another act.

Along the midway, few people seemed aware that Fleischman had even been here. Occasionally, though, you could overhear a conversation:

"Did you hear about that fat guy in the freak show?"

"Yeah. I heard he died or something."

ONE HUNDRED ONE

Love and War

The love and complications and anger and pride between fathers and sons are some of the most fascinating aspects of the human experience. The father-son relationship is not one that is examined as often as it should be; many men find it too personal—or too painful—to talk about.

In Worthington, Ohio, Jane Trucksis, curator of the Worthington Historical Society, came across a letter in the estate of a ninety-three-year-old man who had died in Bucyrus, Ohio. The man, Joseph R. Neff, had been a lieutenant with the American forces in France during World War I. In 1919, Lieutenant Neff's commanding officer had handed him the letter, which the commanding officer had received in the mail from one William Bigley Sr., on the stationery of Bigley Brothers General Trucking Company in Hoboken, New Jersey.

On May 5, 1919, Mr. Bigley had mailed the letter to the commanding officer because . . . well, read the letter yourself:

ZONE MAJOR
St. André de Cobzac
Gironde, France
APO 705, Amexforce

Dear Sir:
I am writing you with reference to a request received from my son, Sgt. William J. Bigley, to give him my

permission to marry a French mademoiselle with whom he is in love.

It would give me the very greatest pleasure to accede to my son's request; but as his father, with maturer experience and riper judgment, I do not feel it wise to give my consent at this time. Realizing, however, that a blunt, direct refusal might prejudice his reasonable attitude towards the matter and, in effect, lead to the very result I am hoping to forestall, I am taking this means of addressing you as his superior officer, in the hope of enlisting your sympathies and interest actively in the young man my son.

I wish you would attempt to show him that the step he is contemplating is bringing grief to his dear mother and myself; and that we are both of us now sick since receiving this news.

It might help you in talking this matter over with him to call his attention to the fact that he is in debt and that to get married at this time would be to handicap his own future usefulness and progress in business with his eyes wide open. It would be opposed to the soundest American business sense and principles. Through you, he should have no trouble in perceiving the logic of the situation.

I should thank you to give him the most kindly counsel such as you would give to your own son under similar circumstances, for doing which I should feel myself under an everlasting gratitude to you. If other appeals fail to reach his mind in determining him to change his plans, at least urge him to postpone the taking of the step until he can return home and find out how his mother and I feel about it. I am sure that we are willing to do everything in our power to pleasure him and bring all the happiness possible into his life.

I believe that the weight of your personal appeal to his reason will be productive of the results desired; and thanking you in advance for the consideration of your favor, and in the earnest expectation that we may soon receive some encouraging news from you and him, I am,

Yours with a burdened mind and an anguished heart,

William Bigley Sr.

Mrs. Trucksis of the Worthington Historical Society gave the letter to me because she wants William Bigley Jr., if he is still alive, or his descendants, if he is dead, to have it. She has no idea how to find him or them.

"There is such a story in that letter," she said. "Of love and war, and fathers and sons. The family ought to have it.

"And the letter is so touching in so many ways. Can you imagine a father today putting that kind of trust in his son's commanding officer—writing to the commanding officer to ask him to literally interfere in his son's life?

"The idea of such a letter today is almost unimaginable. This was obviously a father who expected his son to do what he told him to do. But this was 1919. You can argue about what the father was doing, but it's clear that he loved his son.

"And the language in the letter! So cultured, so carefully worded. The whole story of the letter is from a time that has passed."

Joseph Neff, the lieutenant to whom the commanding officer entrusted the letter, apparently never discussed it with anyone, so when it was found with his papers there was no clue as to the resolution of the story.

But if the family wants the letter, I hope they'll get in touch. Thanking you in advance for the consideration of your favor . . .

ONE HUNDRED TWO

A Legend a Few Feet Away

Pancho Gonzalez died the other day. One of the greatest tennis players who ever lived, and an athlete so charismatic that people could not take their eyes off him, he was sixty-seven when he lost his fight against cancer.

Once, when I was a kid, through pure happenstance, I got to watch him play from about as close as you can get. It's the kind of thing I doubt would happen today, with world-class athletes protected by layers of security guards and business agents and public relations people. On the day it happened, it was as easy as asking.

Gonzalez—his name was spelled Gonzales in the papers back then—won the U.S. national singles championship in 1948 at the age of twenty, then won it again the next year. His serve was frightening, it was so powerful; his flat serve, when it was aimed properly, was almost impossible to return, and his American twist serve leapt from the surface of a court so erratically that his opponents could only guess at which way the ball might bound.

Gonzalez turned pro in 1949, at a time when professionalism was disdained in the tennis world. So during his greatest years, he was forbidden from playing in the world's most prestigious tournaments, including Wimbledon and the U.S. championships, which were open only to amateurs. Still, he remained the most fascinating figure in tennis—the best.

In 1962 Gonzalez was serving as a coach for the United States Davis Cup team (he could not play on the team because he was a pro). The team was scheduled to play a sectional match against Canada in Cleveland. A friend and I rode the train from central Ohio to Cleveland to watch.

Tennis was not a hugely popular sport in 1962; the Davis Cup sectionals did not draw all that large a crowd. Watching the top amateurs play was a treat, but the person none of the spectators could look away from was Gonzalez, standing on the sidelines.

One day, after the Davis Cup matches, my friend and I were hanging around, when out of the locker room came Gonzalez, in tennis whites. He had several rackets in his hand. With him was Chuck McKinley, a member of the U.S. team. They walked to an empty court. It was evident they were going to play.

One of us—I think it was probably my friend—called to Gonzalez and asked if he and McKinley needed ballboys. Gonzalez nodded—we hardly registered in his consciousness, but we could save him the trouble of chasing down balls—and motioned each of us to opposite ends of the court.

Which is where, for the next few hours, we crouched and watched the great Gonzalez play tennis. We were within feet of him; when he would come over to grab a ball from us, we were within inches. No one else was around. For a couple of Midwestern kids who loved tennis, this was a gift that was almost beyond belief. Before we had boarded the train in our hometown, we had hoped only to be able to watch the Davis Cup sectionals. And now here, late on a warm afternoon on this court in Cleveland, there were four people: Pancho Gonzalez, Chuck McKinley and us.

What a tennis lesson. What a day. Almost numb with the thrill of it, we studied Gonzalez as he set himself for his serve, as he tossed the ball into the air, arched his back, brought his racket through and—as the ball screamed toward McKinley—as he rushed to the net, seemingly moving forward and sideways at the same time, covering every inch of the court. He was a craftsman and an idol and a teacher, all at once—and, against all likelihood, when each point was over he would turn to us, look at us, wait for us to toss him a tennis ball.

As I say, I don't think something like that would happen in quite this way today. Gonzalez cussed at us when we were slow in retrieving balls, and admonished us to quit being spectators and start being better ballboys. We loved it. Being cursed out by Pancho Gonzalez? What a great and priceless thing.

At the end of the afternoon, as our payment, Gonzalez gave us the tennis balls he had played with. He was on his way off the court when he did it; he turned toward us and tossed us each a ball. It was like being in a movie, or in a slow-motion dream: Pancho Gonzalez was calling out to us and throwing us his tennis balls. Anyway, he was a patient at Sunrise Hospital in Las Vegas when he died the other day. The best memories never die, though. I can see him leaning into that serve now. So close.

ONE HUNDRED THREE

A Winner in the Only Game That Counts

I hope he won't mind my writing this. We've been friends for too many years for me to ever betray a confidence. I don't think by writing this I'm letting him down. I'm just so moved by the person he's become that I have to say it here.

When I called his house the other night it was an unfamiliar voice that answered the phone. The radio was blaring, and the voice was one I had never heard, and for a moment I thought I had the wrong number. The voice said a few labored words I didn't understand, and then stopped. The rock music from the radio continued, though.

I stayed on the line. Three or four minutes passed, and the music kept playing, and finally I heard another phone being picked up in the house.

"Hello?" my friend's voice said.

And I said hello back, and I said that it had sounded as if a foreign-born person or something had answered his phone, and I asked if anything was wrong.

"Tell you in a minute," he said, and his voice went away and soon enough I could hear it in the room where the other phone was still off the hook. The room from which I was hearing the rock music.

"I've got it, honey," I heard him say. Then: "It's all right. Thank you for answering."

He hung up that phone, and when I heard him again he could talk with some privacy.

"She's really a sweetheart," he said, and then he explained.

He had been out of town on business, he said. When he had returned, the girl—the girl who had answered the phone with such difficulty—had moved into his house.

He and his wife have their own daughter, a bright, healthy girl. His wife is a substitute teacher, and at one school there are children who have severe disabilities.

This little girl was one of those children. She was born with a terrible problem that has affected her both physically and mentally. It is not the kind of thing that medicine or surgery can fix. When my friend was out of town, the little girl with the painful problems suffered another one: There was an accident in her home, and her mother was going to be unable to care for her or her brothers and sisters for a while. The little girl—she is twelve —didn't really understand. One more rotten hand dealt her by life.

Instead of letting her be turned over to a social service agency, my friend's wife arranged through the school to take the girl in until her mother got better. So when my friend returned from his trip, she was living in his house. It had been a family of three— my friend, his wife and their daughter. Now there were four, at least for a while.

"She's just a wonderful child," he said.

This is not a story of historic sacrifice or unprecedented nobility; there are thousands of people in this country who, out of charity or goodness or whatever you may call it, do fine and honorable things every day. But we all start out as kids, with our own circles of friends, and we all grow to be adults and some of us turn out to be good people and some of us turn out to be not-so-good people. You never know, when you're a kid, who among you and your friends is going to turn out to be what kind of person. You never know who's going to win the game in the ways that truly count.

"It was our anniversary," he told me.

Meaning: When he got home from his trip, it was his wedding anniversary.

"The four of us went out to a nice restaurant," he said. "I don't think she'd ever been anyplace like that in her life. She looked so beautiful and so happy. It was like she was a princess in a castle."

He was talking about the girl who is staying with him. She joined his family for that wedding anniversary celebration.

I asked him if even a part of him would have preferred to have had the wedding anniversary dinner be more private. Just my friend and his wife.

"Are you kidding?" he said. "You should have seen her face, looking around the restaurant and ordering from the menu." He was talking about his guest again, of course.

"I don't think I've ever had a better anniversary dinner," he said.

The girl will go back home one of these days. Maybe her life will be richer for having been treated with such kindness and care during her own family's troubled time; maybe she will never really understand.

And my friend doesn't think it's any big deal. Someone needed some help, that's all. He truly doesn't see anything all that special about what he and his family are doing.

You win the game, pal. We were all kids together and we all grew up, and you win the game. I've got to tell you here, because I'm no good at saying things out loud. You're the best of us, and you don't even know it, and this is the only game that counts and you are my hero.

ONE HUNDRED FOUR

The News

A man walked down Michigan Avenue with his briefcase swinging by his side, a smile on his face and a brisk pace to his stride. He was whistling. The exact tune he was whistling was not immediately discernible, but about one thing there was no question: This guy was in a happy mood.

At a newspaper vending box, a woman who appeared to be in her mid-fifties, wearing a heavy overcoat, waited her turn to drop her coins into the slot. In front of her was another woman, approximately the same age, getting her paper. That woman removed the paper from the box and turned around. The woman who was waiting smiled as if slightly surprised and said, "We've got to stop meeting like this!" The woman with the newspaper said, "We must have our clocks set to the same time!" They may or may not have known each other in some other context than this newspaper-machine routine, but they clearly were accustomed to encountering each other here. "Maybe I'll see you tomorrow," the woman with the newspaper said. "I hope so," her acquaintance said, getting ready to drop her own coins into the box.

At the counter of a cigar stand, a businessman paid for a pack of gum with a dollar bill. The clerk behind the counter, in a hurry, slid the businessman his change. The businessman started to walk away, then looked at the coins in his hand. He turned back to the clerk and said, "Excuse me—how much was that gum?" The clerk, a little wary, told him. The businessman said, "I thought this was too much change. Here—you gave me a quarter too much." And he returned the extra money to the clerk.

In a shopping mall, a child was screaming and crying. The child seemed to be tired, and with each passing moment the crying grew louder. Apparently it had been a long afternoon, and the child was throwing a bit of a tantrum. Other people in the mall looked over, some with annoyance, some with concern. The child's mother, carrying two large shopping bags, knelt down next to the child. The mother did not yell, and did not scold, and did not yank at the child's arm. Instead the mother talked quietly with her child for a minute or two; at one point the mother smoothed the child's hair with her hand. Within two minutes the child was quiet, and seemingly in a better mood; the child was even giggling. Hand in hand, the mother and her child walked toward the mall's exit.

At a busy intersection, two pedestrians—both men, both in business attire—waited for the light to change. They were not walking together, but it seemed obvious that they had met before. "I've got one for you," one of the men said. He then told a joke. It was not uproariously funny, but it was neither mean-spirited nor dirty. When the joke-teller got to the punch line the other man chuckled, shook his head—then repeated the punch line, as sort of a combination thank-you for having been told the joke, and an assurance to the joke-teller that the story had been all right. They crossed the street together, then headed in different directions.

On an airplane headed into Erie, Pennsylvania, a young sailor in uniform talked almost nonstop during the whole flight. The recipient of his conversation was a woman perhaps twenty years his senior, who by the luck of the draw had been assigned the adjacent seat.

As the flight progressed, it became clear that the sailor's rapid conversation was the product of three different factors. First, some of his comments indicated that he was a nervous flier; the chatter was his way of dealing with his jitters. Second, he had just completed his Navy training, and he was doing a little macho posturing about the things he had seen and the things that might lie ahead. Third—and most important—he was heading home.

For every tough-guy Navy story he would tell, he would say something about his mother and how much he was looking forward to seeing her. He must have mentioned his mother five times during the flight. As the plane made its final descent into Erie, he pointed out the window and said to the woman next to him: "See that house down there? That's my brother's house." And a few seconds later: "That's my house, right there." And: "I used to work at that McDonald's."

After the plane had hit the ground and was rolling toward the main airport building, he said to the woman next to him: "I wonder if my mom will be at the airport?" The plane stopped and the sailor stood up. The woman who had been riding next to him—she hadn't said much during the flight—reached toward the sailor as if to touch his neck. "Wait a second," she said. "Your collar's up. You don't want to come home with your collar crooked." And she straightened it.

The above stories have only two things in common. One is

that I observed all of them happen within a single twenty-four-hour period. The other is that, by any objective criteria, they are not dramatic or momentous or earthshaking events; thus, none of them would probably ever be deemed important enough to be included in a newspaper.

ABOUT THE AUTHOR

Bob Greene's national bestsellers include *Be True to Your School*; *Hang Time: Days and Dreams with Michael Jordan*; *Good Morning, Merry Sunshine*; and with his sister, D. G. Fulford, *To Our Children's Children: Preserving Family Histories for Generations to Come*.

Greene is a syndicated columnist for the *Chicago Tribune*; his column appears in more than two hundred newspapers in the United States, Canada, and Japan. For nine years his "American Beat" was the lead column in *Esquire* magazine; as a broadcast journalist he has served as contributing correspondent for *ABC News Nightline*. *Chevrolet Summers, Dairy Queen Nights* is his seventeenth book.